AFTER *the* ROOF CAVED IN

AFTER *the* ROOF CAVED IN

An Immigrant's Journey *from* Ireland to America

MICHAEL J. DOWLING
with CHARLES KENNEY

ARCADE PUBLISHING

Arcade Publishing books may be purchased in bulk at special discounts for sales promotion, corporate gifts, fund-raising, or educational purposes. Special editions can also be created to specifications. For details, contact the Special Sales Department, Skyhorse Publishing, 307 West 36th Street, 11th Floor, New York, NY 10018 or info@skyhorsepublishing.com.

Arcade Publishing® is a registered trademark of Skyhorse Publishing, Inc.®, a Delaware corporation.

Visit our website at www.arcadepub.com.

10 9 8 7 6 5 4 3 2

Library of Congress Cataloging-in-Publication Data is available on file.

Cover design by Erin Seaward-Hiatt

Print ISBN: 978-1-956763-77-5
Ebook ISBN: 978-1-951627-25-6

Printed in the United States of America

To Kathy, Brian, and Elizabeth
with love and gratitude

Northern
Ireland

IRELAND

Dublin

Limerick

Rathkeale

Ballingarry

New Castle West

Knockaderry

Cork

CONTENTS

Introduction: ix
Leading Through the Pandemic: How Childhood Adversity Can Prepare Us

Preface: xvii
Voices in the Night: The Irish storytelling tradition.

1. The Village of Knockaderry: 1
"A lone figure waving his cane in the air."

2. Hierarchy and Hurling: 25
"Too bad someone like you could never go to college."

3. Love of Learning: 43
"He's only going to end up sweeping the streets."

4. A Cacophony of No: 57
"I was beginning to believe that the Church was as much about power as it was about religion."

5. A Scar that Never Healed: 67
"What the hell are these exams for anyway?"

6. University College Cork: 82
"Oh, my God, I'm in college!"

7. Joe Is Gone: 108
"What did I do?"

8. Fordham and Failure: 116
"I am returning to Ireland (for good) very soon. . . . It won't be long before we are all together . . ."

9. Hugs All Around: 135
"Did I consider it a terrible loss at the time? I did not."

10. The Mario Cuomo Years: 147
"We had to help people help themselves."

11. The Mission of Northwell Health: 171
"The only way to serve yourself is to serve others."

12. Gun Violence and Climate Change: 189
Two Major Public Health Crises

13. Mam's New Life: 199
"Is that you?"

14. Grand Marshal: 209
"The greatest incubator of opportunity the world has ever known."

15. A Good Ending: 223
"We're lucky we've gotten closer as we've gotten older."

Afterword: 237
A Lifelong Love of Learning

Acknowledgments   253

About the Authors   257

INTRODUCTION

Leading Through the Pandemic:
How Childhood Adversity Can Prepare Us

THE ORIGINAL VERSION OF *AFTER the Roof Caved In* was published in January 2020 just as the coronavirus began its assault on the United States. As I was preparing to promote my memoir, bookstores shuttered from coast to coast as normal life came to a standstill. Almost overnight, the twenty-one hospitals and more than 850 ambulatory sites at Northwell Health, where I serve as CEO, were inundated with desperately sick people suffering from a new, mysterious, and often-fatal disease. So began a medical nightmare during which my organization cared for more than 318,000 COVID patients from March 2020 until April 2022—the most of any health system in the nation.

At first blush it seems that a memoir about growing up in rural Ireland during the 1950s and '60s has little, if anything, in common with experiencing a global pandemic. Yet, I find a particular resonance between the two experiences. My personal story focuses on my life in Knockaderry, a town in Limerick County in the southwest of Ireland, where my parents, four siblings, and I lived in a two-bedroom cottage with a dirt floor, thatched roof, and no indoor plumbing or electricity, and where my mother cooked our meals in an open fireplace.

The details of my story in the pages ahead are about my striving as a boy to find education and opportunity beyond the Galtee Mountains we could see in the verdant distance. But underneath it all, my story is one of hardship. At its core it is about navigating the adversity through which—often painfully—we may discover meaning in our lives.

In the winter of 2020, my colleagues and I were confronted with what the *New York Times* described as an "apocalyptic" assault in which "so many people are dying that the city is running low on body bags." In that moment, I had a sense of true north bequeathed to me by my mother, Margaret (Meg) Dowling. Perhaps more than anything, I am my mother's son. I make no pretension that I am as fine a human being as she was, but I carry her genetic inclination for optimism and a determination to remain steadfast through tough times. Mam, as we called my mother, possessed an otherworldly ability to deal with adversity. Nothing slowed her down—not extreme poverty, alcoholism within the family and violence in the home, her own deafness, or raising five children on a few dollars a day.

Through it all, she never complained. I choose these words with the utmost care, knowing that generally when people speak of those who "never complain" they are really talking about people who *rarely* complain. My mother did not rarely complain. *She never complained.* Every day of her life was fueled by optimism, kindness, a desire to always do for others, and her faith not only in God but in humanity as well. She would often say, "Always remember that people are good. You may see the bad parts of them, but there's goodness behind it. It's there someplace. You may not see it all the time, but it is there."

Growing up under my mother's influence, I came to believe

that for some people hardship is a curse, an excuse to live life as a sullen complainer. We had no shortage of these in the village of Knockaderry. For others, however, hardship is a gift where adversity and reversals that scar our lives also sharpen our ability to find meaning in life. I count my mother and myself in this latter camp. Mam found meaning in caring for others—her children and husband, first and foremost, but scores of others in Knockaderry and beyond. She found meaning in bringing light into otherwise dark lives. When I told her I needed to leave Ireland to pursue opportunity in America, she did not try to dissuade me, though it hurt her to see me go. I left because of my optimism and my belief that better days lay ahead over the ocean. I have always believed that deciding to leave one's home country for something foreign and unknown is in itself an optimistic act. Immigrants, by definition, must be optimists.

As I was writing this introduction to the paperback edition of my memoir, I was drawn to some of the important thinkers through the ages whose views were consistent with Mam's approach to life, including the Austrian psychiatrist and Holocaust survivor Viktor Frankl, author of the seminal work, *Man's Search for Meaning*. In 1942, Frankl and several of his relatives were sent to the Theresienstadt concentration camp in Czechoslovakia, where his father died of starvation. In 1944 he was moved to Auschwitz and then to two other camps in the Dachau complex. In 1945, after Allied troops liberated the camps, Frankl discovered that his wife, mother, and brother had perished in the camps.

What did Dr. Frankl do after suffering on such an unimaginable scale? He soldiered on. He sought out and found meaning and purpose in life. After spending three years in four different concentration camps and losing his family, Frankl served as chair of neurology at the Vienna Polyclinic Hospital, wrote numerous books that made important contributions to psychiatry, and lectured worldwide. He remarried, had a child, and lived to age ninety-two. Millions have received the wisdom found in *Man's Search for Meaning* in which he wrote that "everything can be taken from a man but one thing: the last of the human freedoms—to choose one's attitude in any given set of circumstances, to choose one's own way." Long before I read Victor Frankl I learned from my mother that even amid painful adversity you can find uplifting joy and meaning.

In a recent conversation with my friend and colleague Kevin Tracey, a neurosurgeon who leads The Feinstein Institutes for Medical Research at Northwell Health, he connected Frankl's thinking to the ancient Greek idea of *amor fati*—loving one's fate whatever that may be. This defined the Stoics, those who accepted fate, embraced even the worst of times, and found meaning, nonetheless. *Amor fati* comes from ancient Greek mindset "for making the best out of anything that happens: Treating each and every moment—no matter how challenging—as something to be embraced, not avoided. To not only be okay with it, but to love it and be better for it. So that like oxygen to a fire, obstacles and adversity become fuel for your potential. When we accept what happens to us, after understanding that certain things—particularly bad things—are outside our control, we are left with this: loving whatever happens to us and facing it with unfailing cheerfulness and strength."

The more I reflected upon *amor fati*, Victor Frankl and his writing, the more I thought of my mother. She may not have studied the Greek philosophers or the works of Frankl, but she knew their lessons by heart.

I have been tested many times during my life, but never as my colleagues and I were tested when the coronavirus pandemic landed on our front door in early 2020. Our hospitals went from treating patients with hundreds if not thousands of conditions to treating almost exclusively patients suffering from COVID-19. We had never seen anything remotely like it. No one in the world had. We added 1,600 new beds throughout our health system within several weeks, setting up intensive care equipment in hallways, auditoriums, waiting areas—anywhere we could find space to save a life. There was no playbook for this. Never before had our frontline doctors and nurses experienced such fear. Every day they came to work, they tended to very sick people and worried that they might take the virus home to their children, spouses, or parents. It was a horror movie in which patients on ventilators never moved, never spoke, never interacted with their doctors and nurses; in which some of our doctors, nurses, and other employees contracted the virus and died. At the start, the nation's medical community was flying blind. We did not know that infected people could be asymptomatic. Nor did we know how the virus was transmitted, and that symptoms included loss of taste and smell.

The nation was rightfully alarmed that America's doctors groped for solutions in the early stages. I was concerned, of course, but I confess to having a stoic's constitution. The more ominous the news about the pandemic, the calmer I became. It was not that I forced or willed myself to remain calm; it was more my natural reaction to rising danger. Calmness for me was an instinctive reaction. I believed in the skill and compassion of our people, believed we would figure out the best treatments, believed we would make space for every patient arriving at our doors. I believed that at some point—weeks, months, years, whatever it was going to be—we would get to the other side having saved many lives and learned many lessons. In fact, that is what happened.

As a leader it is essential to remain calm, to be able to think clearly, and to avoid frightening employees and the community. Thinking well during frantic times requires clarity of mind and calmness of spirit. This characteristic has always served me well, but never before had it been as impactful as it was during the COVID-19 crisis. At the start of the crisis my instinct was to go to our hospitals and be with our doctors, nurses, respiratory therapists, and other team members, but I was advised by a senior physician that this would be too dangerous; as a seventy-year-old man I could be vulnerable to the virus. *"You could get infected,"* he told me. *"You could get very sick. You could die."* He was quite upset with me.

But I did go to many of our emergency departments, patient floors, and intensive care units. During the first stop I made, it was recommended that I wear full personal protective equipment (PPE). I did so and went to the nurses' station where the staff members wore N95 masks but no other PPE except when entering patient rooms. I felt ridiculous that I was so heavily gowned and protected when I was not even interacting with patients. From then on, I wore an N95 mask just as the staff did, but no other PPE. I was not about to convey the message that it was more important to keep the CEO safer than anyone else.

My visits with staff members caring for gravely ill and dying patients brought sadness, of course, but it also proved to be one of the most gratifying experiences of my life. I was in the presence of our medical teams and their exhaustive efforts to save lives. I found that my presence on the floor helped calm staff members, who felt that the leader of the organization had their back and appreciated what they were doing. As a leader you must go to where the action is. How can I, in the midst of the worst pandemic we had ever experienced, ask people to go to the frontlines but not leave my office? In light of the danger in their hospitals and the prevalence of the virus in New York City, some CEOs at other major medical centers secluded themselves in their vacation homes in Florida. I took a different tack. I walked the hallways talking with staff, thanking them for their efforts and asking how they were holding up. Did they need anything? What could I do to help? People told me about the deaths and the wrenching experience of being present while families at home watched on Zoom as their loved ones drew a final breath. I talked with doctors and nurses, of course, as well as kitchen, transport, security, carpentry, and housekeeping workers. I was conveying to them, *I am here to support you and do what I can to keep you safe. We will get through this. It will take time. It is the hardest thing we have ever done together but we are strong. We will get through this together.*

The determination of our people to care for overwhelming numbers of sick patients was something to behold. One of our nurses, Emily Fawcett, put it this way: "I wanted to be there for New Yorkers. I wanted to fight COVID for New York. I wanted to defend my city against this weird virus that we knew nothing about. I felt this calling."

Optimism comforts and inspires. It allows people to believe, even amid a global pandemic, that there will be a better tomorrow. As rough as things got at home in Knockaderry, I always believed, even as a child, that there was something better out there in the future, over that horizon. This was pure Meg Dowling—my mother's gift to me.

I also felt a duty to convey optimism and confidence to the greater New York community. During scores of news media interviews, I always said that I was optimistic we would find our way through and that things would be better soon. At Northwell we committed to sustained transparency, sharing publicly what we knew as the crisis dragged on. We never withheld bad news, but we conveyed it with a sense that, yes, it is very bad now, but it will get better; we are learning every day. In a crisis, information is healthy, fear is not.

As I write in the spring of 2022, the pandemic is not over by any means, though in the United States we have made real progress. And yes, I am optimistic about our ability to effectively respond when the next pandemic strikes, for it is *when*, not *whether*. Peggy Noonan wrote in the *Wall Street Journal* words that I thought went to the heart of the optimism I feel: "The hidden gift of this pandemic is that this isn't the most terrible one, the next one or some other one down the road is. This is the one where we learn how to handle that coming pandemic."

The next time could be worse. In fact, it could be much worse—a viral stain more deadly and transmissible than anything the world has ever seen. Now is the time to prepare for that. At the ground level, the doctors, nurses, and other team members are ready. The question is whether the nation's leaders will fund research, encourage manufacturing of essential equipment within our shores, and pursue other steps that will give Americans the optimism and confidence that next time, we will be ready for whatever comes at us.

PREFACE

Voices in the Night

As a boy growing up in the tiny village of Knockaderry in the southwest of Ireland, I vividly recall the stormy sounds of the night. Lying in bed, I would hear the howling wind and lashing rain; protected within our house, I would feel safe and comforted. I loved the sounds of the frequent storms that swept over our village, but the nighttime sounds I loved best were the voices of the adults coming from the main room of our house, near where my brothers and I slept.

My mother and father and their friends would huddle around the open fireplace, the only source of heat in our house, and they would talk of wondrous things—tales of brave Irishmen who had fought against the English so long ago, heroic figures who risked their lives, and often gave their lives, in the cause of Irish freedom. There were stories as well of families who had been lost during the famine more than a century earlier, and stories of others who had fled the country for a new life in America. There was whispered talk about neighbors in the village—troubles in a marriage, wayward children, a notable instance of drunkenness. There were even, on rare occasions, veiled criticisms of the parish priest, scandalous talk that would never go beyond the walls of our home. Sometimes there would be a word or two of derision aimed at Mr. Burke, the notorious taskmaster in the primary school. This I loved to hear!

The best stories were long and meandering, told slowly by practiced storytellers. There would be a story about Patrick Moylan, an Irish hero, who faced off against the British, standing his ground until he was finally captured and hung from the branch of a tree I passed each day on my route to school. To me, such stories were thrilling. I listened to the clinking of teacups and could picture my mother serving tea to friends, her manner always cheerful and welcoming. I could tell who the people were by their voices, all familiar to me. These men and women were patient in sharing their stories, their musical laughter expressing the joy of being together, protected from the storm, comforted by friends.

In school we learned about the ancient Irish tradition—thousands of years old—of the *seanchaí* (pronounced *shana-keeah*—traditional spelling *scéalaí*), the storyteller, who would pass along Irish history and folklore. The *seanchaí*, with their ability to recall and skillfully retell stories conveyed through the ages, were the keepers of our history. Legend had it that the great majority of stories were passed along at night, after the cows had been milked, the horses fed, the peat stacked, the fields harvested. It seemed that the falling darkness brought on a slower rhythm more attuned to the unhurried sharing of time with friends. The storyteller didn't need much—just an attentive audience, a warm fireplace, and a few mugs of tea.

The *seanchaí*'s ability to recall details of historical facts, fictional stories, and folk tales helped inspire a rich literary tradition in Ireland. While storytellers in rural villages shared what they knew with townspeople, the literary lions of Ireland brought storytelling disciplines including plays, poetry, short stories, and novels to life in ways that achieved nothing less than high art. In my village school, we learned that the writings of James Joyce, Samuel Beckett, Brendan Behan, William Butler Yeats, and others were viewed with reverence throughout the world of literature. One of the strengths of Irish education is its focus on great works of poetry, with a particular emphasis on the genius of Yeats. I was mesmerized by his poem "The Second Coming," in which he writes the famous opening lines:

> Turning and turning in the widening gyre
> The falcon cannot hear the falconer;
> Things fall apart; the center cannot hold;
> Mere anarchy is loosed upon the world . . .

I loved learning about Irish playwrights, poets, and novelists, but—and I mean no disrespect here to Joyce, Yeats, and the others—I confess that the nighttime stories I heard as a child thrilled me most. From countless nights of listening to the adults, I learned about the rhythm and tempo of storytelling, but mostly about the joy of conveying a human story about characters who, as a listener, you came to care about and feel somehow connected to.

So Irish stories come not just from the literary greats. Ireland spreads its storytelling tradition generously throughout the populace so that all of us who were born and grew up in Ireland have some small claim to the *seanchaí* tradition. With this memoir, it is my hope to follow in the centuries-long line of countless Irish men and women who have shared their stories around fires and living rooms and thereby contributed in some small way to a record of life in this magical land.

My story starts in rural Ireland in the 1950s, a time when most of the country was stuck in an agrarian world more akin to the 1800s. I am tempted to say that it is my story, and that is true as far as it goes, but it is more than that. It is also a family story, about my parents and siblings—my brothers Joe, Sean, and Patrick, and our sister Mary. It is the story of Ireland at a particular time, before the full force of modernity arrived. It is a story of agrarian Ireland, of deeply and strictly Catholic Ireland, of Ireland under an informal—but no less strict for its informality—caste system. And I suppose that, ultimately, while it is surely an Irish story, it is also an American story about a boy who dreamed of opportunities that were said to exist across the ocean in America, most particularly in New York. It is also very much an immigrant's story: the story of coming to America with nothing but my mind and a determination to work and study; a tale of how this nation welcomed me, as it has so many other immigrants through the years; and how that immigration has made America, in so many ways, what it is today.

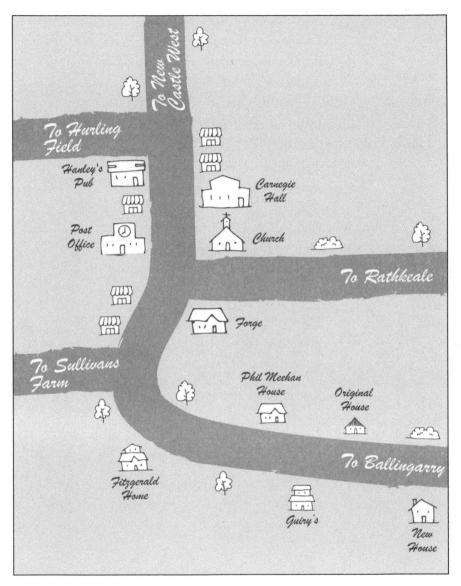

Knockaderry, County Limerick

Chapter One

The Village of Knockaderry

"A lone figure waving his cane in the air."

MY VILLAGE OF KNOCKADERRY, IRELAND, was a place that time forgot, an agrarian community with donkey carts and horse-drawn plows. That was true of much of rural Ireland in the 1950s and '60s, bypassed by the postwar economic boom reshaping the rest of the world. In 1968, Knockaderry had been my home for all of my eighteen years, and though my feelings were sometimes mixed, I nonetheless held a deep fondness for its beauty and its people. In May of that year, I prepared to travel what seemed to me an unfathomable distance—across the Atlantic to New York. I had just finished my first year at University College Cork. I had paid for that year by working a summer in England and in construction during the school year, but in order to continue my education, I would need more money than I could make in Ireland. I planned to work in New York City for the summer before returning to school in the fall.

As I contemplated leaving, I knew I would miss this place. I would miss the sheer beauty of the landscape. The southwest of Ireland is a land so verdant it seems the product of an Impressionist's brush—rolling hills, endless shades of green, cows grazing in the pastures, views over steeples and farms and meandering rivers for miles and miles.

Beyond our house, up a steep hill through a pasture marked with prickly furze bushes, their yellow flowers dazzling in season, was a summit from which you could see forever. To the northeast, with farmhouses dotting the landscape, was Limerick City, twenty-five miles distant. Beyond Limerick City, to the northwest, the valley gave way to the Shannon estuary, running from the Atlantic Ocean on the west coast of Ireland all the way to the split between Limerick and County Clare. From atop the hill we could see Foynes Harbor, one of the country's largest ports. Turning a bit eastward, we could see the peaks of the Galtee Mountains, which as children we were told were enchanted. In the fore distance we could see Knockfierna, "the hill of truth," where the village of Ballingarry lay, a revered place where a group of Irish men and women, having survived the famine of the 1840s, built a small settlement that has been preserved and can be seen today. The deprivation was nearly unimaginable. We could see castles—Belleek and Dromore—as well as ruins of ancient structures from thousands of years ago. Looking to the south, we could see part of County Cork.

Growing up, we would climb to the top of the hill and gaze off into the distance, wondering about these places we had heard about but never visited. The idea of traveling as far as the Shannon estuary, for example, seemed fantastical, even though it was only nineteen miles away. But now I was contemplating, and in fact planning, a trip of nearly three thousand miles across the ocean.

In the days prior to my departure, as I made the short walk from our home to the village center, I took note of the people and places. The village itself hadn't changed in my lifetime, or for several lifetimes, in fact. Along the main road was Saint Munchin's Church (virtually everyone in town was Catholic), a private home across from the church that served as a post office, a small community center next to the church, and Hanley's Pub. Sean Hanley, the pub's owner, was a friendly, though somewhat distant, man who was mad for the sport of Irish hurling. Mr. Hanley lived adjacent to the pub with his sister Peg, who managed a small grocery store attached to the pub. Down the road from the pub was the blacksmith's shop with its raging furnace and the sound of Mike Guiry hammering away on an anvil repairing farm equipment or shoeing horses. As a boy, I would stand in the doorway, gazing through the smoke, marveling at Mike's ability to mold steel into various forms using heat and muscle. The blacksmith's trade when I was growing up was, like Knockaderry itself, much as it had been a century earlier. Behind the pub and down a long pathway was the land dearest to me—the pitch upon which I had played countless games of Irish hurling. I would miss the pitch more than just about anything else.

One thing I would not miss was the house I had grown up in until the age of twelve. My parents, siblings, and I had lived in a thatched-roof cottage made of mud and stone that had hardened through the years to look and feel like cement. There was an art form to constructing thatched roofs, and a skilled thatcher would make it look beautiful from the outside. Inside, a lining of canvas bags, nailed to the rafters and painted white, kept dirt and debris from falling into the room. Our house consisted of three small rooms, all with mud floors—the main room with a fireplace (about twelve by fifteen feet), one bedroom for my parents and baby sister and brother (about eight by ten feet), and another for me and two of my brothers (about five by eight). My brothers Joe, Sean, and I slept in the same bed, and if you rolled over at night and touched the wall, you would get wet from the ever-present moisture seeping through.

While I would not miss the old house, I would greatly miss my brothers and sister. I was the eldest, and we were all separated by three years, with Joe coming after me, then Sean, then Mary, and finally Patrick. When Mary and Pat were born, I was old enough to be able to help our mother—whom all of my siblings and I called *Mam*—with them. I would sometimes push them in a carriage along the village road or I would mind them while Mam went to church or did chores around the house. It was a tight squeeze in the house with five children, but we managed. The living room contained an open-hearth fireplace seven feet wide and so high that you could stand inside and look up the chimney. It served as the home's sole heat source, as well as the place where Mam cooked our meals on pots and pans affixed to iron rods within the fireplace. Just to the left of the fireplace was a bellows, which we would hand-crank to blow air fueling the fire. To make toast, you would place a slice of bread on a fork and lay it on its side next to the fire. Near the house was a small shed where we stored potatoes and other vegetables, as well as turf and wood to be used in the fireplace.

Getting peat for the fire required traveling an hour from home in a borrowed donkey cart with my dad and entering a vast bog of peat, dense with water and difficult to cut. We used a special cutting tool called a *sleán*, basically a turf spade, to slice through the peat, shaping blocks a foot long by about four inches wide and stacking them in the bog to allow air to dry and harden them. We would then return about a week later to collect the dried bricks used to fuel our fire. We had no electricity, indoor plumbing, bathroom, or running water. We hiked up the hill a few hundred yards from our house and extracted water from a neighbor's well. For light in the evening, we relied upon candles and the glow of the fireplace. The only decorations in the house were a couple of religious pictures on the wall of the main room and curtains Mam had made for the home's three windows.

Over time, with frequent rainfall, the thatched roof absorbed moisture and grew too weighty for the support structure. When heavy rains persisted, water would often leak through the walls and we would have to sweep the water out the front door. One night when I was twelve, as my brothers and I slept, a storm settled upon the area and the roof gave way, sending the ceiling in our room crashing down upon Joe, Sean, and me. We woke covered in soaked canvas bags, straw, rafter boards, dust, and who knows what else from the rats that nested up there. There was no shower to hop into and rinse off. Outside, we doused ourselves with a bucket of water and returned inside, where we slept in the middle room near the fireplace. In the following days my brothers, my dad, and I were able to rebuild the section of the roof, and life went on as before.

Housing wasn't the only semi-primitive aspect of life. Growing up, there were no regular health appointments to speak of. If someone was very sick or seriously injured, they would be taken in a horse-drawn wagon or a donkey cart or, on rare occasions, driven in a borrowed car to a doctor in Newcastle West, a town five miles away. Visits to a dentist were rare as well, and were nothing but pure torture. I remember when my younger brother Joe was twelve or thirteen years old, he had a terrible toothache and was taken to the dentist, who feared infection and pulled all of Joe's teeth. I had several teeth extracted at a young age as well. Theoretically, this was done under local anesthesia, but the anesthesia was spotty and the pain of having a tooth yanked out from the roots was excruciating. I vividly recall the dentist calling out as he was about to perform some manner of torture on me: *"Hold on to the bottom of the chair, my boy!"* And a visit to the dentist did not mean coming home with a new toothbrush. In fact, we didn't have toothbrushes at all. We cleaned our teeth with a washcloth dipped in soap and water.

Despite the material deprivations, and possibly in some ways even as a result of them, it was a good life. Just behind our house we had a small garden and grew much of our own food, including lettuce, onions, carrots, parsnips, kale, potatoes, and turnips. Turnips were delicious. Heading out to the schoolhouse in the morning, we would pick a turnip, wash it off, take a pen knife, scrape the outer skin off, and eat it raw. We tilled the garden by hand with shovels, spades, and rakes. The lack of mechanization meant all of the work at home, as well as the work my brothers and I did on nearby farms, was by hand. Like most of the villagers, our means of transport was by foot or by bicycle. The benefit of all this was that we were physically fit and strong. Nobody in the village was overweight, and most of the young people with whom I played sports were extraordinary athletes.

As I took my farewell stroll around the village, already nostalgic, I knew I would miss much about Knockaderry, but the hardest part of going to America, by far, would be leaving my mother, Margaret (Meg) Dowling. As the oldest child, I had developed an extremely close bond with her. Mam was steady through the best and worst of times, upbeat through any and all struggles, even the darkest days in our house. She was one of those exceptional human beings who possessed an irrepressible optimism and always persevered. She was a tall, broad-shouldered woman—attractive and meticulous about her appearance—with dark hair and a warm smile. She was blessed with beautiful skin and never in her life used makeup. She was energetic, curious, and open-minded. Mam had grown up in the town of Glenroe in East Limerick, about thirty miles from Knockaderry, where her father worked a small farm. Her parents, Michael and Ellen Hayes, had ten children who survived, as well as two sets of twins who were stillborn. Born in 1920, my mother completed primary school and then attended secondary school (high school), which was unusual for a girl at the time. She completed two of the four years of secondary school and a first aid course as well, an achievement of which she was justifiably proud.

Her accomplishments were all the more amazing because my mother was deaf. She'd lost her hearing at the age of eleven and remained profoundly deaf for the rest of her life. What caused her loss of hearing, exactly, has long been something of a mystery within our family. For many years I believed that the cause was a tainted medication she was given when she was sick. There was also a story that a virus might have caused her hearing loss. But there was a third story passed down through the years about a schoolteacher—Miss Ray—administering a beating to her so savage it caused her to go deaf. It was 1933, when my mother and her sister Nora (who for some reason was called Dorella) were walking home from school and they passed a man who was burning bushes in his field. It is important to understand that there were still raw feelings in Ireland from the 1921 civil war, fought over a treaty with England that called for breaking off Northern Ireland as a British territory. Bitter feelings still roiled on both sides. Some were ardently in favor of the treaty, others adamantly opposed. Éamon De Valera had led the anti-treaty forces in 1921 and was thus revered by the anti-treaty side and despised by the treaty proponents. In the 1932 national election for prime minister, De Valera prevailed. My mother, being from a household supportive of De Valera, shouted out as she passed the man in the field: "*Up with Dev!*" The farmer found this expression objectionable and reported the incident to the school. Whoever ruled the school was clearly anti–De Valera, because the following day my mother was chastised and beaten—a beating which included blows to the side of her head. Irish families back then typically wholeheartedly supported just about whatever teachers said or did to their children, but this went too far. My mother's father was so enraged by the extent of the beating that he went to the school the next day, withdrew his daughters, and enrolled them in the Kilfinnane School a good distance away, where the teachers were nuns. Whatever the true cause—a beating, a virus, or bad medicine—my mother remained deaf for the rest of her life. But she learned to read lips and adapted to her condition with remarkable equanimity and never complained about her fate.

In fact, Mam was lucky to be alive. One winter day, when she and Dorella were at school in Kilfinnane, a sudden blizzard overtook the area. The nuns decided to let the girls go home early. Most of the girls lived nearby the school, but Mam and Aunt Dorella had a five-mile walk home. They trudged through the blizzard, but about a mile outside Kilfinnane, the drifting snow became too much for them. At Stony Corner, up in the rugged hills of the town, they took cover beneath a rocky outcropping. Shivering, covered in snow, they waited. Our grandfather knew they would be in trouble and he set off with a pony and cart to bring them home. He walked for miles in terrible conditions, calling out their names. Eventually, Dorella heard her father. They had fallen asleep and surely, without my grandfather's intervention, they would have perished there in the snow. He placed the girls under wet blankets on the pony cart and trudged back, leading the pony through the snow until they arrived safely home.

In the late 1930s, my mother entered the Convent of the Sisters of Mercy in St. Albans, London, with the goal of becoming a nun. She was influenced, no doubt, by the Sisters of St. Paul the Apostle, who had taught her in school, but she was also following the path of her two older sisters, who had become nuns. Patricia, my mother's oldest sister, had joined the Good Shepherd Order. Known as Sister Mary Lelia, she served for many years in the Philippines, especially during World War II. My mother's sister Lucy was also a fully professed Good Shepherd nun and worked in Bangalore, India for a time. Lucy left the Order in her early thirties, returned home, married in 1941, and had nine children.

It has to be said that having three nuns in the family was not unusual in Glenroe in the 1930s. Another girl from Glenroe, Maura O'Brien (later Sister Mary Francesca) also joined the convent with my mother. Sister Mary Francesca lived out her life as a Sister of Mercy, but my mother's career as a nun was short-lived. At the convent in London she became unwell at one point and her brothers, Jim and John, who were already working in London at the time, visited and found her sick, undernourished, and miserable. They wasted no time in spiriting her out of the convent and back to home in Ireland. Soon thereafter she met my father, who was then working as a stone crusher in a local quarry. They married, and I was born a year later, November 18, 1949, in my maternal grandmother's house in Glenroe, brought into the world by a local midwife. There were complications of some kind with the birth and my mother was fortunate to survive.

Mam was tireless in body and spirit, working every day to keep the family happy and together. That did not always prove easy, and there were heartbreaking times that remain seared in my memory a half-century later. If it is true that *blessed are the peacemakers for*

they shall be called children of God, then there was no doubt that
Mam was God's child. She was selfless—a good and generous
friend to everybody in the village. She helped her closest friend
Philomena (Phil) Meehan, who had lost both her legs in a horrifying accident as a young girl when her father, cutting a hay field,
did not know Phil was hiding in the grass. Mam was a gifted
seamstress who struggled to make ends meet, to find the material
needed to make our clothing. She struggled with my father, a
proud but difficult man, whose hair-trigger temper frightened us
all. As I grew up, two of my strongest motivations were to excel
in school and at athletics, but what motivated me more than anything, I think, was to try and bring joy and peace to my mother's
life; to never be a source of trouble or sorrow.

Although deaf, she had little difficulty communicating. She was
an expert lip reader, and in the living room of our home you could
get her attention by tapping your foot on the floor and she would
feel the vibration and turn in your direction. She played cards and
bingo, visited with friends, and, of course, took care of our family.
She was a devout Catholic and attended Mass several times a week.
She seemed to believe that any adversity—deafness, poverty, trouble in the home—was something that a person of faith would deal
with and move on. Mam and I shared a love of learning, and she
somehow obtained a regular supply of books for me to read, ranging from Zane Grey's tales of the American West to Shakespeare's
plays and Churchill's speeches. She was an avid reader and particularly enjoyed the work of Maeve Binchy, Tom Wolfe, Robert
Ludlum, Jeffrey Archer, Dick Francis, Vikram Seth, and an Irish
author named Canon Sheehan, whose novel *Glenanaar* was her
favorite. Mam loved this novel, loved the writing and the characters, and particularly enjoyed the section of the book that mentions

a famous hurling match pitting Glenroe, where she had grown up, against Ardpatrick.

Through her example, I learned the power of optimism and kindness. With Mam, the dwindling cup was always more than half full. *The world is a good place. People are good.* She made clear to me that I had potential to go beyond Knockaderry. She encouraged me and, most importantly, she believed in me and my potential. She wouldn't lecture. Her encouragement would come in the normal course of the day, as she was in the garden picking vegetables for supper or gathering red and black currants from nearby bushes, which she made into jam. She might smile at me and utter a few words of encouragement as she worked by the fireplace preparing a meal. She not only encouraged me with her words, but, really, with her entire approach to life.

In 1968, as I prepared to travel to New York for the first time, I was leaving a village where I knew everyone and everyone knew me, where most people helped one another with a selfless sense of community. It was in the community DNA. If rain was coming—it seemed rain was *always* coming—and you saw the Guiry family in their fields, you would automatically drop what you were doing and go out and help. No one needed to be asked. Everybody knew and helped one another—especially during harvest time, when people would show up at whatever farm most needed extra hands at that moment. As the author Niall O'Dowd notes in his book *A New Ireland*, this was consistent with "the old Gaelic tradition of a co-operative labor system where people in rural communities gathered together to help one another." There were plenty of helpers in the village—families ranged from having five children, like ours, to some having more than a dozen. The Gormans, for example, had fourteen children crammed into a house no larger than ours, and they were hardly alone. Older children looked after the younger ones. Helping a neighbor till a field, fix a barn, milk cows, or spread cow manure (which produced the greenest fields you've ever seen) did not result, most of the time, in any direct payment of money. The community ran on an informal barter system whereby anyone doing something for someone else could later call on that person for assistance—to borrow a horse or donkey cart, for example.

My father believed there were many benefits to working, beyond money: helping your neighbor, being outdoors, getting stronger and more physically fit. But more than that, Dad believed that, as some of the poorest people in the village, we had an obligation to help those who happened to be relatively well off. If anyone ever gave me money for helping them, my father would make me return it.

In addition to the barter system, there were other oddities about rural Irish life: an abundance of trust and an utter lack of privacy. On a regular basis, while our family was in bed asleep, visitors would drop by our house—the door was never locked—and make themselves a cup of tea or have a piece of bread. Perhaps these were people who had left the pub but had a several-mile walk home ahead of them. They would think nothing of stopping in at our house or another neighbor's for a bit of refreshment and a relaxing few moments in front of the fireplace. I remember many mornings when Mam would come into the kitchen area and say, "I wonder who was here last night?" She would ponder it, notice that the brown bread was half-eaten, and say: "It was probably Paddy. He likes the brown bread. Yes, it was probably Paddy." (Americans who value their privacy, particularly in the bathroom, will be surprised to learn that in our home you went to the bathroom in a chamber pot in the house—whether you were alone or not. Or you went outside—not in an outhouse—we didn't have one.)

While there was little formal entertainment in the village, Knockaderry was a very social community, where people frequently gathered in the evening to talk and share stories. Traditional Irish dancing was common at the village crossroads near our house, where musicians with accordions, fiddles, and tambourines would entertain late into the evening. The night—without any exterior lighting at all—would turn pitch black, and you could still hear the music but not see the musicians.

Other than sporting events, some of the most important social gatherings were wakes and funerals. Wakes were held in the home of the deceased with family, friends, and villagers gathered together for drinks to talk about how wonderful the dearly departed was (even when they might have thought otherwise). Whiskey was developed in Ireland eighty years before the Scots did it. Its name comes from the Gaelic word *uisce beatha* [pronounced *ishka baha*] meaning *water of life*. But because the pronunciation of *uisce beatha* was so difficult, the word in everyday language became *whiskey*. And at Irish wakes, which went on for days, these waters of life did, in fact, flow like water.

When we were growing up, we were taught that prolonged wakes had an important practical application beyond the drinkers having one free round after another. It was said that back in the seventeenth and eighteenth centuries, people in Ireland would commonly drink a powerful elixir called poitin. This was a home brew that packed a wallop so potent that it was said that some people would get drunk and fall into a coma-like condition for several days. These victims of the drink in some cases lacked a detectable pulse and thus appeared for all practical purposes to be deceased. As kids, we were told the terrifying story that there had been cases where graves were exhumed, only to find that there had been evidence of furious scratching of the casket from within. We were led to believe that people who had consumed poitin and shown no detectable sign of life had actually been buried alive. The story was that the fear of premature burial was so pervasive that at a certain period of time people were buried with a string running from within the casket, up through the ground, attached to a bell above the earth. Thus, the derivation of the term "saved by the bell" for those who, upon waking within the casket, could send a signal that they should be rescued at once. (Whether anyone was spending time around graveyards awaiting the ringing of a bell seems dubious.) The result of this primal fear of premature burial was the days-long wake during which time it was thought that if the person were in a state of hibernation, he or she would have an opportunity to awaken. And if, after several days, it was clear there were no signs of life, the person could then safely be buried with mourners traveling a mile in procession to the graveyard.

While wakes were major social and religious events, so too was Christmas. Midnight Mass on Christmas Eve brought the entire village together, and on the day after Christmas, known as St. Stephen's Day, musicians from the area would visit homes and perform traditional Irish songs. These gatherings—known as the Wren—might include anywhere from three to ten musicians of varying abilities going from house to house throughout the evening. The singers and musicians would wear old clothing and in some cases paint their faces. These talented people were immensely popular and warmly welcomed as they went from house to house entertaining one family after another. Mythology held that the wren connected the world to the afterlife, and the wren, it was said, had betrayed the first Irish Christian, St. Stephen.

Anticipating the arrival of the musicians created a good deal of excitement in the village. As a child at home, I would listen intently in the hopes of hearing the musicians, many highly skilled, playing as they wandered through the village. I would hear their music gradually growing louder as they approached, and then there they were, in our home, playing their violins, flutes, tambourines, and more with a great sense of joy. We would give them food and drinks, and even some money as well, if we had it.

Another oddity about our life was that we didn't own our house. We rented it from Mr. Sullivan, an older farmer who lived a hundred yards from us with his sister, Mariah. My brother Joe recalls that the weekly rent was half a crown—two shillings and six pence. While the vast majority of people in the village were quite social, there were a few—Dinny and Mariah Sullivan included—who were hermit-like. I don't recall either one of them ever speaking to me. In fact, I never witnessed either one of them speaking to anyone.

Starting around age ten, I worked on neighbors' farms, especially in summer and on school vacation, as well as before and after school. I enjoyed the chilly mornings when I was in the pastures with the dogs to round up the cows. I loved looking out over the landscape and seeing the stalks of corn, the expanses of earth where potatoes were planted, and the hay as it grew tall through the warm weather. In the chilly air, the dew looked white, and I would run through the grass, glancing back at the tracks my feet made. In the early morning—typically around 5:30 or 6:00 a.m.—the farms were alive with the sights, sounds, and smells of animals: cows, horses, hens, goats, dogs.

I was taught how to milk a cow when I was eight or nine years old. The trick was to get in very close to the cow, almost underneath it, as a way to protect yourself from kicking or a swishing tail. Early on I learned that different cows had distinct personalities. Some were quite docile and would stand still for the time it took to milk them. Others, particularly the young ones, were a challenge. The first thing you learned to do when milking was to "spancel the cow"—that is, tie the cow's hind legs in a looping rope (known as a spancel) so that you would not be kicked in the face or head. Then you would tuck the cow's tail—this was very important—into one of the loops around the leg. You wouldn't think there was much of a threat from a cow's tail, but a tail dense with dried cow dung could be sharp as a knife edge. There were stories in our village of farmers hit with a cow's whipping tail and sustaining serious damage to an eye.

Once all the cows had been milked by hand, usually by about eight in the morning, the farmers would pour the milk into tankards, then haul it in a tractor or donkey cart to the village creamery about two miles away. With a dozen or so farmers convening at the creamery around the same time each morning, there would be good-natured banter among the men. As a boy on non-school days, I really enjoyed that time of the morning with all the men gathered around. Someone would call out to a neighbor, "Hey, you old fat bastard," which meant *you're a good guy.* Several farmers on the way home would stop at Hanley's Pub for a quick one or, in some cases, for half the day. You always knew who was inside Hanley's by identifying whose donkey was outside.

Typically, farmers and their helpers would head back home after the creamery and have breakfast—tea and Irish soda bread—at around 9:00 a.m. After breakfast I would often head back out into the pasture to spread piles of cow dung on the farm, working with a hand fork. There might be as many as fifty piles of manure dotting the field, all delivered by donkey or horse cart, and I would have a competition with myself as to how quickly I could to spread it. This was hard work, but I enjoyed it. I felt comfortable with the physical nature of it and felt from an early age that it would help make me stronger and fitter for sports, especially for hurling, the sport that became so central to my life.

On a typical weekend in Knockaderry, Saturday morning was for work on the farms, of course, but on Saturday evening the whole village would begin preparations for Mass on Sunday morning. No one I knew had a shower. Without indoor plumbing, there wasn't even an indoor bathtub. On Saturday nights, we would take turns going outside to a freezing cold tub of water, stripping down, dumping a bucket of cold water over our heads, and scrubbing off a week's worth of dirt and grime. Even though we would be in the cool or even cold evening air, we would scrub and scrub until we were perfectly clean. This was doubly important for me to do because I served Mass as an altar boy.

Sunday morning, after helping neighbors milk cows and do other chores, we would change out of our Wellington boots—essential protection against incessant rain, muddy fields, and cow dung—and dress up in our finest clothes, a mix of hand-me-downs from other village families as well as clothing Mam skillfully tailored on her Singer sewing machine to fit each one of us. Mam believed poverty should not prevent us from being clean and well groomed. More affluent townspeople wore sports coats, trousers, shirts, and dresses purchased from stores in Limerick or Newcastle West. Going to Mass in your best clothing was all-important. Every Sunday morning we went off to Mass as a family looking and feeling very good indeed in expertly tailored clothing—short pants for children, white shirt, and polished shoes. People in the village would often say that Mam had a gifted pair of hands, and she used them for the benefit of others, making clothes for people in the community, including the cassocks and surplices worn by the altar boys. Mam was not only a skilled and highly respected seamstress, she was also considered one of the warmest and most caring people in the village.

On Sunday mornings, most people in the village walked to church or rode bikes, but a few of the more affluent would ride in a horse-drawn trap, a simple type of carriage. Families would walk together with the father leading the way, followed by the mother and children walking behind. Couples rarely walked side by side. If a husband and wife did walk together, they would never hold hands. Growing up, I never saw couples holding hands. If it was raining on Sunday morning, which it often was, we would simply get wet. Most women wore scarves on their heads, tied under the chin, and while a few women used umbrellas, men never did. It was considered unmanly. In church, the ritual was the same each week, with women and children sitting in the front section, while the men sat or stood at the rear. Attendance at Mass on Sunday morning was all but mandatory, with any absences noted and questions asked: "I wonder where Mary Meehan was today?" "Is she sick? Is there a family problem?" The ladies would soon get to the bottom of where, in fact, Mary Meehan had been that morning.

The attitude toward women was complicated. Women like Mam were really the glue that held the household together. Women worked on farms, milked cows, tilled the fields, washed laundry by hand, tended the kitchen fire, cooked all meals, made and repaired clothing. Women were the strength and backbone of the community. And yet, the men were clearly in charge.

Once the church ceremony was over, the women went home to prepare dinner, the midday meal, while the evening meal was supper. Many of the men went to the pub to continue the discussions they had begun during Mass at the rear of the church—mostly about farming or sports.

Sunday afternoon there was often a hurling match on the pitch in the center of our village, a short distance from the pub, or in nearby towns and villages. We all played Irish football and other sports, but when I was growing up, hurling was the dominant sport in Ireland, and to me it was everything. My dad, who had been an accomplished hurler in his own right, put a hurling stick—known as a *hurley*—in my hands when I was a toddler. I started playing with other boys in the village at age four. I played on teams from the age of six and continued at an elite level up through college. It is a game of controlled mayhem, played at hyper-speed, requiring skill and toughness, and I loved the intensity of the often violent games and enjoyed competing alongside my friends and teammates. If there was a hurling match Sunday afternoon, virtually the entire village would turn out. Sometimes on Sunday we would hike up the hill behind our house and spend a few moments looking off into the distance—at the Galtee Mountains or the Shannon estuary. And then we would slide down the steepest part of the hill, a rock face that allowed for a fun ride down. We would each find a flat rock to sit on, then position ourselves at the top of the slope, lift our legs in the air, and push off for a wild ride down.

When there was no hurling match, one of the most popular Sunday afternoon activities was fox hunting. Most families had beagles, and on a Sunday afternoon, there might be sixty or seventy people with thirty to thirty-five dogs. Most farmers in the village had draft horses, but these were not suitable for fox hunting.

Instead we hunted on foot. The beagles would be released, find a fox (sometimes a hare), and the chase was on. We learned at a young age that a fox is clever enough to elude capture the great majority of the time. These hunts would go on for many hours as the fox ran through streams, circling back, confusing the hounds. It was not uncommon for us to chase the fox for eight or ten miles, until the fox either was trapped by the dogs (rarely) or succeeded in escaping (nearly all the time). By early Sunday evening you could find yourselves many miles from home and the return trek would begin. One time, I was fortunate to race ahead and arrive just as the dogs captured and killed the fox. I took the pelt and made good use out of it. After skinning the fox, I made a Davy Crockett–style hat out of the fur with the fox tail attached and would wear it to school during the winter months.

Growing up I had, of course, heard many stories about America, but travel anywhere by people in Knockaderry was relatively rare. Since few people owned cars, a distance of even ten or twenty miles was significant. A trip from Knockaderry into the city of Limerick was something our family rarely did, even though it was only about twenty-five miles away. News of the outside world was not easy to get unless you owned a radio. I had read about America and heard stories from people in Knockaderry about relatives who had made the trip—including some of my father's siblings who had gone to America, though we had little contact with them. We benefited from the fact that a lot of Americans and their relatives would visit the village ("the Yanks are coming" was a common expression), and you would hear about life in the states, especially New York (where *the streets are paved with gold!*). The way people talked about it, there was no doubt that life was far more advanced there than in Ireland.

We would hear stories about America and how some people there had a swimming pool at their house. I had never seen a swimming pool and could not imagine that someone could have one at their home. It seemed like a fairy tale.

At the time I didn't understand the reasons for the great disparity between Ireland and the US. Later, as I became more educated, I came to understand the complex forces that left Ireland as an economic backwater for so long. Like so much of what had happened in Irish history, the poverty of the mid-twentieth century could be traced back to conflict with England that had gone on for the better part of seven hundred years. Still fresh in the Irish collective memory was the famine of the 1840s, when Britain did little to help starving people and a million Irish men, women, and children died of hunger and another million emigrated, most leaving for America.

After centuries under the English thumb, leading Irish men and women had had enough and resorted to armed insurgency. Numerous prominent Irish leaders banded together during Easter Week in 1916 and mounted an armed assault on important government buildings in Dublin. Irishmen had pushed back against British rule many times through the years, but this battle was different. British troops attacked, and fierce firefights broke out between the rebels and the English throughout the city. Nearly five hundred people, including many civilians, were killed during the fighting, while more than two thousand were wounded. Fourteen of the fifteen leaders of the uprising were executed by the British. The Anglo-Irish War that broke out in 1919 lasted until 1921 and led to the declaration of independence from Britain. This included twenty-six of the thirty-two counties in Ireland; six counties in the north remained within the United Kingdom. Almost immediately upon gaining independence, Ireland became embroiled in a bitter tariff war with England, which meant that Irish agricultural products could not profitably be exported to Britain. Since Ireland was an overwhelmingly agrarian economy, this created widespread hardship. Things were so bad that between 1945 and 1960, a half-million Irish men and women—out of a population of just over three million—emigrated in search of work elsewhere. Niall O'Dowd has written that in the 1940s a tariff war did great harm to Ireland, "a dirt-poor country almost totally reliant on Britain for exports." O'Dowd observes that in the aftermath of the tariff war, "500,000 emigrated from a country of only 3.5 million," with the result that "Ireland was stripped clean of its greatest asset, its young people."

Our family and our village found itself in the crosshairs of history, living at the bottom of the socioeconomic ladder. The sense of superiority among the English—their arrogance and condescension toward the Irish, looking down on them as ignorant peasants—made for deep resentment.

There was no doubt that Ireland was a kind of father country to America in the sense that many Irish men and women had traveled to America to make a better life. As a boy, I became fixated on the notion that America was a place where, if you were willing to work, you could make real money. More than that—much more important to me, in fact—was the idea that in New York you could become successful, could make something of yourself in a way far more valuable than money. I saw the confidence and prosperity of the people who came from the states to visit our village—saw it in the clothes they wore, in the rental cars they drove, in the very fact that they could afford a two-week vacation to the old country. But they also possessed something more—an air of accomplishment, as though they were doing good and meaningful things with their lives. From an early age I got the idea that something must be great on the other side of the ocean; that if you wanted to get ahead, you had to go to America.

At the age of eighteen, about to leave Ireland, I did not have anything concrete lined up in the US, neither a job nor a place to stay. I had relatives in the states—second and third cousins mostly—but I had no direct relationship with them. A few days before I was due to depart, I competed in a hurling match and took a stick across the face and my forehead opened up, blood everywhere. I got stitched up and looked like hell, but I was ready to go.

I had come to believe that as the oldest in the family I had an obligation to make sure that I could make the family a little bit better off. On one level, I thought that the best way I could do so would be to stay in Knockaderry and help Mam, but I needed tuition money, and from what I could tell about America, it seemed possible to make enough to return to university and then some extra to send home. Whenever I thought about the difficulty of leaving, my resolve was strengthened by what I had come to see as the unfortunate reality of life in Ireland. In Knockaderry, there were many good people, but there was little motivation or opportunity to improve life. There were many cases where a thirty-year-old son would take over a farm from his sixty-year-old father and continue on the identical path his father had lived. There was the farm and the pub, which I had come to consider a kind of black hole. In 1968, my plan was to work in America for the summer and try and figure some things out. I knew—and I think I had known for some years—that I could not stay in Ireland, not over the long term. My dad, who wanted me to become a policeman, would always say "there's a pension" for policemen—a pension was gold. But I was eighteen years old and a pension wasn't my idea of success. I wanted to explore, to see what was out there, what was possible in life.

On the day I left Knockaderry, Mam and I spoke quietly. She reminded me to write regularly and to be careful; to eat properly and take care of myself. She hated that I was leaving, absolutely hated it. I think she must have feared that I would never return. That happened in some cases—people leaving for the states for what was supposed to be a few months and then deciding not to come back. I did not know it at the time, but Mam had already lost one child—a baby who had not survived childbirth. I only learned of this from her many years later when, while I was visiting Ireland, Mam showed me the cemetery in which the baby was buried. Maybe with my leaving she feared losing another child, I don't know, but I knew I would return. I had to continue my education, for one thing. On the day I left Mam supplied me with a package of rations containing Irish sausage, Irish bacon, and homemade Irish soda bread. She was convinced I would need it in the US.

She hugged me in a fierce embrace. This was so difficult for her. I was her oldest child and the closest to her. While it was tough for me as well, it was also exciting to be exploring not only a new world, but a new way of life. My dad was not in the house when I departed, and I wondered where he was. Mam and I went outside and she said to me, "He's up there." I looked up on the hill several hundred yards away and saw a lone figure, my father, waving his cane in the air. I waved back and left for America.

Chapter Two

Hierarchy and Hurling

"Too bad someone like you could never go to college."

SOMETIMES, AT HOME IN KNOCKADERRY, my brother Joe and I would play a game with the rats that lived in the thatched roof of our house. Inside, I would hit the canvas bags on the ceiling at one end of the room with a hurley and send a rat skittering across the bags above us, while at the other end, Joe would bang the ceiling, sending the rat back toward my end. Joe and I would set traps for the rats that would descend into the kitchen at night, and we caught our fair share.

Rats and mice were unwelcome guests in the house, but there were other animals that were invited in. My father's mother Johanna lived down the road from us and I remember when she brought a massive pig into her kitchen so the sow could give birth under the kitchen table. It was important to make sure the newborns—called bonives—were kept safe given their future value in the market-place. Some pigs would have twenty or so offspring, and when a sow would have more bonives than nipples, the young ones would be bottle-fed. I remember sitting in my grandmother's kitchen cradling a baby pig while feeding it a bottle.

My family didn't have animals then, nor did we own land. My dad was a laborer for the local county council, working on county roads filling potholes, putting down blacktop, and improving the roadways. Before he was disabled with arthritis, he would pedal a bicycle to work each morning—about five miles each way—and then cycle home in the evening. My mother occasionally made a bit of money as a seamstress, and I added a small sum working one summer when I was fourteen or fifteen in Nash's mineral water bottling factory in Newcastle West, about five miles away (I walked or rode a bicycle to and from work). The plant made bottled juice and soda and my job was to work the conveyor belt, washing bottles. I liked to work, liked to make some money, and most of all liked contributing to the family. My brothers Sean and Joe would also get summer jobs to contribute to the family finances.

You would think that any and all work would produce income. You would also think that any and all income would be welcomed in the family, but neither of those suppositions were true. A tradition in the village was observed and enforced in our house by my father. One of the unwritten cultural rules was that as a family at the bottom of the social hierarchy, we were expected to work for the affluent farmers for no direct cash compensation. (I use the term "affluent"—they were, comparatively, but I realize looking back on it that although they had much more than we did—for example, they owned land, animals, and their own homes—they were nonetheless families of modest means.) Instead, an informal barter system was customary: We would milk the cows for the neighbor and, in return, we would get milk at no charge. One evening Joe and I went to a nearby farm, where we often worked, to pick up a supply of milk—the barter system in action. When we got there, however, the family dog viciously attacked Joe, biting into the skin on his shoulder. When the farmer got word of what had happened, he got his shotgun, came out, and shot the dog.

Another time, when I was thirteen or so, I was working at the nearby farm owned by Mr. Cantillon. I knew the Cantillon family well and often worked on their farm. Mr. Cantillon was not the friendliest person, although Mrs. Cantillon was quite nice, but even when I was young it was clear that they were at a different level of society. They had helpers working in their house, who I believe lived on the property, but they were not permitted to eat meals with the family. At the end of a particularly arduous day when I had spread dung in the fields, Mr. Cantillon rewarded me with six pennies. I was thrilled to report this at home, but my father ordered me to return the money. This made little sense to me. Here we were, clearly less advantaged than most of the other people in our village, and I couldn't accept six pennies? I was doing the most basic kinds of work—it doesn't get much more basic than shoveling and raking cow shit—yet I wasn't allowed to keep a few cents?

Sometimes my brother Joe and I would make a few pennies selling rabbits to neighbors. Up the hill a few hundred feet above our house was a good-sized sandpit, and there were many evenings when Joe and I would set traps there. These were rudimentary bits of looped wire attached to a ground stake that would capture a rabbit hopping through the sand pit. In the morning we would go up the hill to see whether we had had any success, and on good days we would have a rabbit to sell. Joe and I also sometimes gathered and sold wild mushrooms, which we would string together on what we called a *trelace*—a dozen plump mushrooms from the fields strung together in a neat pile.

I came to understand our lack of standing in the community in a variety of different ways, many quite subtle. At our house, my brothers Joe and Sean and I each had one set of nice clothes, sewn by my mother. There were families such as the Guirys and Cantillons who, rather than having their clothes made at home, were able to buy clothing in Limerick or Newcastle West. I heard a story about a young man in town who, I was told, spilled a drink on his shirt at the pub, most likely Guinness. He looked down at the stain and literally took his shirt off and threw it away. In other words, he had enough extra shirts that he wouldn't miss one of them. To me, this was crazy. Who would throw away a perfectly good shirt? Why would someone be so wasteful? I would be upset—though I wouldn't show it—when I saw families who had much more than we had take their good fortune for granted. But they weren't the only wasteful ones. I knew of families like ours, who were struggling financially, yet the father would go to the pub and spend money on alcohol or cigarettes or both. I didn't get it at all.

I noticed pretty early on a sense of underlying class tension in the community. On the one hand, people with a degree of affluence could be very generous to us. The Dillanes, for example, were one of the first Knockaderry families to own a television set. This was around 1963 or so, and it became the object of much fascination for all of us. (At the time, I thought television was a radio where you could see the people.) Every Thursday evening at 8:00 p.m., a number of us would be allowed to go to the Dillanes' to watch *The Virginian*. We would sit in the living room, fascinated by the program, even as we wondered whether the family was merely tolerating us or actually enjoying our presence. While it was something I looked forward to and enjoyed, at the same time, I was aware of a sense of condescension toward me and my family by others in the village, especially farmers, all of whom had much more than we did.

I admit that this air of superiority got under my skin. One day when I was about sixteen, I walked to the Sullivans' farm (another Sullivan family—not the Sullivan from whom we rented our house) to get milk, and Mr. Sullivan told me that his son was about to head off to college. He was excited about it and proud, of course, but he did not leave it at that. He said to me, "Isn't it too bad that someone like you could never go to college?" And he let the comment sit there, hanging in the air, as though the path of my life, a dreary path at that, had been predetermined. He wanted to make clear to me that his family was superior to ours; that his son was better than I was.

This was part of what my brother Sean would later describe as the "cacophony of no" that permeated our lives growing up. The idea that we were at the bottom of the social barrel and were destined to remain there throughout our lives was a powerful force in Knockaderry. It was all around us. The *noes* came from everywhere and the concept was reinforced by the authority figures in the village—teachers, priests, and other people in town who had higher standing on the socioeconomic scale. Sean said that the implicit message within the "cacophony of no" was a simple one aimed at people like us—*You are working class, at the bottom rung, and that is what you'll always be. It's a fact of life. You'll never be anything else.* I think that message echoed in my dad's head over many years and bothered him deeply.

That day when Mr. Sullivan bragged about his son and insulted me turned out to be a kind of fuel for me and for my ambitions. As I walked back home that day, I felt a powerful sense that Mr. Sullivan was wrong; that I really would be able to go to college. How? I did not know. But I instinctively believed it would be possible. I was fueled by anger not because I believed in his dark vision of my future, but because I did *not* believe in it.

Looking back on it, I believe it was one of the most important things anyone ever said to me. In a strange way, I owe some of my determination to Mr. Sullivan. I was instinctively convinced that I would be able to do something with my life other than repeat what my ancestors had done. I played by the Knockaderry rules and accepted the current reality that it was my obligation to serve the more affluent families, but I was also convinced that at some point I would not be constrained by those rules. I sensed the condescension; felt it even when it wasn't anywhere near as explicit as what Mr. Sullivan had said to me—and I used it as motivation.

The class structure was on display a couple of Sundays each year when British riders—known as Red Coats—appeared in the village for a fox hunt. They did not hunt on foot the way we did, but instead would arrive in a group of several dozen English men and women with wagons and magnificent horses ready to follow the hounds. It was such a spectacle that virtually the whole village turned out to see them, watching them prepare for the hunt, leading the horses out of wagons attached to trucks, and then saddling up. All at once the bugle would blow, the hounds would be released, and the horses would strain to gallop. The riders wore uniforms of resplendent red hunting coats, white trousers, and black riding boots polished to a high shine. They represented the upper crust of society, and in an odd way this evened out the class distinctions in our area, because compared with the Red Coats, everyone in town was poor.

These elites from the upper reaches of British society were a reminder of the centuries-long control of Ireland by Britain, and the way these English carried themselves conveyed an unmistakable air of superiority.

I wondered about these people, wondered where exactly they had come from and what kind of life could they possibly lead where they would have the wealth needed to own such horses and wear such clothing. What kind of homes did they have? How were they educated? Why did the women ride sidesaddle? Many people in the village despised the English, but nonetheless admired these visitors' horses and their glorious attire. You would hear some of the old men say, "Yeah, I hate the bastards, but seeing them in the village in all their regalia is enjoyable."

In school we were taught the history of English domination and the bitterness it engendered. Our primary school teacher, Mr. Burke, was violently anti-English, and that left its impression on all of us as we grew up. He was deeply nationalistic and devoted much of his life to learning and teaching Irish history and tradition, as well as Gaelic, the Irish language. When I was growing up, fluency in Gaelic was a prerequisite for employment by the government (in administrative roles). You were not taught to be anti-English, per se, but by learning Irish history, you naturally took on an anti-English attitude. Anyone studying that long, repressive, exploitative history could only conclude that the English had inflicted generations of suffering on the Irish.

The subject of British rule and cruelty was frequently discussed in Knockaderry. When adults gathered around our fireplace at night, I would often hear, from my bedroom, bitter denunciations of the English. But there was another side to the Irish–English relationship, and that was a fascination among many Irish people with the royal family. If there was something involving the royals in the newspapers, on the radio, or, in a rare case, when someone saw them on television, people in the village would eagerly be reading, listening, or watching the Queen, while at the same time expressing enmity for the royals. In a way it is the Irish personality: We hated the Red Coats, but people would say, "Let's go see them, they're nice-looking."

Hatred and the violence it generated had a history in Knockaderry, and not just Irish versus English. In the nineteenth century, feuds among various families in the village were not uncommon. A Knockaderry history recorded that the "village was the scene of many faction fights in the 1830s . . . fueled by alcohol. The major faction in the area was the Curtins who were joined on occasion by the Haughs and Mulcahys who fought the Connors, Longs, and Lenihans. Some of the factions could muster large numbers to appear for them. In September 1835, the Connors factions numbering three to four hundred strong paraded the main street of the village. The Curtins, who were few in number, withdrew."

The most tangible sign of our family's standing in the community was the thatched roof cottage we lived in. It was among the least appealing homes in the village, and it became clear as we grew up that my father wanted something better for the family. By the time I was twelve, there were five of us. The thatched roof house wasn't large enough, and over time it had grown unstable. In 1961, only months after the roof caved in, my parents found a new home a short walk from the old house. We moved into the new house, which was subsidized by the government, and my parents paid weekly rent to the county.

The *new house*, as we always called it, was great. It was constructed of concrete with three small bedrooms and a kitchen area with a range fueled by coal and wood. There were two doors, one front and one back (there had been only one door in the thatched-roof house). And there were half a dozen windows, twice the number in the old house. The new house also had an outhouse and electricity! I was fascinated by the idea that, my God, all you had to do was flip a switch and the lights came on. There was no indoor bathroom, no shower, and no sink. We had running water from a tap outside, and my mother would draw water from the tap, boil it, and use it for cooking, and she would use boiled water in a basin to wash dishes. I thought the new house was really grand—we all did—and I remember how happy it made my mother and father.

When the new house was under construction, I spent some time working with the Hickey Brothers crew that built it. We wound up moving in before the new house was fully ready. We were forced to leave the old house when a storm caused the entire roof to cave in on the rooms below, rendering the house unlivable. I went there the following morning with a local farmer in his donkey cart to retrieve some furniture, but there really wasn't much left to salvage. With the new house, our overall family status hadn't changed all that much, but we were living in a much improved setting, and the family income inched up slightly thanks to the gift of a cow from a generous neighbor. We sold milk at the creamery, and soon enough we had the money for a second cow and later a third. The problem was that we needed land for the cows and didn't have enough, so my mother went to a bank and borrowed the funds needed to purchase a parcel just down the road. The building on the property was the old schoolhouse where I had attended primary school, recently abandoned in favor of a new school nearby. My dad, brothers, and I tore it down and sold the pieces for scrap.

It took many years for my mother to make the weekly payments to the bank, but the new land enabled us to have not only three cows, but also chickens and hens, which allowed us to sell eggs. We also had a pig every year that we would fatten up and slaughter, selling parts to others in the village and keeping the bacon for our own meals. I remember killing pigs and making sausage with local farmers, then hanging the salted meat from the ceiling, careful to preserve the pig's tongue, which was my father's favorite dish.

At Christmas one year, the plan was to have a fresh turkey, which my brothers Joe and Sean were assigned to kill and pluck. Joe was going to do it, but Sean insisted he had a better method of dispatching the turkey. Sean grabbed the bird and snapped its neck and he and Joe plucked all the feathers and hung the turkey out back to dry off. No sooner had they done so, however, than the turkey jumped down from the line and began running away. Evidently, Sean's method wasn't quite as effective as he had led Joe to believe. They chased after the naked turkey, caught it, and finished the job.

Not all that far from the new house, along a main road out of Knockaderry, there was a vivid reminder that there were people in Ireland less well off than we were. On the side of the road for a period of time was an encampment of what were known in Ireland as travellers (also referred to as travelers or gypsies). These nomadic people roamed the countryside in colorful, horse-drawn wagons and set up camp at random locations along the way. The travellers were not particularly well liked by most people in Knockaderry. They camped outside, cooking over open fires, and the encampments, over a short period of time, would be covered with trash.

For the most part, travellers were insular and avoided mixing with the other residents of the community, although some worked for local farmers. It was said that the children of travellers were kept in the camps and not permitted by their parents to attend school. People in Knockaderry were generally wary of travellers fearing theft or violence. Travellers were known as excellent bareknuckle fighters, and as kids we were warned to stay well away from them, and we knew not to get into fights with them unless we had many of our friends nearby, for travellers always traveled in packs and were ready for a fight at any time. There were people in the village and beyond—Mam included—who had a more generous view of the travellers. Sometimes she would share some food with a traveller family and she warned that we should be careful not to judge.

You never knew exactly when the travellers would move on, but, invariably, the day would come when they would load up the wagons and depart for a new location, leaving the roadside area in Knockaderry a mess of discarded trash. People in the village were always happy to see them leave.

While there were hardships while I was growing up, there was much joy as well, and my greatest joy in life at a young age—along with pleasing my mother—came from hurling. Hurling was once described in the *Daily Mail* this way: "Several broken sticks, two broken heads, and two bruised fingers were part of the afternoon's play, for hurling, the Irish national game, is the fastest and probably the most dangerous of sports. It is a combination of hockey, football, golf, baseball, battle and sudden death. It [is] a real Irish game." The famous hurler and hurling coach Donal Óg Cusak wrote in his autobiography:

> I believe hurling is the best of us, one of the greatest and most beautiful expressions of what we can be. For me that is the perspective that death and loss cast on the game. If you could live again you would hurl more, because that is living. You'd pay less attention to the rows and the mortgage and the car and all the daily drudge. Hurling is our song and our verse, and when I walk in the graveyard in Cloyne and look at the familiar names on the headstones I know that [they] would want us to hurl with more joy and more exuberance and more . . . abandon than before, because

life is shorter than the second half of a tournament
game that starts at dusk.

Hurling may well be the fastest, most violent field sport played
anywhere on earth. A number of years ago, a sports reporter at
CNN put together a list of the sporting events every true fan
should aspire to see live in a lifetime. The Olympics came in
first. In second place was the Irish Senior National Hurling
Championship. Invented by the Celts before the birth of Christ, it
has endured as an essential part of Irish culture for three thousand
years. I started hurling in Knockaderry when I was six years old.
Everybody played and everybody tried out for the local teams, a
hundred or more kids going for fifteen spots on a team. You competed to move up to the next level every two years. There was an
under-ten team, then under-twelve, and so on up until the senior
league, which was eighteen and older. The team I played on—with
essentially the same roster through the years—won championships in 1962, '63, '64, and '67.

Hurling requires razor-sharp hand-eye coordination, speed,
dexterity, and fitness, as well as physical and mental toughness. It is
played on a rectangular field that looks like an American football
field but is much larger—140 to 160 yards long and 90 to 100 yards
wide. There are goal posts at either end, and you score a single point
by hitting the ball between the goal posts *over* the crossbar, whereas
a three-pointer is scored by hitting the ball past the goalie between
the posts *under* the crossbar. There are fifteen players on each team:
six forwards, two midfielders, six defensemen, and a goalkeeper.

Hurling is similar to lacrosse in that it is played with a hard
ball and a stick used to control and shoot the ball. A hurley, which
made for a great birthday present when I was a kid, is made of

a piece of flat, hard ash wood, ranging from three to four feet in length. Unlike lacrosse, there is no protective gear and no web in which to catch or cradle the ball. A player is allowed to hit the ball while it is on the ground or in the air. You may also catch the ball in your free hand as you are moving up the field, but then you must shift the ball to balance on your hurley. Each player has a particular feel for their hurley, much the same way that baseball players break in their gloves just exactly the way that best suits their needs. For a player, the hurley has to feel just right—the correct length and weight—so that it feels like an extension of your hand. Hurleys were generally made of ash wood and when two players came together and the hurleys collided, it was known in the game as the "clash of the ash." These collisions were often quite violent. Thus, players typically affixed a steel strap around the wide part of the hurley to prevent it from breaking.

Here is the challenge in hurling: Can you take the ball, balance it on the flat part of your stick, run down the field while the other team is hacking at you with their sticks—which often results in broken hands, fingers, arms, noses, cheekbones, and a fair amount of blood on your face—and still manage to get the ball over or, better yet, into the goal? Try running at top speed, controlling the ball on the flat of your stick while being assaulted from all sides, and then, on top of it all, learn to flick the ball up in the air and take your stick back, swinging it like a baseball hitter, and drive it on to the goal. Some games—hockey and lacrosse, for example—are rough. Hurling is violent, and when I was playing, no one wore a helmet or any other protective gear (there is a rule now requiring all players to wear a helmet with a face mask).

As a boy I carried my hurley with me everywhere, learning to balance the ball on the stick no matter how quickly I was running, no matter how much zigzagging I did as I ran. When I wasn't working on someone's farm or going to school, I was playing or practicing. Because it stays light very late in Irish summers, I could practice until 10:00 or 10:30 p.m. Our local team practiced several times a week after school when we would arrive at the pitch and change into our uniform shorts and shirt, bundling our school clothes and tucking them under a furze bush to prevent them from getting too wet if it rained. After practice—there were no showers or lockers— we would change back into school clothes and head home.

I practiced every day, whatever the weather. It was the one predictable, ever-present constant in my life. I did it because I loved it—loved everything about it. Learning how to pick the ball up off the ground while running at near top speed and then maintaining control of the ball on the flat stick required hundreds of hours of practice. Over time the hurley becomes part of your hand, an extension of your arm. I learned early on that you cannot play the sport if you are fearful that you may get hurt—you have to accept that you *will* get hurt. I had no problem with this. When you competed to make a starting role on a team, it was essential to accept the fact that you would get injured and to play with courage and determination because if you failed to do so, the coach would very quickly find someone to take your place who would do whatever it took to get on the field. A number of years ago researchers at University College Dublin studied teams representing various counties throughout Ireland and found that during the course of one season, 82 percent of all players were injured at least once. The injuries included bone fractures, concussions, muscle strains, and a number of injuries to players' eyes, including damage that resulted in partial blindness.

Knockaderry was a hurling-mad community. Being selected for the local team was an honor and playing well brought respect and admiration from everyone in town. In youth leagues, there were hurling matches at least a couple of times a week, including weekday evenings and Sunday afternoons, and our teams won many local and regional championships. Hurling was the great equalizer in Knockaderry. I was on the team with boys from more affluent families, but being teammates placed us on the same level. We were fifteen boys proud to wear the Knockaderry colors and we took care to look as sharp as possible in our uniforms. Your teammates were your club, your social group. For the big games on Sunday afternoons, the town would shut down—everybody would be there. I never wanted to be on the fringes watching the play, and was fortunate to play center field and center forward, key positions where I was in the middle of the action. I always wanted to be exactly where the most intense play was happening.

Our coach, Paddy Hennessey, a stout, red-faced individual, was fanatical about the game and never let us forget that Knockaderry had a rich legacy of hurling excellence that was our responsibility to uphold. He cut you no slack. He would be screaming, "What the hell is the matter with you?" It wasn't, "Well, you tried hard." No. It was, "You played like shit. You were actually terrible out there." We players were a little bit afraid of him, but he was a great coach. Two of his sons—Paddy and Jack—were on the teams with me from ages eight to eighteen, and they were great hurlers. Other talented teammates included Jim Begley, John Corkery, Sean Maloney, Paddy Lyons, and Moss Walsh. As teammates we had the sense that we belonged to something special; that we were engaged in something that, to the Irish people, verged on the sacred. When we went to games, we always presented ourselves in clean, well-cared-for uniforms—shorts and shirts and well-polished shoes. Before games, especially big tournament games, there was a palpable sense of tension and excitement. In the days before a big game, just about everyone in the village turned their conversation to our team. Winning was sweet, and after big victories there would be songs written about the game and the players who had participated. (One song, written when I played in the senior league, spoke of "Mike Dowling of the famed UCC"—University College Cork.)

I remember very clearly a famous game we played in 1967—Knockaderry versus Ballingarry for the West Championship. It was, as anyone who witnessed it will confirm, a particularly brutal contest. Both teams were outstanding that year and both sides were determined to do whatever it took to prevail. There were a few fist-fights on the field, as well as in the stands among fans who gave new meaning to the term rabid. At the other extreme were fans who would get so nervous during games that they would look away from the action. These fans would hear the cheering and ask some-one nearby—*Did we score!? Did we score?!* The Ballingary team were known for their toughness. The lads were a bunch of farmers' boys with snarls. You earned anything you got against them. The game went down to the wire, to the final minute, until we pulled it out.

Back in Knockaderry, the celebration ensued. These were the best of times in our village, when we won a major match, and everybody would gather in front of the pub for a big celebration with music and dancing. The farmers would assemble old truck tires, pile them up on a hill near the pub, and light a bonfire. Team members were paraded around on shoulders. Men would recall details of the game, specific plays, and it was just fabulous to be part of the elite group.

Being recognized as an important player on the team made my family quite proud. In Ireland, every mother hoped to have a son who would enter the priesthood, while every father's desire was for a son who was a great hurler. My father, along with my siblings, would come to the home matches in Knockaderry—the hurling pitch was a ten-minute walk from our home. But my mother rarely came, and she stopped coming altogether after one particularly brutal game where I got hit with a stick that split my forehead open. I was near the sideline, not far from where she was standing, and I dropped to one knee to gather myself. There was blood everywhere. That, as far as I can recall, was the last time she joined the spectators at a hurling match.

While winning was great, losing felt like it was the end of the world. I remember a game when I was fourteen years old and we were playing the team from Rathkeale, a town a few miles from Knockaderry that we could see from the top of the hill. They were a very good team, although we were favored. I was playing against this other guy and he just did a job on me, just made me look stupid. You know you have those days when not a damn thing goes right. Every ball that dropped between us, every ball that we went at together, he seemed to get. That day, either I was a step too slow, my hand-eye coordination wasn't sharp, I didn't hit him the right way, or maybe all three. It's an awful feeling when you lose, especially if you lose when you've played poorly, when you know that if you played well your team might have won.

I always worked hard to improve, but never harder than when I felt that I had not performed up to my capability. Those were the times I drove myself hardest. I would stay outside in the evening and practice hitting the ball toward a tree in an effort to improve my accuracy. I would see how far I could run with the ball balanced on my hurley.

Along the way, as I grew more mature, I realized that hurling teaches you about life. No matter who we are or where we come from, we all face difficult challenges along the way, and the ongoing nature of those challenges tests whether we have prepared in a disciplined way to take on whatever happens to lie ahead. In hurling, as in life, study, preparation, and hard work pay off—maybe not always, but certainly more often than not. Central to the lessons of hurling is that once you have practiced and improved your skill and fitness levels, you have to look within yourself. Fear prevents you from being your best—fear of getting injured, fear of failure, fear of the unknown. Conquering fear is freeing. It enables you to play with joy and a sense of freedom, just as it enables you to try new things in life, some of which will surely fail. But with those failures comes an understanding of teamwork and grit and the kind of lessons we treasure.

Chapter Three

Love of Learning

"He's only going to end up sweeping the streets."

BESIDES HURLING, THE OTHER GREAT joy in my life was learning. From an early age, I loved reading, studying, and school. Looming over the Aughalin primary school was the intimidating presence of Mr. Burke: principal, teacher, and disciplinarian, a large, menacing man, stern, with a heavy gait and sour disposition, who was one of the most prominent citizens in Knockaderry. There was talk that he had been in the Irish Republican Army at some point, and he certainly acted as though he had a military background. In the morning before school you had to line up and march into class—*left-right, left-right*—and God help you if you fell out of step. Transgressions in Mr. Burke's class were often met with the business end of a four-foot-long hazelwood stick or even the thick wooden leg from a stool.

As enthusiastic as he was about Irish history, sports, drama, and the Gaelic language, he was fanatical about penmanship (an obsession I share to this day) and insisted upon flawless homework from every student. One of his many rules was that all students were required to write with their right hand, which meant any natural left-hander had to adapt. This was unfortunate for a new boy in class, perhaps unaware of the rule, who was writing with his left hand one day. Noticing this, Mr. Burke moved behind the boy and swung the stick, striking the boy in the head.

In the morning, you had to line up with your homework and hold it up like a sign in front of your body at chest height. Any imperfection, such as a smudge or crossed-out letter or word, would bring punishing blows—to the backs of the knees, hands, head, or back. When striking a hand he seemed to aim for the thumb, which would numb your hand for some time.

There was a kind of ritual to Mr. Burke's administration of the hazel stick. There was one boy, Edzy Connors, who stuttered, but to Mr. Burke such a disability was impermissible. When a rule was broken—a stutter from Edzy, for example—Mr. Burke would stand up straight and stretch out his arms slowly in a theatrical fashion. He would then remove his sport coat, carefully drape it over a clothes hanger, and place it along the wall. He would roll up his shirt sleeves, first one arm, then the other. All of this would be in what felt like slow motion, clearly intended to build the fear in his victim. He would then spit on his hands, get a strong grip on the hazel stick, and swing away, his face tensing as he did so. It was as pure a form of cruelty as I could then imagine.

When my brother Joe would get out of line, which was infrequent, Mr. Burke would be scathing. When Joe was only nine or ten years old Mr. Burke said to him, "Dowlin', you'll never amount to anything." Mr. Burke was so feared and despised by most students that my brothers Joe and Sean and their friends engaged in discussions where they talked about the idea of murdering Mr. Burke. They weren't sure exactly how they would accomplish this, though they thought that beating him to death with his own sticks might be best.

With Mr. Burke, you were never sure in advance exactly where the strike would come. It could be on the back of the legs, hands, back, or even your head. I remember being hit by Mr. Burke on several occasions, especially on the hands and thumb, although I do not recall the beating he administered to my back. My brother Joe, however, remembers it vividly. Joe says that when I was around twelve years old I came home from school one day and my mother noticed that my back was tender to the touch. She asked me what the matter was and I said there was nothing the matter. However, my mother had me remove my shirt. She saw a series of stripes across my back—ten or eleven swollen red welts from Mr. Burke's stick.

Looking back, this sort of violence against children seems criminal, but at the time, it was an accepted part of the culture. Not only did parents not usually object when their children were struck, but quite often, when parents found out, they would administer another beating themselves. Joe received a terrible beating from Mr. Burke at one point and soon thereafter became ill with a fever, but even then Joe feared telling our father what had happened because our father's attitude was, *Well, you must have done something to deserve it.*

There was one beating in particular from Mr. Burke that Joe and I remember all too well. The Guiry family lived in Knockaderry, diagonally across the road from our home. John Guiry was probably my closest friend. His father owned a pretty big farm and the family was comparatively well off. The Guirys were very good people and John a particularly nice boy. In primary grades we would walk the short distance to school together in the morning. Later, we would ride our bikes to secondary school together and we hung out together in our free time.

One day in primary school, John did something—I don't recall what—to earn Mr. Burke's ire. Mr. Burke then staged his fear-inducing preparatory charade, took the thick leg of a stool he kept in the back of the class, and hauled off and smashed John across the side of the head with vicious blows, causing the side of John's face and head to swell up. John was never the same after that. It was clear Mr. Burke had crossed a line, because the next day Mr. Guiry, John's father, showed up at the school and he and Mr. Burke met privately and punches were exchanged. Some years later—in his late teens, I believe—John passed away. His death was stunning news in the village and no one knew at the time what the cause was, at least none of the kids knew. There was talk that it was something wrong with his brain, and in retrospect it might have been some sort of brain tumor, but at the time my brother Joe and our friends and I all wondered whether it was Mr. Burke's beating that had somehow contributed to John's death.

As crazy as it sounds now, I thought at the time that this was a perfectly normal, traditional way to mete out discipline. Though I disliked Mr. Burke, I nonetheless respected his intellectual ability; respected his facility with the traditional Irish language and his demands for academic rigor. And despite some beatings, I had the sense that Mr. Burke appreciated the hard work I put in. I always did my homework well and often studied via candlelight, late into the night.

Mr. Burke was revered in town as an educated man. He lived a half-mile from us in a spectacular house where you walked up a steep set of stairs to reach the entrance. I worked at his property trimming hedges and doing other odd jobs. The one time I was invited into the house was in connection with a school play Mr. Burke directed, in which I was one of the actors. In the house I was struck by the display of trophies—row upon row of them— Mr. Burke and his students had won in various theatrical and other competitions around the country where scholars competed on their knowledge of Gaelic and Irish history. During the visit, Mr. Burke was entirely altered from his schoolmaster persona.

He was actually quite nice to me and introduced me to his wife, a soft-spoken, friendly lady. What was so striking about this was that I had never before heard about any student being invited to Mr. Burke's home. That evening, I was the only student present. We sat in his living room amid the trophies and he conveyed to me that I had the ability to perhaps one day win competitions, as he had. The mere fact of being invited into his home gave me a sense of confidence. While he was a tyrant, he was also a good teacher who demanded discipline and hard work. He also showed a preference for boys who were good at sports, and by the time I was twelve years old I was known throughout the village as one of the leading hurlers in my age group.

Mr. Burke had just one child—highly unusual in those days—a son who entered the priesthood. He also had nieces and nephews who came to live with him. Joe, Sean, and I thought there was something a bit off about the son. Maybe we made that assumption because we found the idea of having Mr. Burke as a father so harrowing. Over the years, however, the son—known as Fr. Peadar de Buirce (the traditional Irish spelling of Burke)—proved to be a caring and spiritual man. My sister Mary, who still lives in Knockaderry, knew him in later years when Fr. Buirce came to be a beloved figure in the village. He was afflicted with some sort of speech impediment and he was an excitable man, but he also, Mary recalls, possessed a good heart and a firm conviction that all people were inherently good. The best testament to his character was that Mam felt he was saintly.

When we were in the seventh or eighth grade, the school staged a production of a one-act play drawn from a short story written by Patrick Pearse (1879–1916), a poet, author, and political activist who was executed by firing squad for his part as a leader of the Easter Rising in 1916. The play, entitled *Íosagán*, is deeply spiritual. It features an elderly man, Old Mathias, who is quite ill, receiving a Sunday morning visit from the character of Íosagán, the character I played in the drama, who is the embodiment of Jesus Christ, and who appears as his father's envoy to the dying Old Mathias. It is a wonderful old Irish story with a deeply religious feel to it that was very much consistent with the teachings we received in school. The story, from which the play is adapted, is also characterized by a spare writing style and a sense of wonder and mysticism.

Mr. Burke was also focused on having us learn how to speak publicly. Standing up in front of a small class of students doesn't seem like much, but it was nerve-racking, especially when you had Mr. Burke observing. Thanks to his insistence that we work at it and improve, I grew increasingly comfortable speaking in front of the class, and it would prove to be an invaluable skill.

In much the same way, my passion for reading, learning, and studying, which deepened at a very young age, has served me well in everything I have done since then. My mother encouraged my interest in school and learning, but unfortunately my father took a different view. For a long time, Dad could never understand why I spent so much time studying; why school was so important to me. It may have been because he'd never had a chance at any sort of formal education for himself. My father was a very intelligent man, a natural at math as well as highly skilled at building and construction, but his lack of formal schooling left him with a deep suspicion about the value of education for someone in our social stratum. He said things like, "You should be out working. What the hell are you studying that shit for?"

I was the odd man out about school as far as my brothers were concerned. Neither Joe, who was three years younger than I was, nor Sean, three years younger than Joe, had the interest in studying that I did. Quite the opposite, in fact. Joe was exceptionally bright, especially in math, and a very caring brother, but he didn't have a great deal of drive in school or in sports. He was a naturally gifted athlete and could have been outstanding, but just didn't want to put in the effort. He wasn't interested in training or fighting to get on the teams. He was shy as a boy, more reserved than I was, but he was solid and reliable. Sean was a terror—skinny, energetic, tough as nails, willing to fight at any moment. He was also an outstanding athlete in Irish football as well as rugby and hurling. Sean had a powerful intellect, and through the years he developed a passionate love of learning, which included an uncanny ability to remember verbatim quotations from some of the great Irish poets.

Things were going quite well for me through my final year of primary school. I was thirteen, and I was very focused on performing well enough academically to move on to secondary school. My work paid off, and I achieved the standard necessary to continue my education, but there was a glitch. Mr. Burke loomed over all and, in an incident that shocked me, he attempted to head off my move to secondary school. In fact, his idea was to have me repeat the final year of primary school, at which time I would be fourteen and old enough to quit school and get a job.

The issue came to a head when my parents and I met with Mr. Burke one evening and he told my parents that it would be a waste for me to continue to secondary school because, as he put it, "He's only going to end up sweeping the streets anyway. He'll get a job sweeping and never anything more." It seems entirely irrational that Mr. Burke at one point admired my work and complimented me by inviting me to his home, only to later try and bring my formal education to an end. But at that time in rural Ireland, Mr. Burke's view reflected reality—that children like me from poor families did not generally go on from primary to secondary school. What Mr. Burke was proposing was not at all out of the ordinary. What was unusual, in fact, was my desire to move on in my education and my mother's determination to make sure it happened.

My mother knew how important education was to me. She shared that aspiration for me. She did something quite unusual for parents in Knockaderry—she stood up to Mr. Burke. She pushed back, saying that I had performed well academically and had every right to continue my schooling. Unfortunately, my father, who thought that life would be for me much as it had been for him, agreed with Mr. Burke. This both infuriated and saddened me. Dad could never grasp the determination I had to find another pathway in life. My mother, on the other hand, understood completely, and she fought on my behalf until eventually Mr. Burke yielded, and I was allowed to move on to secondary school.

I had one last mission as my final year in primary school came to a close. One day when Mr. Burke was elsewhere in the building, I took hold of his hazel stick and, using a small knife, cut it into small pieces and disposed of them by putting them through small holes in the school's wooden floor. I knew, of course, that he would just go out into one of the fields and break off a fresh branch to inflict misery on future students, but I felt a measure of satisfaction in getting away with one of the few seditious acts I ever committed in school.

The closest secondary school to Knockaderry was St. Ita's, a school for boys located in a large two-story building in Newcastle West, about five miles from Knockaderry. There was no public transportation, of course, so attending required riding a bicycle five miles each way to and from school. I usually rode from Knockaderry with my friend John Guiry and other boys, and we would race along the twisting roads by pastures with cows and horses grazing, passing farmers in donkey carts or on horseback. John and I would talk as we rode—about sports, farming, people in the village. Every once in a while, we would talk about the future, and I would share with him my thought that, some day, I would leave Knockaderry to go to college. I might even head off somewhere else to work. John once expressed a wish to do the same, but his family was rooted within Knockaderry on the land they owned and farmed. The farm is run by his brothers to this day.

Sometimes we would stop our bikes along the way to school to walk along the bridge railing spanning the River Deel. This was thrilling, though dangerously reckless after a storm, when the river would swell over its banks and the water would rush just six or eight feet below the bridge. It was exciting to see the raging waters, almost rapid-like, swirling below and the giddy feeling that came when crossing—*very* carefully—for fear of tumbling in and being swept downstream. There were accidents, of course. Kids would fall in every once in a while, but they would just swim a short distance to the bank, continue the ride to school, and try and explain why they were soaked from head to toe. Usually, when John and I would pause here on our route, I would sit on the railing and contemplate the water, watching its swirls and the reflection of the sun off the surface, seeing whether I could spot a trout or salmon.

One of the highlights of cycling to school was the ride along a frightening stretch of road past what was known as the "crooked tree," about two-thirds of the way to school. This was a tree off the side of the road with a long branch parallel to the ground about ten or so feet up. The often-told story was that an Irish hero, Patrick Moylan, had confronted the British here in 1732 and been hanged on this very tree. My friends and I were sometimes spooked by the thought of it and we wondered, *Who else was hanged there? What had they done wrong?*

But there were days—many days, in fact—when the dark clouds gathered, the skies opened, and the rain poured down without letup for the full ride from home to school. The worst was a hailstorm where bits of icy rain would sometimes be so sharp they could cut your ears or the skin on your face. Often, we arrived at school soaked to the skin and then sat in class, steam rising from our clothing as we dried out.

The headmaster of St. Ita's was Mr. James Breen, a demanding but fair man who cared deeply about the students—a significant improvement over the reign of Mr. Burke. Unlike Mr. Burke, Mr. Breen treated us with respect and sought to guide us on a rigorous but enjoyable educational journey. St. Ita's had been founded in 1935 by Mr. Breen and other teachers. It was a simple structure with bare rooms and poor science facilities, but what the school lacked in outward appearance it made up in the caliber of students. The classes were a mix of boys from the town as well as many, like myself, from the surrounding villages and countryside. The school's reputation was that the students were bright, hardworking achievers. I was proud to be there.

At St. Ita's I got involved a bit in student activities and got on well with Mr. Breen. He and I developed a good relationship because we were both interested in solving problems, rather than pushing a particular ideology. But not every teacher was as nurturing as Mr. Breen. There was Mr. O'Donnell, a nasty little man with a bad attitude and a penchant for throwing things at students and belittling them in class. He had a steel-encased compass he would sometimes throw, aiming at boys' heads. Once, when he picked on one of the smaller boys in our class yet again, I stood up and challenged him. Of course, I was punished for that, but it was worth it. Mr. Breen pretended to be upset with me, but when we were alone, he confided, "I don't like him either."

At St. Ita's, I felt like I was on the right path in my life toward more opportunity. Even from the start of secondary school, I had an eye toward the intermediate exam in the third year and the secondary exam in the fifth year—two crucial tests that determined whether I would be eligible to go on to college. I paid close attention in class and always completed my homework assignments to the best of my ability, never arriving at school unprepared, whatever the subject or assignment. I was passable in math and excelled in my favorite subjects—history, geography, science, and English.

I was fixated on the idea of college. The truth was, though, I didn't really know what college involved, other than more education. My assumption was that college prepared you to become a teacher. I was entirely unaware of the fact that in college you could major in a variety of subjects and choose any number of professional fields after graduation. I had never seen a college, nor did I know much of anything about how a college education worked. I only knew—and I knew it with absolute certainty—that by going to college I would have opportunities beyond the village. I knew that college would mean not having to think about being a policeman who would eventually gain a pension in thirty-plus years.

To get into college you had to score in the top echelon of the secondary school final exams, which was a rigorous process. I fell into a steady rhythm. After cycling home from school each afternoon, I would do whatever chores were necessary at our house or for a local farmer, then head off to hurling practice in the village. After supper, I would study for the rest of the evening. This was my favorite time of day, quietly reading and studying until I fell asleep, often as late as midnight. These were joyous days for me.

When I was sixteen, I decided to start saving money for college, and it was clear to me that significant amounts of money could not be made in Knockaderry. I had heard about job openings at a steel factory in Crawley, a rough town in England, not far from London. Needless to say, I had never been outside of Ireland, and for that matter, had rarely been to other parts of the country itself. Nonetheless, I was determined to get one of the jobs at Crawley, and in June 1966, I made the trip to England, where I landed a job in a steel factory that made parts for train carriages and locomotives.

It was my first time leaving Ireland, my first time using a telephone (when I first picked it up I wasn't sure which end to speak into), and it opened up a whole new world to me. I had never been on an airplane before, but a cheap flight from Shannon to London was striking in how quickly it was possible to move from one place to another. For my whole life until that summer, traveling anywhere—to a nearby town or the twenty-plus miles from Knockaderry to Limerick—was slow and tedious on foot or bicycle. But that summer I traveled 500 miles in a couple of hours!

For the first week or so in Crawley I stayed with one of my aunts, but she was so unpleasant—constantly making belittling comments to me—that I quickly moved out and found an inexpensive room to rent not far from work. The rooming house had a shower—the first time I had ever seen one—and I worked as a laborer within the plant doing a variety of menial jobs. I would work eight-hour shifts and accepted any overtime offered to me, which required, on some occasions, that I sleep overnight in the factory bunkroom. There were some raw characters working in the factory, and one night, one of them attacked me, no doubt intent on beating me senseless. I defended myself with a nearby wrench and sent him crashing to the floor. He never bothered me again.

The only question that summer—the uncertainty that loomed over my life—was whether I would score well enough on the standardized exams required for college admission. It was known to be a very challenging test on a series of subjects, including Gaelic— and you could attain perfect scores in math, English, history, and science, but if you failed the Gaelic portion of the exam, you failed, period. This "leaving certificate examination," or "leaving cert" as it was commonly known, was the final test administered at the end of secondary school, and a certain level of performance was required on the exam in order to be able to attend an Irish university.

There was a neighbor in Knockaderry, a farmer named Ned Fitzgerald, for whom I had done some work. One day, when I was about fifteen and was helping him build a cement yard, he told me he believed that I had some potential and that at some point I would need to leave Knockaderry. He said to me, "Mike, you've got to get out. There is no future here." This had a real impact on me, and affirmed the instinct I had developed some years earlier that I needed to do something different than follow the traditional path of Knockaderry life—farm, church, pub, repeat. The only way out was through education. The very few people I knew in Knockaderry who had college degrees—teachers and priests—were considered important. They seemed somehow above the rest of us, occupying a higher tier in society that was more worldly and sophisticated.

I was in my rooming house in England when I got the envelope, forwarded to me by my mother, containing the test results. I opened it slowly and there it was—five honors-level scores out of seven subjects. I had made the cut for college. At summer's end, I traveled from England back home to Knockaderry and the promise of more education that would lead me I knew not where—I just knew it was the right pathway forward.

Chapter Four

A Cacophony of No

"I was beginning to believe that the Church was as much about power as it was about religion."

WHEN I WAS GROWING UP, Knockaderry was a very Catholic place. Many if not most people in the village—women in particular—were devout practitioners of their faith and, like my mother, attended Mass multiple times each week. Mam and these other women believed in the power of faith and prayer to affect the course of their lives and the lives of their loved ones. They believed that God listened to their prayers and chose, in certain situations, to answer those prayers. They felt an intimate relationship with the Almighty. Catholic teachings came directly from the pope in Rome, and it was accepted dogma among Catholics that the pope was infallible in matters of faith or morals. These devout Catholics were blessed with what the Church referred to as "the gift of faith," an ability to discern the truth of Catholic teachings, absent tangible proof. For many people in the village, the Church served as the center of their lives, providing a set of rules and principles to live by. Most people in Knockaderry—though certainly not all—followed those rules.

For Mam, faith in God was an immensely positive force within her life. She was guided by Church culture and rules and she was inspired, even energized, by the sense of connection she felt to God through prayer, the Mass, and other elements of Catholic tradition. She went to Mass frequently, not only to pray for her family, but also, I think, because it afforded her that rare luxury of peace and solace, a much-needed respite where she would sit and pray and perhaps light a candle that represented the offering of a specific prayer for someone else. It was her own time, a getaway, a private period of meditation.

There is an undeniable spiritual power to the rituals within the Mass—soulful hymns, incense lending a mystical feel, and the joining together of all the people in a singular act of worship. And, of course, the heart of the matter—the Eucharist, where worshippers consume the body and blood of Christ. When I was very young, I felt this connection and was moved by the experience of the Mass. Did I believe in it in a visceral sense? I am not certain, but it was so deeply embedded within the culture of our family and our village and our country that, as a boy, I believed.

No organization reached the same level of prestige as the Roman Catholic Church, and this gave the parish priest a unique standing in the community as a conduit to the Almighty. One of our priests, Father Lyons, lived in a grand house and was cared for by Ita Collins, who worked as his live-in maid. He was also one of the very few people in Knockaderry who owned a car. The priest was not only an iconic religious figure, but also a respected intellect whose views on almost any issue—farming, marriage, hurling, anything—were taken seriously. In a very real sense, the priest and the Church were at the center of life in Knockaderry.

Catholicism had long been deeply embedded within the DNA of most Irish men and women. While there were many Protestants in the northern reaches of the country, the vast majority of the rest of Ireland was Catholic, and there was no question that the Roman Catholic Church was the most influential organization in the country, and that influence was pervasive. In Knockaderry, the entire village went to Sunday morning Mass—either at 9:00 a.m. or 11:00 a.m.—the biggest event of the week.

At its most elemental level, Catholicism gave people in difficult and even desperate times something to hold on to; something to believe in: *Yes, life is difficult and sometimes brutal, but if we follow some basic rules, we will be rewarded after we die with a place in heaven.* A common theme was that suffering on earth had a purpose—gaining the celestial reward in the afterlife. I had the sense that people believed that the tougher life was on earth, the better the heavenly afterlife. In Knockaderry, it was so rare to find anyone who was not Catholic that when we heard of a Protestant man living in the area, my friends and I went over to his farm to see what he looked like.

The reality in Ireland throughout much of the twentieth century was that Catholicism was officially supported by the Irish national government, as stipulated in the country's constitution. In Ireland, the Church was embraced by leading civic figures, including Éamon De Valera, the Irish statesman. De Valera was one of the organizers of the Easter Rising in 1916 in Dublin, when all the uprising leaders were executed, except De Valera. He was spared because, having been born in the United States, he was considered a US citizen, and English authorities feared the reaction of the United States if they executed an American. De Valera went on to become the leader of Ireland for another four decades.

As president, De Valera was a social conservative who believed in the primacy of the Church, the Irish family, and Irish agriculture. He presided over the writing of a new constitution for the free state of Ireland, and Article 44 of the constitution recognized "the special position of the Holy Catholic Apostolic and Roman Church" in Irish life. The Irish prime minister at the time, John Costello, expressed it this way: "I am an Irishman second, a Catholic first, and I accept without qualification in all respects the teaching of the hierarchy and the Church to which I belong." The constitution noted the need to protect Catholic teachings, including the responsibility to "guard with special care the institution of marriage," thus the prohibition against divorce. The government followed the constitution with a law in 1935 outlawing the sale of contraceptives in the country.

During my lifetime, especially in the 1950s and mid-1960s, the Church reached the height of its influence within the country. Yet at that very same moment, the seeds of the Church's demise were sown by the institution itself. There was evidence of it in my own home, where, at night, I would hear conversations my parents had with friends. Every once in a while, someone might say something critical of the priest or of a church policy. These occasions were rare, but they had an impact on me because they were so contrary to everything we had been taught. When I was growing up, you would see pamphlets aimed at young people promoting church policies:

> The Young Lady Says No!
> What to Do on a Date?
> Shall I Be a Nun?
> Divorce Is a Disease!

At some point I wondered, why are these necessary if everyone is doing what the Church teaches? As I grew older and progressed in my education, it became clear to me that church policies had unintended consequences. The prohibition on birth control, for example, meant people had large families. And since tradition mandated that families pass along the farm to the eldest child, it meant that in some families, eight or ten or more children were left without a way to support themselves and their own families. An obvious result was that a large number of Irish men and women emigrated to other countries, particularly the United States, in search of work. This not only drained Ireland of workers, it also reduced consumption, productivity, and tax revenues, thus decimating the economy.

The unquestioned authority of the local priest also meant that errors in judgment by the priest resulted in harmful consequences. Let's say a farmer wanted to till his field on Sunday, after a spell of bad weather. In that case, the farmer would be required to go to the priest and seek permission, which was not always granted. The fact was that if Sunday was the only sunny day in the week, farmers had to work the fields then or risk losing crops. It was particularly important to hay the fields at the right time, but if the priest denied permission for Sunday work, that was the final word. Nobody argued because the priest was so powerful.

The priest was not only the conduit between the people and God, he was also considered wise and just, and his influence extended over the behavior of people throughout the village. In our house— as was the case in every other house in the village—there was no arguing with the priest, but pretty early on I began to think that there was something off kilter. I was quite young, maybe twelve or thirteen or so, when I first heard about a farmer who was denied permission to work on a Sunday, and I remember arguments with people saying, "Well, till the field, you got to feed your family. Till the field. The heck with the priest and his opinion." This bordered on blasphemy. The Church, in retrospect, seemed to benefit from the large numbers of poor—and poorly educated—Irish people during the middle of the twentieth century.

By age thirteen or fourteen, I had grown increasingly skeptical of the authoritarian way the Church ruled. I remember once as a kid we wanted to raise some money for the local hurling team by staging a collection across the street from the church as people left Mass on Sunday morning, but the priest wouldn't allow it. I thought, *Who gives you the right to tell us we can't do something, not on church grounds, but across the street?*

What most damaged my relationship with the Catholic Church was when the priest would publicly humiliate my family. This happened several times each year, when the donations to the parish from each family in the village were read aloud by the priest during Mass. I dreaded those mornings. I would be sitting near the front with my mother and siblings and I would grow tense as the names and amounts were read off. *Mr. Sullivan* (the farmer) *gave five pounds. Paddy Cantillon* (another farmer) *six pounds. John Dowling* (my father) *two shillings and six pence.* As the priest announced our contribution publicly, I could feel people around us in the pews looking at us. I sat there fuming.

There were other incidents through the years that gradually turned me away from the Church—but not from religion, not from faith. I remember going to Mass with my mother and my wife, and Father Lyons made reference to a recent airline crash. A commercial aircraft with more than 150 people on board had gone down off the Irish coast, killing everyone on board. During the homily, Father Lyons mentioned the crash and asked the congregation to join in a moment of silence "for all the Catholics on board." I was actually stunned. *For all the Catholics?* How about for all the *human beings* on board?

This happened when I was visiting home from America, and I remember my impulse was to get up and walk out of the church. I was so disgusted with what the priest had said that I was on the verge of doing it, when it occurred to me that such an action would confuse and embarrass my mother, who was sitting next to me in the pew. Because she was deaf, of course, she had not heard what the priest had said, so she would not understand my reaction. That moment seemed to crystallize for me my feelings of antipathy toward the Church. This was no small matter. I was calling into question one of the cornerstone beliefs on which I was raised—in fact, *the* cornerstone belief.

With the benefit of hindsight a half-century later, I know the extent of the Church's influence over people's lives was excessive. As a child, I instinctively felt a sense of mistrust toward Father Lyons. He was hardly in the image of Jesus Christ, a generous, loving person with a particular sense of empathy for the least among us. In contrast, Father Lyons carried himself with an imperious air and, it seemed to me, looked down upon people as lesser beings. Rather than seeing himself as a servant of the people, he viewed himself as a master of sorts. The theory of celebrating each human soul was a pretense. I could never understand how mature adults would take direction from him. They actually feared him, as if bad things would happen if they confronted or challenged him.

An important part of the culture involved the select boys in the community who had a vocation—who felt called to the religious life and were ordained as priests. This was a huge deal in the village, for whenever a boy went away to study for the priesthood and was subsequently ordained, that Knockaderry family gained enormous respect and admiration. Mothers whose boys became priests or whose daughters became nuns could hardly contain their pride and joy. Many boys in the neighborhood at least thought about it, and a number went on to be ordained. I thought at the time that in a number of those cases the boys did it to make their parents—especially their mothers—happy and proud. A number of those boys who were ordained later left the priesthood after their mothers passed away.

I never considered entering the priesthood, even though I felt almost as though I was letting my mother down by not doing it. My cousin Vincent became a member of a teaching order, the Irish Christian Brothers. The Brothers took vows of poverty, chastity, and obedience like priests, but unlike priests, they were not allowed to administer the sacraments. The rules in this particular order permitted his parents to visit him no more than once per year. Even though he was not far away at a school in Cork, he was essentially removed from their lives. What this accomplished, I wasn't at all sure.

I was a dutiful Catholic boy for the most part. I served as an altar boy, anticipating every step in the Mass in harmony with the priest. I also signed a Church-sponsored pledge to join the Pioneers, an organization devoted to sobriety. I even signed the Pioneer pledge in the summer of 1966, promising that "I will abstain for life from all intoxicating drinks."

But at a certain point during my late high school and college years, I realized something about myself that had never before been clear in my mind. I had always conformed to whatever the societal norms were—I was diligent about following the rules at home, in school, on the playing field, and everywhere else. But I was gradually changing, no longer willing to blindly follow the rules. I was beginning to believe that the Church was as much about power as it was about religion. The imperious nature of the parish priests put me off, as did the hypocrisy of their affluent living arrangements despite their vow of poverty, a level of affluence that virtually no one else in the community could ever hope to attain.

As I grew older I also learned about some of the harsh measures the Church had taken, especially as it related to women and sexuality. Niall O'Dowd has noted that in the Republic of Ireland the use of contraception had remained illegal since the 1930s. And in what seems in retrospect an utterly bizarre move, in the 1940s the Catholic bishops of Ireland, according to O'Dowd, informed the government that they wanted Tampax banned "on the grounds that insertion might stimulate women sexually." Tampax was banned.

The pub was another core social institution in Knockaderry, and I had no use for it. The fact that some farmers—certainly not all, but some—would head there directly from the creamery in the morning seemed absolutely crazy to me. I understood that the pub was relief—and temporary relief, at that—from the dreary reality and monotony of day-to-day life. Farming was a glorious life for many people, but there is a relentlessness to poverty, to living on the edge day after day, year after year, that can wear down even the sturdiest soul. For farmers, the future encompassed a short horizon, where each day resembled the day before and all the days to come. I knew when I was just thirteen or fourteen years old that I couldn't live in that kind of environment. I couldn't live in an environment where the Church had such a commanding power over people, where a farmer would acquiesce to a priest telling him he couldn't work on Sunday and risk his crops rotting, his livelihood disappearing. I knew this life was not for me, that there had to be better opportunities out there somewhere.

When I joined my brothers and sister in Knockaderry in the fall of 2019 for a family gathering, we talked about the Church and the class structure in town. My brother Sean, who now lives just north of Dublin, observed that the Church had been central to amplifying the "cacophony of no" in our lives. "This idea of no,"

Sean said, "was hugely reinforced by the Church because they've always thrived where they have an opportunity to do social control where you have a largely uneducated population. In those years the school teacher and the priest were the only people who were educated." And these figures of authority would make clear that our aspirations really didn't count for much. "Even at ages thirteen or fourteen we had dreams which were driven by the situation we found ourselves in. Our background was pure working class, poor working class. I can remember, as a very small kid, being aware of the fact that it was a farming community, with a lot of what I considered to be big farmers, like the Sullivans, who had forty or fifty acres. We weren't like that. We lived a subsistence lifestyle."

Sean said that when the priest would read each family's donation amounts aloud at Mass, "that was the *cacophony of no* emphatically putting you in your box. The message from the Church—or at least from the parish priest—was, *Look, you are working class, and you'll always be working class. That's what you'll always be. It's a fact of life—you'll never be anything else.* But we sought to change the outcomes that were expected of us. Because there's nothing more motivating than somebody telling you that you can't do that. That's motivation. You tell us we can't do something, now you're looking for serious trouble. We all rebelled against that attitude, and we all succeeded in clawing our way past that expectation. We would not accept the notion that there were limits on what we could achieve. None of us would. None of us did."

My biggest conflict, however, was not with the Church, the pub, or any local customs or social norms. It was within my own home—with my father.

Chapter Five

A Scar that Never Healed

"What the hell are these exams for anyway?"

MY FATHER HAD A DIFFICULT upbringing. Jack Dowling was the youngest of seven children in a disciplined household. His mother, whom he loved and respected, was a tough taskmaster. When I was a boy, I once got a cut, and she called for the rural Irish disinfectant: "Just piss on the goddamn thing," she told me. "It's fine, stop complaining."

Although my father was a very intelligent person, it was clear early on that education was not in his future. He left school during the primary grades and devoted himself to his family's very small farm. While his older siblings emigrated to England or America, my dad worked milking cows, tilling fields, spreading dung—doing whatever was necessary, and doing it so well that he built a reputation as an excellent and tireless worker. He would help neighbors at any time and work as hard or harder than anyone else, no matter the task. People respected him for this.

But when we were growing up, there was something not quite right about my father. He was angry much of the time, and that created near-constant stress in our home. He was as intemperate as he was unpredictable.

Our parents used to host card games at our house, and one evening the parish priest came by to play. This was an honor, an occasion when the family was blessed with the presence of the most important person in the village. Who knows what happened exactly, but there was some sort of disagreement that escalated quickly when Dad ordered the priest out of our house, telling him: "Get your stuff and leave." Naturally, this humiliated Mam, but that was the reality of our dad. Something—anything—would set him off, and he would scream at you or belt you or both, and you would be left wondering, *What just happened? What did I do wrong?*

I don't want to place all the blame on Dad's shoulders. Circumstances mattered. Those years in the 1950s and '60s, when Ireland was essentially a third-world country, were frustrating times with few good jobs, poor infrastructure, and little social welfare—all of which helped explain the Irish exodus to America. However difficult the circumstances, though, my father's behavior too often crossed any reasonable line.

One night, when Joe and Sean were building a concrete wall, Dad walked into the room. They had put up about four or five rows of concrete blocks and he said, "That's not straight. Take it down." It wasn't just the one small crooked section that had to be torn down—it was the whole thing.

My father was a complicated man. His rigid nature actually helped make him a gifted builder with a remarkable eye. Even when he was crippled with rheumatoid arthritis later in life, the local farmers would get him in when they were doing a project, because if Jack Dowling said it was right, it was right. He was fanatical about order and precision. For example, the garden behind the house had to have perfectly straight rows. We plowed those rows with a hand plow and a borrowed horse. As a kid, you're plowing with this giant horse and Dad behind it, and then, if anything was crooked, you were to blame.

"There wasn't much laughter in the house, not that I can remember," recalls Sean. "There was stress always—that was a given." These days, when Joe, Sean, Mary, Patrick, and I get together for a few days, we spend most of our time telling stories about the old days—not the painful stories so much as the funny ones. We laugh for hours. Sean said he thinks that our joy of laughter is "almost like a new skill we've learned in later years." Grim circumstances generated stress and anxiety. My father's angry temperament pervaded the house like toxic clouds from the cigarettes he chain-smoked. You never knew when his temper might flare—it could happen at any moment, triggered by almost anything. As a result, we tended to walk on eggshells around him. If you stepped out of line, made a mistake, banged the door—he would pounce.

Dad was not a big drinker, like some men in the village who gravitated to the pub nearly every day. Of course, he didn't have the money to go to the pub, but on the occasions when he did drink, we knew there would be trouble. It took only a modest amount of alcohol to make my father drunk—he just could not handle his liquor. At weddings and funerals, when there would be ample free alcohol, he would drink too much and then angrily stagger around. There would be screaming matches. You knew there would be things thrown, and that there was probably going to be violence. You knew that Mam was going to have an awful time.

Uppermost in my mind was to avoid doing anything to upset him, but you never knew what the triggers might be. If you were doing carpentry or stonework with him and you didn't do it right, he would lose it. One time, he got so angry that he hit me in the head with a shovel. I had gone to work helping a neighbor on some project and I hadn't told him I was doing it, and when I came home he was waiting for me. When I walked around the side of the house, *boom*. He swung a shovel like a baseball bat, striking the side of my head, knocking me senseless. Blood everywhere. I was thirteen years old.

He and I often worked closely together, and these were times when, for the most part, we got along well. We worked in a focused, disciplined way, quietly going about our business. We worked side by side expanding our new home, and we worked on a major project helping take apart the old school building. We worked bringing stone from a quarry as filler for the backyard of the new house. We also traveled regularly on a donkey cart out to the bogs to dig out chunks of peat for the fireplace. The peat, soaked with water in the ground, was heavy, and the work exhausting, but we usually got through it because I did exactly what he told me to do and because I had learned from him how to be an efficient and tireless worker. Sometimes we would burn wood in the fireplace, but Ireland's forests had been cut down long ago, so peat became the preferred choice for most rural families.

My father kept any emotion, other than anger, to himself. As I got older, I realized that he really did care for all of us, but he would rarely show it. I never remember Dad saying *I love you*. I never heard him say those words—ever. I don't remember him ever hugging me. My brother Joe, who now lives outside Newcastle West in County Limerick, recalls that whenever I would leave home for a trip overseas to New York, my father would disappear. Joe says that if I was scheduled to leave "at three o'clock Dad would go missing at half two, be off up the hill somewhere. He just couldn't say goodbye. He didn't want to show emotion. That was the way it always happened."

But there was tenderness somewhere inside my father, and sometimes it would show. If he knew you were hungry, for example, he would give you his food, but he would be curt about it. He would say, "Hey, eat that." Talking at meals was frowned upon. The attitude from my father was explicit: *Shut up and eat and get back to work.* "He would give you anything, but he had a very short fuse, too," recalls Joe. "In the old house, Mam would be keeping his dinner warm over the fire when he came home. And she put the potatoes into the ashes to keep the skin glowing—how beautiful. But she'd get us out of the house when he came in because if we were there, he'd give us the meat. We didn't have much meat other than bacon unless we would catch rabbits. And he'd end up giving it to us. He was very generous."

The violence, anger, arguing—all of the toxicity that pervaded our home—took its toll on everyone, but perhaps no one more than my sister Mary, who still lives in the village of Knockaderry. In the early years, when Joe, Sean, and I were in our teens, she was just a child, innocent and vulnerable, and so deeply shaken by Dad's rages that she would slip out the back of the house and retreat to her hiding place in the shed. "I was so scared," she recalls. "I was *so* scared . . . I used to hide in the coal shed, or if I was in bed and our father would come in late at night and he had been drinking, I would just cover my head and pray that it wouldn't get bad or, if it did, it would stop fast. He was just unreasonable. You made a joke about something today, he could laugh. If you made it tomorrow, he could take exception. There was always that insecurity there and kind of vulnerability that you had to test everything." When Mary met her husband, Pat, and first visited his family home, she had a revelation. "It was a beautiful summer evening and I was in the kitchen with Pat and his brother and his mom. We were looking at photographs at the table and as we were poring over this photo album, the back door opened, and it was Pat's dad coming in from working in the garden. I froze. His father came in and he said, 'Hey, guys, what are you looking at?' And he just put his arm around his wife and leaned in to look at the pictures and I thought, 'My God, if that was our father, he would just go crazy. *What are you doing in here? I'm out doing the garden. Why aren't you out doing some work?'* He was so volatile, so, so volatile. The volatility was there all the time. It was very difficult to cope with. He had a great heart. When he was good, he was very good. When he was in good form, I loved him to bits, but the days he wasn't, I hated him. I knew I was happier with my mother on my own. I was happier when our father wasn't there. One night, before I fell asleep, I remember thinking and being afraid to think it because Catholicism was so inbred into us: *Something's going to happen to me if I think this.* And I remember thinking, *if my father was dead, our lives would be so much better.* And when you're twelve or thirteen that's a scary thought to have."

Christmastime was the worst. There was more liquor available during the holidays, which meant Dad would drink more, which meant he would be even angrier and more violent than usual. There was a lot of drunkenness in the village around Christmas, and the combination of a lot of foolish drunks and Dad's anger gave me a deep distaste for Christmas throughout most of my life. There would be wonderful treats, it was true. We would get a present, for example, such as a new hurley, and as a special treat my mother would make Jell-O, which was thrilling. But invariably, something would go wrong to make the whole thing miserable.

Sean remembers that Dad "was never capable, really, of actually opening up, and being caring, but then again, that was his generation as well. You didn't hug your son. I feel strongly that he was limited and incapacitated by that inability, as were many of that generation, the inability to be expressive and to show that they cared. Because that was weakness." My brother Patrick, who now lives in Kilkee, County Clare, had the same view, that Dad "shared his frustrations through anger. I never remember our father telling me he loved me. Oh God no. No, no, no that wouldn't have been. That wasn't our father." Patrick's view of our father's violence, however, differs from what Joe, Sean, and I experienced. By the time Patrick came along—a dozen years after I was born—Dad had mellowed just a bit. Mary had been born three years before Patrick and Dad never hit Mary, nor did he strike Pat. "He never laid a finger on me because he wasn't able," said Patrick. "He was with a walking stick."

Every once in a while, when we were kids, we would catch a glimpse of the softer side of his personality, something he was a master at concealing. On perhaps two occasions that I recall, the family would pile into a car borrowed from a neighbor to drive from Knockaderry to Glenroe, where my mother's family lived. This was quite the adventure. First, my father had to crank the front of the car to get the engine going, and then he would have to do his best at something he very rarely did—drive safely over the narrow winding roads of rural Ireland. My father was not only an inexperienced driver, but a nervous one as well. We would look forward to these trips, while simultaneously fearing possible explosions from Dad. Almost anything we said or did could set him off, especially during the tension of driving. At the same time, there were tender moments on our drives. He loved pointing out a particular house where he had stopped during his long bicycle trek to and from work back when he was a younger man. He would tell us, "I would always stop at that house because Mrs. So-and-so would always make me tea and it was halfway so I knew I had another ten miles to go. She would give me tea and a bit of bread, and then I would continue on." As Mary observed: "He did love us, but he was not able to show it at all."

The ugliest side of life in Knockaderry was rarely spoken about, and then only in the most confidential terms. It involved violence, especially by drunk husbands against their wives. When you heard about the wife with the broken nose, or the wife with the black eye, you always knew it was alcohol-related. You would hear people say, "Well, she must have deserved it, she must have done something wrong to get him mad." I remember, as a kid, being appalled by that thinking. I rarely remember people saying, "He was wrong, and she was right." The typical attitude was the opposite: He was always right, she always wrong. She probably didn't have the dinner ready when he got home. Or maybe the dinner wasn't hot enough. The excuses would be along the lines of *He's a hard-working guy, he's under a lot of pressure, he's working two jobs, he's working long hours.* So, what should he have done? If it was an extreme case where the husband's violence crossed some line, you would hear people saying, "Well, he's a real bastard."

While violence against women was certainly not universal, it was not uncommon. In the Dowling household we were not immune to this, especially on those occasions when Dad got drunk. Sometimes he would strike my mother—a horrific thing to see. When I saw it at a very young age, my instinct was to hurt him, but I was just a little boy. Through the years, Joe and Sean and I did what we could to keep our father from hurting her, and we were often successful, though not always.

One time when he came home, my mother was painting a wall in the house, because she loved to try and keep the house as neat and attractive as possible. We had very little, of course, but she took pride in what we did have. Dad came in as she was painting the wall, and I don't know why he got so angry—maybe the dinner wasn't ready because she had been painting. Whatever the reason, he just totally lost it. He picked up the open can of paint and flung it at my mother, striking her with the can and splashing paint. I watched this, and I was so stunned I did not know what to say or do. I only knew at the time that I wished I was older, bigger, stronger. It seemed like something that was beyond reality; something that no one would ever do to someone they loved; something you could only do if you were possessed of demons so powerful that they would consume your entire being. And after such events, what did my mother do? She cleaned up the paint, restored order in the room, and went on with life.

Did my father love my mother? I absolutely believe he did, and my siblings share that view. "There were arguments and all that," says Joe. "I mean she loved him very much and I suppose in his own way, he loved her, but his temper let him down." Every once in a while, Dad would be the one hurt in a confrontation. When my brother Sean was about six or seven years old, he got into a physical confrontation with our father one night. It started in the kitchen area, but soon moved to the bedroom, Joe slammed the door on our father to protect Sean. As our father lunged forward to strike Sean the steel latch from the door sliced into Dad's hand. Sean and Joe escaped out of the window and ran up the hill beyond our father's reach.

By far the biggest problem between my father and me was his view that education was a waste of time and my view that it was probably the most important thing in my life. One night when I was in secondary school, with exams scheduled for the next day, Dad had me working on repairing a steel water tank in the back of our house. He had me using a drill bit that wasn't made for steel, which made the drilling job next to impossible. I worked at it for a long time with Dad watching over me. It was getting late—after midnight—and I had to study. My mother urged him to put off the work for the night and pick it up the following night after exams, but he gruffly dismissed her. It was willful ignorance and incredibly stubborn. My mother was furious, but she was carefully restrained in the way she spoke to him. "You really should give him a break so he can study," she said to him. "And he's got to sleep as well. The exams are important." He grumbled a response and told me to keep working. As it grew later, she pleaded with him again, but my father replied, "Goddamn it, he's got work to do. What the hell are these exams for anyway?" My mother was the peacemaker and she knew not to go back at him in an angry tone, knew that would only escalate the confrontation. I was always bothered by his attitude. He had really made clear his true feelings about my education back when he had sided with Mr. Burke, recommending that I repeat the final year of primary school and then quit school for a job as a laborer at age fourteen. That stuck in my mind, for not only had he not supported my desire for an education, he had actually opposed it.

As the night wore on and I continued drilling, my mother pleaded with him until finally he relented, and I was able to study and get some sleep. But my mother and I were both so furious over that incident that our anger did not soon dissipate. Dad's view was that for people like us, school was a waste of time. He'd say, whenever he saw me studying, "You should be out working. What the hell are you studying that shit for?"

I'd be upset. I would be furious. I remember walking around the house saying, *I've got to get out of here. I'm getting out of here. I can't do this. I cannot live like this.*

When he was around forty years old, Dad's arthritis worsened to the point where he was pretty well crippled and could not walk without the aid of a cane. His swollen joints left him in constant pain. His feet swelled, his hands twisted, and his joints restricted his movement. As a result, he had to stop working altogether. He lived an additional twenty years and remained ill during all of that time. This was sad to see, because Dad had always been a strong, tough man and an excellent worker, but now he was left unemployed with a very small disability allowance.

This meant my mother had to work more intensively as a seamstress, and she did so, hovering over her beloved Singer sewing machine—a manual model requiring her to crank it to make it work—for hours upon end, filling orders from people and organizations throughout the region. She was not paid much, but any amount she earned helped the family get by. She made wedding dresses, vestments for priests and altar boys, and curtains, as well as coats and dresses for women.

I was working in America by then, but my brother Patrick recalls that our mother kept the family alive. He recalls hearing her sewing until three o'clock in the morning. When the county housing administrator came to our house each week to collect the rent, my mother made the payment required and was never late. Patrick remembers well our mother's enjoyment of creating. "She would measure fabric and the next thing you'd see would be a wedding dress and four bridesmaid's dresses hanging up on the wall."

By this point, Mary and Patrick were the only ones at home. They remember how our mother handled the challenges around her, including Dad's dark moods. Mary also saw how Mam was there for him no matter what. She would do simple things such as walk him into the village to the pub, although she would not go in, as women were not allowed in the pub. She would walk home and wait for him to come back, and God only knew what way he would be. At some point later in her life, Mam said to Mary, "I married him. I promised to live with him. I loved him, and I never want to share my life with anyone after him."

Pat thinks she dealt with Dad's issues "by being a sponge. She absorbed, never fought back because you didn't fight back with our father. You just absorbed . . . So really how did she deal with it? She was strong. She was stronger than anybody else, and when there would be stupid stuff going on, she'd be there trying to make peace and she'd always love the weakest link more than any other link. And where there were difficulties and weaknesses that's where she zoomed her attention. If you're strong you're fine, you're grand, but I'll help the weakest piece in the jigsaw and there were a couple of weak pieces, including Dad."

Experiencing one of my father's angry or violent episodes required all of us to steel ourselves. In the moment, we thought only of getting through it, but time has a powerful effect on the need to try to understand the past. Which led my siblings and me, when we were gathered in Knockaderry in the fall of 2019, to share some thoughts about what had hitherto been something of a mystery: the question of *why*. Why did our dad behave in the way that he did? What fueled the anger and rage that animated so much of his life? We all have our thoughts, but in the end, we believe it was a combination of two things. The first was a profound bitterness that he did not inherit his family's farm, as he quite reasonably expected to do. Second, we are convinced he suffered from depression.

My father's family had a small farm in Knockaderry village. He grew up on that farm, the youngest of seven siblings, and he worked on the farm from childhood. Through the years, his siblings emigrated to England and America, leaving him as the sole child at home. He continued to work the farm, and essentially devoted his life to it upon quitting school at age thirteen. Years passed, and he expected that he would inherit the farm and the house that went with it. But in a shocking development, the farm was not given to my father, but rather to my father's nephew. This was a crushing blow. Dad had worked it night and day into his late twenties and then, quite suddenly, he was out, and the path of his life was forever changed.

Why did the farm go to his nephew rather than to my father? It has remained something of a mystery, but through the years we have heard bits and pieces of the story, and my siblings and I have pieced together our understanding of what happened. All of Dad's two brothers and four sisters have long since passed away, so we cannot be absolutely certain of this, but we have been led to believe that it was our father's siblings who made the decision to deprive him of the farm. He was the youngest child, it was true, but he was also the only sibling who remained in Knockaderry on the farm. My siblings and I have been led to believe that when the time came to decide the fate of the farm, he and his siblings gathered to discuss the matter. My father's siblings spoke with one voice, contending that their nephew should inherit the farm, and during the course of the evening conspired to get my father drunk enough so that he would agree to relinquish any rights to the property, leaving it clear for his nephew. This left my father with nothing.

"I think we have a better understanding of him now in the sense that it drove him to extremes of behavior that was largely prescribed by the fact that he didn't have an opportunity," says Sean. "He never got one." That failure to have an opportunity—to own and run the farm on which he had grown up and worked so hard—ate away at him. "I think Daddy was a victim of his upbringing, and being let down by his family," says Patrick. "He'd worked on the farm until he was well into his late twenties. No schooling, just farming. That's all he knew and then the next thing they say, *By the way, the farm is being given to somebody else.* That left a scar and a wound that never healed. Towards the end, he became very sad about a lot of stuff in his life such as the farm and that played in his mind when he was at his lowest, very ill."

Shortly before Dad passed away, Mary happened to overhear a conversation between him and his nephew, who was in the process of selling the farm. The prospect of a sale saddened Dad greatly, to the point where Mary heard our father begin to cry. With a farm of his own, the course of my father's life might have been very different. He would have had an income, as well as the respect in the community typically afforded productive farmers, and he would have had the chance to pass the farm on within his own family. He would have been able to make donations to the Church in amounts that would not have humiliated the family. He would have had the joy—and to him it would have been such a great joy—of working his own land.

Instead, Dad moved out of the farm to the old thatched-roof house, one of the worst residences in the village, and eventually found work as a laborer for the county council repairing roads— one of the lowest jobs on the socioeconomic totem pole in our community. For a long time, he worked twenty miles away in East Limerick, requiring him to bike to work each way no matter the weather. When they were first married, my parents lived with my mother's parents in Glenroe. To get to his job, Dad would leave home after dinner on Sunday evening and cycle thirty miles to

Knockaderry to stay with relatives for the night. Early the next morning, he would cycle another twenty-five miles to work. He would work the week, including a half day Saturday, after which he would cycle all fifty-five miles home.

My father never got over being rejected. My brother Sean, who trained as a nurse with a specialty in psychiatric counseling, gained a keen understanding of patients with emotional disorders through his work, and he believed that our dad suffered from depression during his life. "I believe that his frustration and his behavior was largely driven by the fact he felt that life had passed him by," says Sean.

My father's mother had remained in the family home on the farm, but when she grew sick near the end of her life, there was a plan to put her into a nursing home, but Dad would not hear of it. He brought his mother to live at our house, where she passed away soon thereafter.

Chapter Six

University College Cork

"Oh, my God, I'm in college!"

DUE TO MY SCORES ON the leaving certificate test, I was automatically eligible to enroll in public university in Ireland. I chose University College Cork, about sixty miles from Knockaderry. As I prepared to leave home for my first semester, I knew very little about what to expect. There had been no counseling or mentoring in secondary school to prepare me for the experience, not in the way high school students are typically prepared in the US and in Ireland today. I knew very few people who had attended college. After secondary school, only a few of my classmates continued their education, and those students tended to be from relatively prosperous families.

In England, the summer before my first year of college, I had earned enough money to pay for registration and tuition. But I knew I would have to work weekends and over Christmas vacation to pay for food and other expenses. When the time came to head to Cork, I bid goodbye to my mother (my father was not around), picked up my small bag of possessions, and walked a few miles to the main road, where I hitchhiked.

I was fortunate to catch a ride on a white tanker truck carrying milk all the way to Cork City. The driver was a friendly guy, and as the truck meandered along bumpy, potholed, narrow country roads that wound slowly through one little village after another, we engaged in conversation about a variety of subjects—including hurling, of course. However, when he learned I was headed to college, he studied me closely and asked a series of questions. He did not run into many boys from our area going to college, so he was naturally curious. He lamented not having had more education himself and asked me about the details of higher education. What he didn't understand was that I really didn't know much more than he did. I'd never set foot on a college campus, and my level of naivete would soon be fully on display. What I distinctly remember about that trip was that friendly stranger—a fellow Irishman—who seemed genuinely excited for me.

When we finally arrived in Cork City after half a day's drive, he dropped me off and told me that the college was on my left. I thanked him as he wished me good luck and I headed off looking for a building that would be readily recognizable as the college—perhaps a building with the word "college" on a sign. But no, nothing like that. I walked along side streets, past manicured lawns and beautiful buildings, but I could not find the college, because I wasn't sure what it would look like. I was anxious and feared I would look as out of place as I really was, and I was too embarrassed to ask any young people walking by, who I took to be college students. I didn't want to look stupid.

Finally, divine intervention. I saw a nun coming toward me who I thought would be understanding, and she was. When I asked her if she could possibly direct me to the college, she replied, "You are in the middle of it. It's all around you." I then realized the college was not just one building, but a collection of many buildings clustered together.

Soon enough, I found one of the buildings with a registration sign and a line of students. I learned that in order to register for classes, you had to have a cap and gown. I bought them in a school shop and returned to the registration area, and as I did so, I saw a large notice above the sign-up area that read LIBERAL ARTS. I was confused by this, because I had neither interest nor ability in any kind of art.

This level of naivete seems comical now, but at the time I had entered a universe beyond anything I had ever known, where nearly every custom and practice, the very language, were foreign to me. It was explained to me that "liberal arts" meant the study of a variety of academic disciplines. I signed up for classes in history, science, geography, math, and English.

It was explained to me that the relatively few dormitory rooms on campus were already reserved, but many families within a mile or so of campus took in student boarders as a way to increase household income. The college provided a list of such families. I soon found a room with Mrs. Turnbull, a short walk from school. She was a friendly lady who provided breakfast and evening supper as part of the rental fee. At Mrs. Turnbull's small home on a pretty side street, I had my own room on the second floor with a single bed, dresser, chair, desk, and reading lamp, with the bathroom just down the hall. After I hung up the few clothes I had brought with me, I set out my hurling clothes and my hurley and returned to campus to scope it out a bit.

I felt delighted with this step I was taking into the unknown. No, I did not know much. Not yet, anyway. But I trusted the process of education, and I was confident that in a short time I would get the hang of it. My only real concern was whether I was smart enough to be here, smart enough to keep up with the other students who seemed, as I walked past them on campus, so perfectly comfortable in this place. I was determined to work hard when classes started and block out distractions such as drinking.

In fact, I never once consumed alcohol while I was in college. As a Pioneer, I had signed a pledge at the age of sixteen, committing to lifelong sobriety. More than that commitment, though, I had seen firsthand in the village and within my own home the destructive power of alcohol, and I wanted nothing to do with it. I knew without doubt that I did not want to be like those men in the village who would stumble out of Hanley's Pub, then stagger off to do a half-assed job on the farm. It would have been difficult to think of anything less aligned with my goals at the time than drinking.

That first day, as I took in the buildings around me and the campus full of students and faculty, many of them in academic caps and gowns, I felt as though I had been carried through time to a place I never knew existed but that had now welcomed me. I couldn't stop feeling that this was just fantastic.

On the first day of classes I sat among seventy-plus students in a lecture hall, and the professor said, "Look to your left, look to your right; only one of you will be here next year."

Once classes started, I read my assignments carefully and was well prepared each day. Yet I could not shake a vague sense of not belonging. I had no friends yet, and I could not help but notice on campus that most students were dressed in clothes a good bit nicer than my own. I also noticed, to my astonishment, that there were students who had their own cars. This I could not fathom. More important than these outward appearances was my nagging uncertainty about whether I was as intelligent as the other students. I felt awkward among all of these young men and women who seemed to carry themselves with ease and confidence. All of this uncertainty was fuel for me, just as it had been rocket fuel when Mr. Sullivan had told me a few years earlier that it was *too bad a boy like me would never be able to go to college*. I worked and worked. And I enjoyed every moment of it.

While I was studying hard, there was also the matter of finances. I had enough to enroll and pay for tuition and had paid for the first few weeks of my digs, as housing was known among students. But I had to work to make enough to pay for my room for the rest of the semester. Although things were very tight at home, Mam had given me money out of the coffee can in which she saved whatever came into the house. That money, which I later paid back, helped pay for my digs that semester. In a way, the whole family helped me that year, for the coffee-can money had been earned through the labor of not only my mother, but also my brothers Joe and Sean. Most of what they earned went to Mam, and everything Mam got went into that can.

To earn the rest of the money I needed, I would hitchhike back to Knockaderry on weekends through the fall to work with Mr. Barry, the owner of a small construction company specializing in building residential homes, mostly in Limerick City and Newcastle West. We would put down sewer and water lines, digging and mixing cement for hour upon hour. I liked working with Mr. Barry—obviously for the money, but I also liked him personally. He was energetic, friendly, and a guy who was making something of himself. I really admired that. (Tragically, on a rainy day a year or so after I stopped working for him, Mr. Barry slipped and fell forward into an industrial power saw and was killed.)

The one indulgence I allowed myself was hurling. There were a number of intramural teams that competed on a field in the middle of the college grounds. The Quarry, as it was known, was the scene of games pitting Liberal Arts against Medicine or Engineering against Agricultural Science. The teams may sound genteel, but students displayed a level of aggression and outright violence that made for vicious contests with frequent injuries. There was something about the competitive atmosphere of college that prompted these young men, all of whom had been hurlers at one level or another prior to college, to bring a particular malevolence to the contests. Everybody there, it seemed, wanted to show that he was the toughest.

In addition to the intramural teams, there was the university varsity team, where play was at a more elite level. In the fall of my first year, I played on the Liberal Arts intramural squad and thoroughly enjoyed myself. I was also selected for the university's varsity squad. One of my teammates was a student my age named Mick Bond, an excellent hurler and a strong student. Mick and I hit it off from the start, and we began hanging out in our spare time, mostly studying together or discussing various things that came up in class or in the assigned reading. He was very bright and we had many thoughtful exchanges, during which I learned a lot. He and I remain friends to this day.

As we spent time together during the first semester, Mick Bond introduced me to his good friend Mick Lane, a friendly, very funny guy. (At the time, I was also called Mick.) Mick Lane wasn't much of an athlete and didn't even play hurling at all, but he entertained us for hours on end with his razor-sharp wit. These guys were terrifically positive influences on me. They were kind, good people and fun to be with, and we learned from one another and helped each other study and prepare for exams.

Around that time, I met another student who would become part of our foursome of friends for years to come. Willy McAuliffe had spent a number of years studying for the priesthood before leaving to attend University College Cork at the same time Bond, Lane, and I started there. We would sit around together having tea and talking about courses and the work, and it quickly became clear that we were of like mind. We were all there to work hard and learn, while making the highest grades possible.

Prior to enrolling at UCC, McAuliffe had not only studied for the priesthood, he had also gotten involved in politics, particularly efforts aimed at improving social justice in society. In the second half of the year, the four of us decided to move in together to a house not far from campus in an area called the Lough. We were all very similar in that we didn't socialize much and didn't hang out with other students at the bars near campus. There was a whole group of people in college who partied all the time at a bar just down the street from campus that we four walked past on our way back to our digs. The bar would be full of students drinking, but we never stopped there. Drinking, dating, parties—they were all distractions from the work we were there to do.

The truth is, I could not have afforded to go out drinking even if I had wanted to. Would I have liked to have attended some of the dances? Sure. But it was a pound to get in and there was no way I could afford that. A small part of me felt I was missing out, but when I thought about it I'd say, *Well, what am I here for? I'm here to get an education.* This helped me stay focused on what was important.

There was one dance I was determined to go to, however, although I cannot recall exactly why. In any case, I was all set to go, dressed up nicely, and I realized that the laces in both my shoes were frayed and broken. I was resourceful enough to figure out a solution: I took a couple of lengths of cord and applied black shoe polish to them, then inserted the cords into my shoes and tied them. The unintended consequence of this, of course, was that I managed to smear black shoe polish all over my hands. In spite of intense washing, I had little choice but to show up at the dance with my hands shoe-polish black.

My first year of college was both hectic and illuminating. I studied diligently, figuring I had to out-work most of my classmates to keep up with people from higher income groups who had always had college in their plans. During my first year, I discovered that there were other academic areas besides teaching that you could major in. I had never heard of an MBA or law degree. I recall meeting a student on the hurling team who was focused on agricultural science. It was a marvel to me.

That first year I missed my family. I missed Mam in particular, of course, but I also missed my siblings. I would often wonder about everybody at home and think, *Do they know I'm okay?* There were no phones available for the kind of instant communication so common today. But I realized during that year what a peaceful environment felt like. It was truly something I had never experienced. At college, people were calm, kind, generally thoughtful. Very rarely did I witness people who were angry or violent. I found a sense of comfort and peace that made everything in life more enjoyable. It was a revelation to me—a way of living so very different from our family home in Knockaderry.

While I thought a good deal that year about my family, I remained focused on the task at hand, which was to prove beyond doubt that I could measure up academically. This was an unbelievably exciting opportunity. I would regularly think, *Oh my God, I've made it. I'm in college.* The process of studying was comforting to me. I had always been calmed by quiet time reading and I had always loved to learn. I enjoyed all my subjects, especially the history of Europe in general, and the Renaissance in particular.

I was doing well as the year progressed, but the prospect of taking final examinations was looming. The talk around campus was that the finals were quite difficult. As hard as I was working, I was apprehensive, because I had never been in this type of environment and never taken a year-end exam at the college level. Of course, neither had anyone else in their first year, but I didn't think about that at the time. My default setting that first year—you might call it my obsession—was that everyone else was smarter and more sophisticated than I was. I worried about exams, wondered what they would be like, wondered whether the questions would be beyond my comprehension or more complex than I could process—fears both rational and irrational.

Final exams were held in a cavernous hall within the Aula Max building, a dreary space where supervisors roamed the aisles in an almost menacing fashion, looking to make sure no one cheated. One exam per day for a week. When the exams were finished, all of the results were publicly posted in the hallway of the Aula Max—large sheets of paper with names and grades listed. A sea of students would arrive en masse, the hallways jammed with people rushing to find out how they had performed. You would see some students study the list, lower their heads, and slowly walk away. Some people burst into tears. Others were beaming, hurrying away to share the good news. Everybody knew who passed. Everybody knew who failed.

When I waded through the crowd and got to the wall, I was thrilled at my results—so thrilled that it would take time to fully absorb, for they answered some of the most fundamental questions I had been wrestling with, and the answers were everything I could ask for. *Yes, I was smart enough to be here. Yes, I belonged.* No matter that I was from Knockaderry, where we had very little, or that I came from a home that was nearly always filled with tension, where Dad disapproved of whatever I was doing here at the university. None of it mattered. I had succeeded in making it through my first year and not just getting by, but actually performing quite well.

As I look back, fifty years later, I can say that that moment was one of the most important in my life. Standing there in the Aula Max looking at the list, seeing my name and my grades, and realizing that yes, I did belong and yes, I had joined the elite society of educated people. It had been a glorious year—I had made some good friends, been selected for the university hurling team, and passed my exams. I was on top of the world. And now, as the summer approached, I was ready to go to work. I considered returning to England, but it seemed to me that job opportunities in the US were more plentiful, and so I prepared to head off to New York to try and earn the money for my second year at UCC.

I remember my first experience in New York as if it were last week. The city felt so vibrant and alive. It was pulsing with a level of energy I had never experienced. Like any newcomer, I was fascinated by the diversity and scale, by the din, the endless flow of humanity, the bustle, the tall buildings, the air of optimism, the possibilities.

For the first few days, I stayed in a room at the Penn Garden Hotel, a hulking structure across the street from Madison Square Garden. As I recall, the hotel room was part of the package that came along with purchasing an airline ticket. But it was only for a few nights, so I knew I had to move quickly to find a place to live and a job. I had to learn some new things first, however.

On my first day, I went to get breakfast at an eatery near the hotel. I looked at the menu and was intrigued by an offering called "Pigs in a Blanket." Coming from a farming community, it was funny and confusing. I wanted tea, but was taken aback when I was given a cup of water and a small bag with a string attached. What on earth could this be? Not knowing what to do, I looked around to see what others in the restaurant were doing, but they were drinking coffee, not tea. After pondering for a while, I decided that the only logical thing to do, since I had never before seen a tea bag (at home in Ireland we used teapots to brew tea), was to break the bag and empty the contents into the water. You can imagine how that tasted.

That first day I spent many hours just walking around Manhattan, observing the remarkable spectacle that is New York City. The size and scope, the noise, the colors, the speed of everything—I was amazed by it all. I was by myself in a place that seemed more foreign than anything I had ever experienced or imagined. The prior summer I had been to England, of course, but the only place in London I ever saw was the train station as I traveled to Crawley for my job.

I made my way along some of the crowded sidewalks, fascinated by the speed at which people walked—the determination of nearly everyone to move *faster*. It was all both wonderful and intimidating. I was, of course, well aware that there were unsafe areas, as there were in any city, but I was not certain which areas those might be, so as I walked mile after mile I wondered whether I was in a safe district. I also had really no concept of the geography. I didn't know how Manhattan related to Queens, or to Brooklyn, and I don't think I was even aware that there was a Staten Island. There was one oddity about my geographic knowledge: in school, we had studied the Hudson River in a geography class, so I did know about the surrounding topography there, including the Palisades in the upper portion of Manhattan.

The one relative I knew of in the US was my cousin Chris O'Meara, a wonderful guy who worked as a bus driver up in the Bronx and New Rochelle. We connected when I arrived in the US and he referred me to some possible jobs. I asked at a bus-cleaning service west of Times Square, but they had no openings. There was another industrial place near Times Square where I inquired as well but, again, nothing available. I made my way down the lower West Side to where the Circle Line boats were docked. Chris had once worked there and said that the Circle Line had hired many Irish kids to work on the boats during the summer months.

I went into the office and the fellow there said he thought they might have something at some point, but he wasn't sure when. I was about to leave, planning on returning a few days later, when the boss came out and said that in fact, there was an opening for a job below decks in the engine room—was I interested? I said I would take anything, and I started work a couple of days later.

I picked up the routine pretty quickly. I would arrive early in the morning and oil the engines, which were set apart in two rows. I would clean the engines and start them as well. Sometimes there would be a leak in an engine that needed fixing, or sometimes a bilge pump would malfunction. Other than those sorts of issues, which were easily fixed, things on board ran smoothly. The equipment was of high quality and well cared for under the engineer in charge. He taught me what I needed to know and gave me more responsibility over the course of the summer. It got to the point where I learned how to operate the controls from below decks— how to turn the boat, reverse course, and slow the speed when approaching a dock. When the boat was out on the open water and there were no obstructions it was all quite simple, but when you were coming into dock, things could get tricky. Over time I learned to judge the speed of the boat easing into the dock by the sound the hull made when contacting the dock. There was a certain squeak where, if the pitch was just so, you would ease nicely into the dock. But if the squeak was off—too soft or too high pitched—you knew you had approached too quickly or slowly. All was forgiven as long as the boat was undamaged.

The job was great, with one exception: It was always over 100 degrees in the engine room, sometimes 110 degrees or, on rare occasions, even hotter than that. For the entire summer, I was covered with grease, oil, and sweat. All through that summer I worked seven days a week, up to one hundred hours weekly, with not a day off from May until September (one week I worked 111 hours). I was making really good money, enough by summer's end to pay my full second year of college expenses. I spent virtually all my time in the engine room as the boat circled Manhattan or crossed New York Harbor. The only people I met were coworkers, and I didn't get to know them very well because I had no time for socializing— it was all work all the time. I was not only fine with that, I loved it, because I knew I was making the kind of money it would have been impossible to earn in Ireland. I spent so much time below decks— and so little time exploring the city—that it was weeks into the job when I realized that the room I had rented, which I thought was in New York City, was actually in Jersey City. I was living in New Jersey and didn't realize it!

There was an oddity about American life I discovered that summer. To my great surprise, I discovered that Americans kept alcohol in the home for consumption there. This led me to believe that Americans actually drank a lot more than the Irish who, in my experience, never drank at home, except for special occasions. In Knockaderry, there had never been alcohol in our home except for a wake, and I was never in any house in the village that stocked alcohol. When men wanted a drink they would go to the pub, the only place where liquor was available. I found it amazing that someone in America could open their refrigerator, pull out a beer, and drink it.

That summer was about the money. My brother Joe remembers distinctly that I returned to Knockaderry after that New York summer with 1,100 Irish pounds—"like a millionaire." In those days, that was a small fortune. Not only was it enough to pay for my university tuition, housing, and food, it left a considerable amount that I was able to give to Mam. The New York summer and the money I made afforded me a level of freedom to take full advantage of college in the second year. I was free from having to work weekends or vacations. It meant I had the luxury of immersing myself in my studies, while also enjoying hurling. It meant I could also get involved in a variety of extracurricular activities that interested me.

When I returned to campus after the summer in New York, I knew the layout, the people, the students and faculty. I knew the athletic facilities, the best places to study in the library, and the places to avoid (bars). I had enough money the second year to buy a voucher for a local Indian restaurant where I'd go in every day, have my voucher stamped, then eat Indian food while filling up on rice. I picked up where I left off with the hurling team as well.

One of the best parts of that experience was traveling with the team to away games. We would spend time together on the bus and in the locker room, getting to know one another and bonding as a team. There is nothing quite as much fun as traveling with your teammates to a challenging away game. We would go to Galway, Limerick, and even to Dublin to play games. Being a part of an athletic team—the camaraderie, the feeling of connectedness and reliance upon one another—is special. Before games the team members grew quiet, everybody in his own space, everybody a little tense. I remember driving through Dublin on the bus with the team, getting to the locker room, putting on our uniforms, shirts and shorts with polished shoes, hearing an inspirational talk by our coach. It was a great feeling to be part of something that special.

That second year I was delighted to be reunited with my friends Mick Lane, Mick Bond, and Willy McAuliffe. We returned to our digs in the Lough within walking distance of campus and picked up our pursuit of disciplined study right where we had left off the prior spring.

Willy had a big influence on me throughout the college years. He was a socially conscious individual who had been involved in political causes for some years, and he encouraged me to get involved as well.

In our third year, Willy ran for president of the UCC student government, and he encouraged me to run for vice president. I was thrilled to be asked, and I jumped into the campaign. Although this was a very new experience for me, I was able to overcome my initial nervousness about public speaking. Here I have to give credit where credit is due: I adapted quickly in large measure due to the paces Mr. Burke had put us through back in grade school. Within a few months I was pretty comfortable speaking to groups of students, confident in my ability to convey my sense of what the student government might accomplish. Running for office forced me to stand up in front of students and be harangued and screamed at and to deal with that. When you run a campaign in college, you've got to get used to being shouted down and ridiculed. It's great training, and I found that I really enjoyed the intensity of the give-and-take of opposing views.

College students can be funny about university politics. There was a certain segment of the student population who looked down on those of us seeking office. They affected a superior attitude and dismissed any involvement in student activities as beneath them. Running for office was deemed essentially uncool, particularly to students who were well off financially. I was still extremely class conscious, although having seen New York City's Park Avenue and Fifth Avenue and the stately residences along Central Park, it was clear that there was a class of people in America whose wealth was unimaginable.

One of the great things about college was that it helped blur class divisions. College was an equalizer. You could have a car and money and friends and time to spend at the bar, but the reality of college wasn't in the bar or a bank statement—it was posted on the wall of the Aula Max. And those grades did not take into account whether you were rich or poor, or anything else. And I loved that. I loved the flattened class lines. At UCC, people didn't much seem to care where you came from or what your father did for work, whether you owned your home or rented. It did not matter. You got in, you were here, you were smart enough. Who cared? The only measurement that mattered was up there on the wall of the Aula Max.

There were times I could not help but sit back and think, *This is crazy, this is amazing. How the heck did this happen?* College offered so much opportunity for academic achievement, for friendships, for leadership, for athletic competition. It was everything I wanted in my life at that time. The first year, the great bulk of my learning was in the classroom or studying. The second year, I recognized that there was a lot I could learn beyond the classroom by getting involved in student government. In the first year, I was finding my way. My regular trips back to Knockaderry to work for Mr. Barry interrupted the flow of the year. In my second year, I had the financial freedom to spend all of my time at school.

Willy McAuliffe and I campaigned energetically for leadership roles and student government and any trepidation I might have had about public speaking and interacting with audiences all but evaporated during the campaign. Willy was elected president of the student government and I was elected vice president, which included the role of chairman of the student government finance committee. It was, to say the least, ironic that someone who grew up with no money was in charge of the student government account. But the truth was, I had learned through necessity how to manage money and I felt comfortable in that role.

One challenge of being in student government was dealing with activists on campus who were energized by leftist movements across Europe and the United States. During the late 1960s and early '70s, student movements across much of Europe and the US engaged in protests concerning civil rights, women's rights, colonialism, and of course the US war in Vietnam. Most of the students at UCC were liberal, but a few were quite radical. Among the radicals on our campus were a group of passionate followers of Mao Zedong, the Chinese dictator. It seemed they were won over by the People's Republic of China's rejection of capitalism and embrace of collective work, where the state made all decisions in people's lives. These students were among the millions worldwide who had read quotations from Mao's "Little Red Book," in which he promoted armed struggle and set rules for Communist governance of China. These supporters of Mao were not particularly large in number, but they made up for it by their ubiquitous presence around campus and by their raucous chants and cheers while they marched past classrooms where students were trying to learn.

It is interesting to think back on that time, when students in the United States were taking over administration buildings and shutting down whole universities, while students in Germany were firebombing academic buildings. The protests in Ireland were quite tame by comparison. I remember very clearly that the overwhelming majority of students were respectful of campus property. We had a beautiful lawn in the central quad, for example, and nobody walked on it. Everybody would walk the path to make sure the lawn remained pristine. In general, most Irish students were respectful of authority.

The Mao enthusiasts latched onto a particular issue: they wanted a room on campus to accommodate their Mao-focused association, and they argued that if other student organizations were allotted space, they should have their own space as well. Their demonstrations grew larger, noisier, and increasingly frequent. One day the president of the university convened a meeting of a number of us involved in student government to discuss various issues, including the Mao club. The consensus in the room was to continue to hold the line and deny the group space, but I felt confident enough to speak up and offer a different point of view. The president of the university, Mr. McCarthy, was an affable guy, a good listener, and I felt comfortable sharing my thoughts with him.

I told him I thought that by rejecting the Mao students' request at every turn, the administration was giving them grievances to protest about. "They're marching all over the place, and it has gotten pretty disruptive and they are fired up about being denied room on campus," I said. "I would suggest just giving them a room, a place where they can gather and discuss Mao and whatever else. By giving them a room you take away their major grievance and maybe they calm down and stop all the demonstrating. They've argued, they've lobbied, they've marched up and down looking for room. Why not give them a room?"

It was an interesting moment. The man who led our entire university fell silent to reflect upon what I had said. Finally, he nodded his head and turned to one of the deans and instructed that the Mao followers be given their own space on campus. The result was that protesters were elated with their victory. Their activity around campus all but halted now that they had a space of their own in which to discuss and debate the merits of Mao's murderous repression.

In part as a result of that interaction, the president and I developed a strong working relationship where he regularly called on me to meet with him in his office to discuss a variety of issues. He was a kind individual, a relaxed and down-to-earth person. I always tried to be the conciliator, tried to reach consensus. My view was, *All right, let's fix this. Let's figure out how to do this.* He came to trust me because I sought sensible solutions. I think he liked the fact that I wasn't strictly ideological, as many students were during that turbulent time. Instead, I was pragmatic. I worked to find compromise, to figure out practical ways to solve problems. He did not always do precisely as I recommended, of course, though he did do it a fair amount. But he always listened to me, and the fact that I was respected by the president was a huge boost for me.

As my time at UCC progressed, I got to know him better and spent more time in meetings with him, particularly after he invited me to join the president's council, a relatively small group with whom he met regularly. Sometimes we would have one-on-one discussions, and I would ask him questions about different aspects of how he managed the university, how he dealt with problems, how he sought opinions from different groups of people, how he tried to reach consensus. He never flew off the handle, never reacted in a knee-jerk way. He stayed calm under pressure. I was learning important lessons from him, watching how he dealt with challenges and crises, wondering, how does one man run a university this big and complex, with all the different kids? How does he handle the faculty, the students, the politics, etc.?

One of the issues I worked on with support from the president involved large groups of travellers camped by the side of the road about a mile off campus. When I was growing up, like most people in Knockaderry, I viewed the travellers as a menace. They would arrive suddenly and camp along the roadside, caring not at all about how they were scarring the landscape. They kept to themselves in almost hostile fashion and some of them would steal, while others looked for trouble. I wondered what was wrong with people who chose to live outside or in wagons, settling here for a few months and then suddenly moving on and settling elsewhere, and so on through the years.

In college, I learned that the travellers although Irish, had roots among gypsies in Eastern Europe going back many generations. And because I was a bit more educated, and with education comes understanding, I began to look more closely at the circumstances of the travellers especially those related to health and education. The idea to help the travellers came up at a couple of student government meetings, and I said I thought we should do something to help the children.

Some other students and I decided to pay a visit to the travellers' encampment to discuss the possibility of our trying to help. We went to their camp and met with a number of women (the men were otherwise occupied) and talked about their children and whether the mothers would like us to create a tutoring program to teach the kids some basics. The mothers were quite receptive to this idea. The other students and I put out a call for help to the student body and the response was tremendous. Dozens of students volunteered. It was so successful that the following year, some other student leaders and I suggested to the mothers that we could have premed students conduct some basic health assessments of the children.

The elevated social consciousness of the time was exciting. Students saw that poverty and ignorance were endemic to the traveller community, and they wanted to help. Faculty members encouraged us and some of them pitched in as well. It was a time when those of us fortunate enough to be getting a top-notch college education felt a responsibility to help people less fortunate than ourselves. This notion was something of an awakening for me.

Clearly, for most of my life, I had been on the lowest end of the socioeconomic scale, but now, in just a couple of years, I found myself in a position of privilege at a fine university. More than that, I found myself in a position of power in a student government leadership role, where I could muster the considerable forces of the student population to address a social need. Over the next few years, we organized hundreds of students from UCC to tutor traveller children in reading, writing, and math, while other students went out and conducted physical assessments on the children. Since the children typically did not attend school, their academic needs were very basic—simple reading, writing, and basic computation. They were generally healthy physically, although they had significant dental needs due to years of neglect. We were able to help with all of this.

As I progressed through the years at UCC, I became acquainted with many students from across the campus. Most of these young men and women were interesting, smart, and friendly. Many were quite talented as well. In my senior year, I was scheduled to go to a formal dance and was looking forward to it, but there was a problem: a couple of weeks before the dance was scheduled, I was struck during a hurling match and my two front teeth were knocked out. It was not a great look for an important college soiree.

I knew a girl who was in her first year of dental school and I asked her for help. She said she had never made teeth before but thought she might be able to do it. One night she took me into the dental lab and she fashioned a mold for a set of replacement teeth to fill the gap in the top front of my mouth. After the plaster and whatever else she used had hardened a few days later, she worked on refining the shape. When she had finished, she put the new teeth in with some sort of cement. They hurt like hell initially, but they did the trick for the dance. Not only that, over time they grew more comfortable. I ended up wearing those teeth for another ten years!

One of the more important lessons I learned while at UCC was that there was another side to the Roman Catholic Church, a side that I had not seen growing up in Knockaderry. I happened to be in church one day when Father Eamon Casey was saying Mass and he gave a sermon that was very different from any sermon I had ever heard. Typically, Irish priests spoke in Mass about the specific day's gospel, about how Jesus had taught his disciples a particular lesson or performed a miracle of some kind, but Father Casey was different. His sermon that day was rooted in the real world of the day, rather than in more ethereal, spiritual concepts. He spoke of helping the poor in practical ways, and although I am not sure whether he mentioned the travellers specifically, his message surely could be read that we as a community had a responsibility to help take care of those in need, travellers included.

Father Casey was a charismatic guy, down to earth and approachable—very different from any priest I had ever encountered in Knockaderry. I wasn't much of a churchgoer in college, but I went whenever he was offering Mass because his sermons were so powerful in calling upon all of us in the community to follow Christ's example of caring for the least within our society. His sermons were about the application of Christian values in daily life, a message that resonated deeply with me then and has continued to resonate with me these many decades later. Tragically, Casey turned out to be a fraud who did not practice what he preached. A number of women accused him of sexual abuse and his niece accused him of raping her as a child and abusing her for years. He resigned as Bishop of Kerry in disgrace.

One of the advantages of being in student government was that I was invited to join the Union of Students in Ireland, a national organization that would hold meetings, usually in Dublin. At these sessions, I would serve as a representative of University College Cork and meet with students from all over the country, including Belfast. The national meetings, where we discussed various public policy issues, were exciting. I remember one huge meeting in particular in Killarney where I walked into the room, surrounded by student leaders from across Ireland, and knew without doubt that I belonged.

What was perhaps the highlight of my final year took place on the hurling pitch. I was very proud then—and remain proud to this day—to have been chosen for the college squad. Making the team was incredibly competitive and only elite players were chosen. On top of that, our UCC team that year won the Fitzgibbon Cup. This was a huge thing in Ireland, something close to the equivalent of the annual March Madness NCAA college basketball tournament.

There were many articles in various newspapers about the hurling teams, profiling players, including photographs of our team members. My crowning achievement in hurling came when I was selected for the Limerick county team, which was the equivalent of an all-star team of college players from the county. It was a thrilling year in the sport that had given my life so much joy (and pain!).

That year I also took on the role of coach of the women's team. Women's hurling is known as camogie, and I was privileged to coach these wonderful athletes playing the sport at an exceptionally high level. Some of these women were renowned players, including Mary O'Brien and Anne Roach, who were as good as any man I ever played against—skilled and tough as nails. It was exciting and challenging to coach the team, trying to figure out the best combination of players to put on the field, identifying the most effective way to communicate both with the team as a whole and with individual players, all of whom had different personalities. The team actually did very well. We made it all the way to the national collegiate finals in Dublin and lost in the final game.

I graduated from University College Cork in May 1971. I left UCC with many things, including what would be lifelong friendships, an excellent education, and a college diploma (a BA and a high diploma in education, HDE). I applied to graduate school in social work at Fordham and received a number of recommendations, including one from the president, Mr. McCarthy, which read in part: "I would regard Mr. Dowling in regard to his social activities generally in the college as being one of the best students we have had in recent years," while another faculty member wrote that I was "one of a small band of hardworking people, which fortunately emerges almost each year from the student ranks." The chairman of the philosophy department wrote that I had distinguished myself "as a man of high moral caliber who is regarded with respect by both staff and students."

Finally, there was this letter from, if you can believe it, the notorious Mr. Burke back in Knockaderry:

> Aughalin Ballingarry County Limerick 29 May 71
> To All Whom It May Concern, Sirs,
>
> I have known the Bearer—Michael Dowling from infancy. He received his primary education up to the age of 12 at my school at above address, and all during his secondary university courses he has kept in close touch with me.
>
> I can strongly recommend him as honest, sober and hardworking, attentive to his duties and upright in his dealings. He comes from a sound family background, is well conducted, well disciplined and of sound moral upbringing.
>
> I can very strongly recommend him for any position to which he may aspire.
>
> Signed,
> Head Teacher, Michael De Burca[1], D.E.A.J.E.

By the time I finished college I was more convinced than ever of the immense value of education, and in my final year, while I was home from UCC on vacation, I convinced my mother that we should send my sister Mary away to boarding school. Mary was a very bright girl with great promise, but I feared that if she stayed in Knockaderry she would not get a good education and she would

---

1   De Burca is the Irish spelling of Burke.

be trapped into staying at home, as so many other Irish girls did, to care for our parents in their old age. I wanted more for Mary, and my mother agreed.

I don't recall the details exactly, but we made arrangements for her to attend a rigorous school for girls in the town of Templemore, about seventy miles from Knockaderry. Tough-minded Sisters of Mercy made up the faculty. Mary started there at age twelve, a few months after I graduated from college. She performed very well academically, although she did not love the regimented nature of the life. She remained at the school—coming home for vacations and summers—until she graduated at seventeen. After a year of college, she had had enough of academia.

While she was away at school, I went away again as well— back to New York to work, but also, as it turned out, to pursue an advanced degree.

Chapter Seven

Joe Is Gone

"What did I do?"

ON THE NIGHT OF HIS sixteenth birthday, my brother Joe went with our nine-year-old sister, Mary, to attend a concert in the Carnegie Library hall next to the church in the center of Knockaderry village. Part of the show was to include young Irish dancers, Mary among them. The plan was for Joe to walk Mary home after the show, but there happened to be a girl at the concert who invited Joe to go to a dance in Newcastle West, and Joe agreed. Joe arranged for someone else to walk Mary home after the show, but somehow there was a mix-up, and Mary walked the short distance home alone. For some reason, Mary hadn't been included among the Irish dancers on stage and she was disappointed. When she got home, crying from disappointment, her sobs were loud enough to awaken our father. He got up and asked what had happened, and Mary told him. He asked where Joe was, and she told him. Dad took a chair from the house and went outside and sat waiting for Joe. At quarter of three in the morning, when the temperature outside was dropping rapidly, Joe arrived at the house to be greeted by our father. He was very angry. "He told me to get out," Joe recalled. "He told me to get out and don't come back. So I did." Joe didn't like conflict or confrontation, so he left with just the shirt on his back. Everyone expected him to be back home by breakfast, or certainly within the next day or so. But the days turned to weeks, then months, and he did not return. Joe had vanished.

I was a freshman in college. I came home and joined in the search. We put out the word throughout the community that he was missing, but no one had seen him. He had left in a rush with no extra clothes and no money. How far could he go?

My mother and father and I, along with Sean and Mary, scoured the village. Nothing. We looked everywhere, roaming the hills and valleys in and around Knockaderry. A neighbor suggested retaining the services of a diviner, someone who practiced the ancient art of discovery via supposed supernatural powers. The diviner, using some of Joe's clothes as guidance, searched the area until he came upon the River Deel, a few miles to the west. The diviner informed us that he believed Joe had drowned in the river and that we should search for his body. Searching the Deel was the worst—the idea that Joe might have drowned in these waters was unthinkable.

Joe and I had been joined at the hip since he was born. We did everything together—went to school together, worked together, slept in the same bed together. We had to find him, and I believed we would. Maybe it was hope rather than belief. While I was searching for Joe, Sean, who was only twelve at the time, hitchhiked to Cork and wandered the streets, asking people whether they might have seen our brother. When that failed, Sean hitchhiked across to Dublin and searched there as well. No sign of Joe. Even Mary, at nine, joined the search in Knockaderry. Nothing.

The sense of heartbreak that hung over the house was overwhelming. Mam was so devastated. She always focused most on the weakest link, on whoever was down or hurt in some way, and now the worst—one of her children gone without a trace. Dad was devastated as well. "He cried for a week," recalls Sean. "With our father not a lot of thought went into certain things. He was reactive to a point of being totally irresponsible. No thought for the outcome or no thought for what it was going to be over the longer term. But he was devastated, my father, as well, because he realized, 'What did I do?'"

Soon I returned to college and resumed my studies, but it was difficult to get Joe off my mind. We all moved on in a way, almost as though there had been a sudden death. The difficulty was there was no closure, no memorial service, no gathering to say, definitively, goodbye.

And then, one day about a year and a half after he left, there was Joe at the house in Knockaderry. "I remember the day he came back," Mary recalls. "I was in the sitting room and I happened to be looking out the window and I saw this guy walk along the road and he had a pair of white wide pants with black splashes like paint. I remember being speechless. I couldn't talk. I remember just being completely overwhelmed when I saw him coming back. I tried to say something to my mother but I couldn't talk."

Even fifty years later, as I write this memoir, the events surrounding Joe's disappearance are painful to recall. It was the most traumatic thing to happen to our family. My siblings and I all agree on that, but, strangely, we had barely discussed it over the years and never in much detail. That changed fifty years after Joe's disappearance, when we gathered in Knockaderry for a reunion—when we all learned a bit more about what had happened. Within our family, besides our mother, no one had been more deeply affected by Joe's disappearance than Mary, who blamed herself for Dad's fit of rage that ultimately caused Joe's departure. "And that's how it started," Mary recalls. "When Joe came home, my father just lost it. And then Joe was gone. Sean would probably have fought back and said, 'I'm not going.' So would Mike, but Joe went. My mother was distraught. I don't know what the relationship with my mother and father was at the time. I just remember my mother being—all of us being just totally distraught. It was a horrific time. I remember people coming to the house, then searching for him, walking the roads, the ditches, the dykes. It was a horrific, horrific time. I think my mother lost a baby at that time. I hated my father so much. My heart broke. My heart broke and my mother's heart broke."

From Joe's perspective, there had been a miscommunication that night about who would bring Mary home. When he returned home from the dance in Newcastle West it was 2:45 a.m. and our father was waiting. Dad told him to get out and not come back. "So I did. I walked eighteen miles to Foynes, down near the coast. I knew a guy down there who was going to England. So off I went to England." From Foynes he hitchhiked to Dublin, where he caught a ferry to England and made his way to London. "For the first few days in London I slept in a park at night. But I got a job in a bar collecting glasses—they're called pot men. And then I got behind the bar and then I worked for a record store." He was working in the Kilburn section of London, staying at a bed and breakfast in Raynes Park, just outside Kilburn. Joe knew, of course, that Mam would be worried sick about his disappearance. After some time—a few weeks as he recalls—he posted a letter to her explaining that he was in London and that he was okay. I didn't learn about this letter until our family gathered in Knockaderry in the fall of 2019. This was news to me. I had always been under the impression that there had been no contact between Joe and my parents while he was away. But it turns out that in response to his letter, Mam traveled to London to talk with Joe, to plead with him to return home and to continue with his education—to get on with life, in other words. Joe says he was very bitter at that time about our dad, but one day, at the house in Knockaderry, there he was.

Strangely, Mary and Joe, though they are extremely close, never talked about the events of that night. "I don't know why we haven't talked about it," says Mary. "I really don't know. It's the biggest thing that ever happened to him in his life, but we've never talked. Maybe it's just I don't want to bring it up for him, that I don't want to bring back memories. I'm sure he has them anyway. Sometimes digging it up is maybe too painful and we have gotten through it and we are very close. We love each other dearly. And maybe that's enough not to have to go back and dig it up. He's a fantastic guy who I firmly believe, if that had not happened to Joe and if Joe had continued with education, *wow*. He has a brilliant mind. Mathematically, Joe is brilliant. But he was put on a path that took him in a different direction. Joe is very kind, maybe a little like me in the line of being a little sensitive. He is really kind and genuine and has achieved an awful lot, even though I believe he could have achieved a lot more." Joe didn't go back to school. He worked in a chicken hatchery—a dirty, arduous job—but it wasn't long before he traveled back to England to work. The fact that Joe veered away from his educational pathway troubled our mother and bothered me as well. As Mary says, Joe has a brilliant mathematical mind. To me, education was the key to the future—to an opportunity for a fulfilling life—and I wanted Joe to see it that way too. He certainly had the brainpower to excel academically, but he went back to England to work before completing secondary school.

After he returned home, the relationship between Joe and Dad remained difficult. As Sean recalls, "There was pressure, stress, a great degree of animosity, people out of control, really, and then Joe went away again." Says Mary, "It was the most horrific time and then there were a lot of fights after that even. But there were nice times, too. You have to think of the nice times. But there was a lot of not nice times." Mary carries a sense of guilt for the whole affair to this day. "I had to go and get help for that. And someone said, 'What age were you? You were eight, nine. How could you have been responsible for somebody else doing what they did? Your father did what he did.' But it took me a long time. Things weren't really much better when Joe returned home—not between Joe and our father."

Drink has taken a terrible toll on our family. After his return and throughout his twenties, Joe was troubled by a dependence on alcohol. He spent quite a bit of time at the pub—in the back of the pub, actually—with friends who didn't want their fathers to catch them drinking. "I did drink quite hard," Joe said. "I had a big problem." Sean recalls the situation with Joe's drinking as being "very bad, very bad."

"It was funny," Joe recalls. "When I got married, there was an incident with our father. We were at the hotel before the reception, I went to the bar and he was giving me a lecture about drinking. I was drinking heavy at that time. That day I was only drinking a mineral because of the wedding, but then he says to me, 'Have a drink on me.' I said, 'All right, I'll have mineral,' and he said, 'No, no, have a whiskey.' So," Joe says with a laugh, "I had a whiskey."

Joe's decade-long alcoholism threw him off track, damaging important relationships, including the extremely close bond between Joe and me. Besides my mother, when I was growing up, Joe was the closest person in the world to me, and then our bond was broken. From the time I was twenty-two until I was thirty-two, it seemed that every time I went home, Joe's drinking had yet again upset Mam. I couldn't understand why Joe would do this—why he would disrupt the family like that. I was furious with him.

During my summer breaks from college, I would return to New York, and I would think: *I'm working my tail off in New York a hundred hours a week. I'm not socializing. I don't have girlfriends. I'm busting my ass and what does he do? I'm trying to help out at home. He's causing distress at home.* One time when I was twenty-one or twenty-two and Joe eighteen or nineteen, I came home from New York with a rented car from the airport and I drove to Newcastle West to extract him from a bar. He was very boisterous. I tried to bring him home and get him out of the car, but he wouldn't get out. I lost my cool and I hit him hard, but he wouldn't fight back, which infuriated me even more. That may have been when I decided, *I've had it. I'm not dealing with him anymore.*

Even when I would return to Ireland, I would make a point of not visiting Joe. We didn't speak for years. My wife Kathy was immensely frustrated by this, urging me to sit down with Joe and try to work things out in a calm, loving fashion; to forgive whatever past transgressions there had been; to be, in other words, a loving brother. I refused. I was too stubborn. Is it possible Joe might have quit drinking sooner than he did if I had been more determined to be an integral part of his life?

Finally, my brother Sean, God bless him, intervened. While Pat stayed with Joe in Knockaderry, Sean came from Dublin, took charge, and was a steady guide helping Joe get into and through rehab. After rehab, Joe, God bless him, has not touched a drop in thirty-plus years. I think of Joe's quitting as nothing less than a heroic act of selflessness. Alcoholism is a disease, a selfish pursuit in the extreme. Alcohol doesn't care about the drinker's loved ones. Joe quit for himself, of course, but he also did it to improve the quality of life for everyone. Joe went on to have a distinguished career in the Irish Army, including serving with the UN peacekeeping force in Lebanon. Joe is a strong man with enormous willpower, and the strength he summoned to quit—for the sake of his family and himself—was impressive. He was helped and continues to be sustained by a strong faith that has become a central part of life for Joe and his wife Kay.

I wish I could say that Joe's sobriety solved the lingering problem between us. But our relationship did not mend for years. I regret that very much to this day. Why did we keep our distance, exactly? Maybe in part it was my impatience and judgment that Joe had been wrong not to continue his education when he returned from England the first time. Maybe my resentment of the trouble he had caused Mam would not let me reconnect with him. During that period I would visit Knockaderry, spending time with Mary at the family home, and we would sometimes literally drive by Joe's house, but I would refuse to stop. I am not proud of this stubbornness, this coldness. I am not proud of whatever within me prevented me from reaching out. But I am very thankful we both figured out how to bridge the gap between us.

Chapter Eight

Fordham and Failure

"I am returning to Ireland (for good) very soon. There is much more I could say but words do not really express it . . . This trip home I think is the turning point in my life. It won't be long before we are all together . . ."

MY MOTHER SAVED SOME OF the letters I wrote home when I was in America, and it is striking to me in retrospect how certain I was back then that I would be returning to Ireland for good once I completed my education in New York. As I look back on that period, I am struck by the intensity of my desire to return home—and in all my correspondence I invariably referred to Knockaderry as *home*. I missed Ireland and I very much missed my family.

Joe was in the Army, Sean was pursuing a degree in nursing, Mary was working in Newcastle West and caring for my parents, and Patrick was at the University of Limerick. I knew what they were doing through occasional letters, a periodic phone call, and my infrequent visits home, but my life for the moment was in America and I felt very far removed from everyone.

My longing for home was particularly acute during weekends and holidays. There were many times, especially in summer or during breaks, when I wanted to go home but couldn't afford it. In one letter home while I was in graduate school at Fordham, I wrote that school "is what I stayed here for and I know that when its finished it's back to Ireland . . ." I remember saying, on a number of occasions, "I will definitely go back permanently a year from now." But a year from now would come and it would be exciting in New York and something good would happen—I would get another job or teaching opportunity.

My first year of graduate school at Fordham cost $2,500, which I had saved over the summer working on the Circle Line boats. For the next two years, I would divide my time between classes—I was studying for a master's degree in human services policy—and a variety of jobs that would enable me to pay for tuition, housing, food, and other expenses. I was in my fourth year working on the boats, but that job was restricted to the summer months, so I had to find other work in winter.

One of my more lucrative jobs was cleaning out bars in Queens. I would go in at around 4:30 a.m., when everybody had left the bar, and clean up—put the chairs on the tables, mop the floor, take out the bottles and trash, whatever needed to be done. For a while, I took care of four or five bars in the early morning before going to class—including McLaughlin's Bar, where the juke box was always blaring, even at six in the morning. There were weeks when I would make as much as fifty dollars from each of three or four bars. I also worked Thursday and Friday nights from 5:00 p.m. to 10:00 p.m. as a janitor at a high school in Queens, cleaning out the classrooms and bathrooms, etc. For several months I worked in Mill Basin in Brooklyn, a neighborhood that juts out into Jamaica Bay, where I cleaned out the holds and bilge tanks of tugs and other boats. I also got a job taking minutes at the weekly meeting of the board of the United Way of New York, an influential human services agency. I made very little money from the United Way, but by listening to the various experts at these meetings, I learned a lot.

All of these jobs enabled me to spend two years immersed in graduate study of human services policies related to health care delivery, welfare, child nutrition, the disabled, the unemployed, the mentally ill—a wide array of afflictions and challenges. The vast majority of the work focused on broad policy questions, but field work was required as well, and in my case that meant counseling children in a high school. I could relate to these kids. It reminded me of the work I had done with traveller children while I was at University College Cork. Like the traveller children, many of these kids in New York had faced a difficult road. I enjoyed working with them. Many were from poor families and lived within a toxic environment at home. There were drug and alcohol addiction issues, family violence, child abuse—the full spectrum of horrors that afflict too many poor people.

The work was important, but it was not what I was interested in doing in the future. I was more interested in policy aspects of health and human services, which required learning about an array of difficulties people face in their lives—many through no fault of their own. In the social services world, the expression that "it takes a village" certainly applies. To have any chance to tackle a problem such as health care access or welfare reform, you had to have a really good team of social workers on the ground at the front lines. At the same time, you needed a team of policy people who understood the nuances of the problem and were creative enough to find solutions that actually worked. I think of it as working at the micro and macro levels simultaneously, and I was definitely more suited to the macro level. I liked thinking broadly about problems and working on ways to improve life for large numbers of people.

I suppose it seems obvious why I was drawn to this field, rather than to medicine or law or business. This was what I *knew*. In the Dowling family, our lives were defined, in some respects, by a combination of poverty and violence. Mam's deafness and Dad's arthritis were defining aspects of their lives, although it must be said that I am not at all sure that Mam's inability to hear had that much of a negative impact on her life. My father was a different story. Although he did receive some pension from the county, it was a woefully small sum. But we had benefited from additional help in the form of subsidized construction of the new house, which made a world of difference to our day-to-day existence. I never knew the details of exactly how the program worked, but I saw the tangible evidence of how that house—in which my sister Mary and her husband live today—improved our lives. At the same time, my mother, while grateful for this assistance, knew that she had a responsibility to make as much money as she could as a seamstress to support the family. My siblings and I pitched in as well, and our family hung on financially.

In graduate school, it became clear to me that social welfare benefits for people in other countries—particularly in Scandinavian nations and the US—were much more generous than in Ireland. Through reading, class work, the influence of professors, and of course my own personal experience, I came to believe in the idea that a benevolent society has a responsibility to help those in need. While in graduate school, I got a job in health care policy for the United Church of Christ, a national umbrella organization for many different Protestant denominations. This organization believed in the mission of Jesus Christ to help those at the bottom of society. I worked within the organization's policy arm, where we were committed to equity in health for all people. The United

Church of Christ believed that there should be a safety net under everybody, that nobody should suffer unnecessary deprivation, that everybody should have access to affordable health care, and that Christians should take an active role in serving the poor and causes of social justice in the world. This was quite different from what I was used to in the Catholic Church. I was never personally aware of work the Church did in Ireland to improve the overall plight of the poor. Working on the details of public policies and lobbying governments at all levels for the United Church of Christ gave me the opportunity on a number of occasions to travel to Washington to lobby Congress on proposals designed to help people gain access to health care. It also exposed me to one of the most influential people in my life up to that time, Rev. Hobart Burch, General Secretary for Health and Welfare, United Church of Christ.

Hobie Burch was in his mid-forties, twenty years my senior, when he took me under his wing and mentored me in the world of social welfare policy. A graduate of both Princeton and the Union Theological Seminary, Hobie was an ordained minister who had also received advanced degrees from Columbia and Brandeis, where he earned a PhD. For a time, he worked at a senior level in the US Department of Health, Education, and Welfare. He was articulate and very smart, and he took it upon himself to share some of his knowledge with me while giving me an opportunity to work on policy research on health care and welfare.

My relationships with Hobie and with Jim Dumpson, dean of the Fordham Graduate School of Social Services and former commissioner of welfare for the city of New York, were extremely important to my professional development. They also became good friends. As Jim Dumpson and I got to know one another, we spent more and more time together professionally as well as socially. At one point I invited him to join me for a trip to Ireland, and when we arrived in Knockaderry—this was the early 1970s—children in the village gathered around, astonished to see a person with black skin. Most of the people in the village—adults and children—had never seen a black person, and a number of children approached him asking whether they could touch him to see whether there was white skin underneath. At the end of our visit, people in the community threw a party for their new friend from the United States.

These men played major roles in the human services world, and working with them gave me an appreciation and understanding of the kind of intellect and skills needed to operate at a senior level. I learned from both of them about policy, but I also learned how to handle myself while working in teams and dealing with policymakers in government. I gained as much confidence from working with them as I did knowledge—and that has made a difference in my life.

I served as a member of the United Church of Christ Interreligious Task Force in Health Care, which was led by Hobie. The purpose of the task force was to advocate and lobby for national health-care reform. I wrote some articles back then for academic publications such as *The Journal of Current Social Issues*. It is fascinating to look back at some of those pieces and see how similar the challenges in health care remain today—not in the quality of science or medicine, but rather in the inability of all Americans to access the health care they need when they need it.

In 1975, my colleague at the United Church of Christ, Grover C. Bagby, and I wrote an article entitled "The Time Has Come for Action: National Health Care Reform." I was twenty-five years old at the time, with limited experience in the health-care world, but I had invested time researching the latest information. It seemed, in 1975, quite likely that some sort of national health insurance plan was about to be enacted into law. There was a growing awareness that too many Americans were without coverage, and traditional political opposition to a national program, especially from the American Medical Association (AMA), had softened. In fact, the AMA had come out in favor of such a plan after many decades of staunch opposition. In the article, Bagby and I wrote that it was crucial to carefully construct a national plan "based on sound social development principles . . . that is geared to benefit mainly the consumers of health services rather than the providers; that distributes the cost in accordance with prevailing notions of equity; that encourages efficient use of resources; that is publicly accountable; and that will make the right to health care a growing reality for *all* Americans." Incredibly, this sentence could easily apply to health care in the United States today, almost half a century later!

Another recurrent theme has continued to resurface in the national health care debate—the notion of the US as a health-care outlier in the advanced world. "The United States," Bagby and I wrote, "is the only major industrial nation in the world without a system of national health insurance. Instead, we have placed our prime reliance on private enterprise and private health insurance. Whether or not we continue to do so will be the central and probably the most controversial issue in any future proposals for health care reform." Looking back through the years, I think we were somewhat prescient, although it would be a mistake to suggest there has been no real progress on the health care front. In 2020 Medicaid insured more than seventy million people, while forty-four million were covered by Medicare, with that number steadily rising as the population ages. Since the passage of the Affordable Care Act, an additional fifteen million Americans have

Mam with me as a baby.

Dad on his trusty bike.

Age one with Mam and Dad.

My First Communion. Joe on my left, Sean on my right;
Mam made our clothes on her Singer.

WEST LIMERICK MINOR HURLING CHAMPIONS 1962, '63, '64.

Back row - left to right:
W Chawke, J Meehan, M. Walsh, P Dowling, T Frawley, D. O'Sullivan, J. Hennessy, P.J. Chawke, M. Meehan, P Hennessy, Trainer (R.I.P.).
Front row left to right:
W Hickey, T Butler, J. Collum, M. Dowling, P Hennessy, J. Mackessy, M. Moloney, J. Guirey.

Photo is of 1964 Champs. Defeated Newcastle West in 1962 West Final, defeated Feohanagh in 1963 West Final, and defeated Dromcollogher in 1964 West Final.

'71 Limerick team; I am bottom row, third from left.

My University College Cork ID.

UCC 1970—L-R Me, Mick Bond, unidentified, Willy McAuliffe.

With Mam. Being together made us both very happy.

With Governor Mario Cuomo (1993). Working with him for 12 years was one of the great honors of my life.

With Governor Mario Cuomo.

With Governor Andrew Cuomo during coronavirus pandemic.

Happy to be with my siblings.

Grand Marshal with Cardinal Dolan.

My son Brian's wedding with his wife Ashley, my wife Kathy, and daughter Elizabeth.

Honorary degree at University College Dublin with my siblings L to R: Patrick, Sean, Mary, Joe.

gained insurance coverage, to the point now where 91 percent of all Americans have public or private insurance. And the progress made in recent years for treatment of stroke, heart disease, cancer, and so much more has been nothing short of historic. Unfortunately, the challenges of cost, access, and equity that we wrote about in that article have only grown more daunting.

In addition to writing articles, I wrote a short book entitled *Health Care in the Church*, which required immersing myself in the topic, reading everything I could get my hands on, and talking with many experts. It was great foundational preparation for the work I was to do later in government and for the role I now have leading Northwell Health. The book, which I wrote when I was twenty-seven years old, made a strong case for access to quality care for all. During this period, I was also hired as a consultant at the Urban League, where I was fortunate to work briefly with Vernon Jordan and Andrew Young, who went on to become US ambassador to the United Nations and mayor of Atlanta, respectively.

After receiving a master's degree at Fordham in 1974, I was asked by faculty whether I might be interested in teaching a social welfare course to graduate students. I readily agreed, in part because I would be paid to do so, but also because the idea of teaching intrigued me. I thought it would be a challenge, and it certainly was. I enjoyed the give and take with students, and I liked bringing the subject to life for them—focusing in on real-world aspects of dense policies about welfare, for example.

My greatest lesson as a teacher was how difficult the job was—how much preparation was required. Teaching forces you to learn at a different level. For me, being a teacher was the greatest tool for self-learning, because before I stood in front of a class, I had to study like crazy to make sure I knew the stuff—*really* knew it. Sometimes there were topics coming up in the course that I really didn't know as well as I should have, and I would study more as a teacher than I ever studied as a student. I think I got more of an education by teaching than the students did listening to me, but I think they got a sense of my authenticity—my visceral understanding of the subject matter. I think they could sense that these subjects were drawn not only from my academic work, but also from my life experience.

The Fordham administrators asked me to teach two additional classes, a total of three per week, which allowed me to cut back on some, though not all, of my outside jobs. I was comfortable at Fordham and enjoyed my colleagues and the students. I was surrounded by bright people also pursuing deeper knowledge in a variety of fields. Over time, I was promoted at Fordham and given new responsibilities, including administrative roles, in addition to my teaching position. I was also appointed adjunct professor, and then full-time faculty, and was soon teaching not only at the Fordham campus adjacent to Manhattan's Lincoln Center, but also at the Tarrytown satellite campus in Westchester. Eventually, I was serving both as assistant dean at Lincoln Center and the head administrator of the Tarrytown campus, which meant I was supervising every aspect of the operation.

During my years in graduate school, Dean Jim Dumpson introduced me to a variety of different leaders in the policy world. I was somewhat starstruck when I first met and started working with Jim at Fordham. My initial reaction was excitement—*Wow, I'm working with a man who was the commissioner, who knows the mayor and the governor—this is amazing!* At Columbia, where I pursued a PhD after earning a master's degree, I worked with a number of renowned faculty members, including Professors Alfred Kahn and Sheila Kamerman. Dr. Kahn was a pioneer and a recipient of the first doctorate in social welfare policy awarded at Columbia back in 1952. Under the tutelage of these deeply knowledgeable people, my studies focused on inequality and the importance of building a strong safety net. This included studying the roles of both philanthropic organizations and government at all levels—federal, state, and local. At the time, though I believed in many liberal solutions based upon proposals for significant government spending on human services programs, I never lost sight of a central tenet I have held on to throughout my life: the essential nature of work in any productive life.

I believe that government has a crucial role to play in helping those in need, but that individuals also have a responsibility to do whatever possible to help themselves. I was guided by the idea that government support should never deprive you of the incentive to help yourself. (In my PhD work, I focused my original research on European taxation systems and their impact on human service programs. While I completed all of the course work, passed my orals, and submitted a draft of my dissertation, I never ended up submitting the final version because I was contacted by the Cuomo administration to see whether I was interested in taking a job in Albany. The dissertation found its way into the trunk of my car where it stayed, unfinished.)

Something unfortunate happened as a result of my gradual rise in the academic world. When I was teaching at Fordham, after I had progressed to the level of full-time faculty, I continued to hang out with the same group of guys I had gotten to know at Irish bars in Queens. When I first met these guys, I was going to school and working various blue-collar jobs to make ends meet. These men were bartenders, bus drivers, construction workers, and I identified with them; I was one of them.

But after a few years, as I progressed academically, one of the guys heard that I was not only studying at Fordham, but that I was a member of the faculty, no less. When the guys learned this, I felt their attitudes toward me changed. It was subtle, but there was something different: *Did I think I was better than everybody?* Now, in their eyes, I was no longer one of them, but somehow separate and apart. I also grew dismayed at the racial attitudes among many of them, though certainly not all, and I was frustrated when a guy would come from Ireland having never met a black person in his life, yet declare anti-black sentiments.

I respected the bus drivers, bartenders, and construction workers very much. I identified with them. I have a deep reverence for work—any type of work—and have demonstrated that throughout my life. I'd held every type of manual labor job imaginable, from spreading dung in the fields of Knockaderry to cleaning out dive bars at night's end. Even though I was working as both a teacher and an administrator, I still considered myself no different than the Mike Dowling I'd always been (I still do). But the guys didn't feel that way. I sensed their thinking: *Well, you're trying to be above your station. Who the hell do you think you are? You're a big deal now, are you?*

Ireland has produced brilliant writers, poets, political leaders, scientists, and more. In America, many Irish men and women have risen to the top ranks of business, philanthropy, sports, and government, yet there are stubborn pockets of people from Ireland who tend to aim pretty low in their aspirations. Where I diverged most sharply with these men whose company I had so enjoyed was in ambition and aspirations. I remember being terribly frustrated at the very Irish attitude some of them had: the idea that they did not expect an Irishman to be successful. My attitude was that *they* were lowering the bar. *You mean you're comfortable and happy just being a bartender and making sure you get good tips on a Friday and Saturday night? That's your goal in life?*

Well, that was not my goal. I was aiming higher. My Irish friends seemed to imagine the stereotypical Irishman as someone struggling, laboring, toiling at the bottom of the economic ladder. Certainly, there were Irishmen who fit that description. But I imagined the Irishman as an intellectual, literate, as a highly educated leader in business, science, education, and the arts. That's where my eyes were fixed.

I gradually decided to go my own way—to not hang out as much with these guys anymore. This was a fork in the road for me. How could I be working with a great mentor like Jim Dumpson at Fordham while at the same time tolerating openly racist views from some of my friends at the bar? I knew that life was not for me. I had been one of the guys and then, suddenly, I wasn't anymore. It was time to move on.

While I spent a significant amount of time working in graduate school—both at school and in jobs to make extra money—I also enjoyed more of a social life than I had in some time. In the summer before my senior year at University College Cork, I had met a young woman in New York, and we started dating.

Dympna Smyth lived in Queens with her mother, who was originally from Ireland. Dympna and I met at an Irish dance in the Bronx and hit it off right away. When I returned to New York the following year for graduate school, we continued dating, then got married in December 1971. My mother and father, along with Mary and Patrick, traveled to the states for the wedding. It was wonderful to be with them.

During the visit, Dad and I spoke a good deal about John F. Kennedy, whom my father, like most people in Ireland, considered an almost-mythical character—the Irish Catholic president of the United States with his Irish background, Irish heritage, family from Ireland. One morning, soon after my family arrived, Dad got up, dressed, put on his overcoat, grabbed his cane, and said he was ready to go. Somehow, he had come to believe that JFK's gravesite was within walking distance of where we lived in Queens. He was declining a little and had no concept of the scale of the United States. Instead of traveling to Washington, which was beyond my budget at the time, we talked a lot about Kennedy. I was thirteen when he was assassinated, and it was as though the whole of Ireland died. I remember everybody in the village talking about how the Communists did it, that it must have been a Communist plot because at the time it was America versus Russia. People would say that the Communists killed Kennedy like it was a fact. As kids, we worried about whether the world would end in a fight between the two superpowers with nuclear weapons.

During my parents' trip to the states for our wedding—what would be my father's only visit to America—there was a funny incident. There were some nuns from the US who knew friends of my parents and visited our home while traveling through Knockaderry. It was a pleasant visit, and the nuns made Dad promise that he would telephone them when he traveled to the states. My father explained this to me, producing a slip of paper with the phone number, and I showed him how to dial the phone (something he had never done before). He exchanged pleasantries with the nun and then she apparently went on for some extended period of talking. Dad was a man of very few words, and this didn't sit well with him. Unaware that she could hear him even if he spoke aside to me, he said, "Is she ever going to shut up?" We all got a good laugh out of it, including the good-natured nun.

During the trip, my dad and I had some pleasant conversations. I learned from my mother and my siblings that he had expressed pride in what I was doing. I was pursuing my doctorate at Columbia at the time, and he would tell people in Knockaderry that I was studying to be a doctor. He would tell people in the pub, if there was a medical issue, "Don't worry, Mike's coming home and he's studying to be a doctor—he'll take care of it." I kept hoping none of his friends would get sick, at least not while I was home. He would tell people how well I was doing, and I was sure he conveyed this with a sense of pride in me, but needless to say, he never conveyed any of those feelings to me.

I had just turned twenty-two when Dympna and I married. In retrospect, I was not as prepared for marriage as I could have been. We moved into an apartment with her mother in Astoria, Queens. Looking back, living with my mother-in-law maybe wasn't the best idea in the world. Dympna was a wonderful person, kind and smart. She was an excellent schoolteacher and very much devoted to her students. The problem was that I was a workaholic at the time—working on my master's courses during the day and then working to make money either at night or in the early morning before school. As a result, I wasn't around much, and my obsession with educating and improving myself left little room for the relationship.

During this time, I also am not terribly proud to say, I liked to take a break and have a few beers in the Irish pub, then at times a few more, and sometimes in a bar one thing would lead to another and the Dowling temper would flash and I would get into some kind of scrap. That sort of behavior isn't exactly a prescription for marital bliss.

We parted after several years, with a lot of respect, and stayed in touch occasionally through the years until her untimely death during her early fifties after she had gone to live in Ireland.

After Dympna and I divorced, when I was twenty-five, I entered one of the darker periods in my life—probably *the* darkest period. I believed ending the marriage was the right thing to do—I could clearly see that it would not work over the long term. Even so, it felt like a huge failure on my part. What had I done wrong? What could I have done to strengthen the relationship? Failure in a marriage takes a toll.

In addition, I had moved into a very small apartment with a friend up in the Bronx in a fairly tough neighborhood. One night I came home from work and found that our place had been broken into and everything, including all of my clothes—everything—had been stolen. During this period I had no personal life, no family life. I missed everyone in Ireland, but didn't have the money to go visit. I think for the first time in my life I slipped into a depression, like one of the black moods that had dogged my father for much of his life. For a couple of years, even though things were going well at work, I felt down, not myself.

It was one of the first times in my life that I had experienced a major failure. Most of what I had tried to do through the years had worked out okay. But this was a crash, and a painful one. I turned quite negative on life in the states and longed for the beauty and simplicity of Ireland. In one letter home my bitterness showed when I thanked my parents for sending me a shamrock right before Saint Patrick's Day. I wrote that "I wore the shamrock but these stupid people over here did not have an idea of what it was," adding that "the sooner I get [my education] done the sooner I'll get back to Ireland for good."

Depression is a powerful force—"the Great White Shark of pain," as the writer David Foster Wallace once called it—and I learned firsthand how it can knock you down. I am glad in a way that I did, because that experience helped me to be more empathetic and understanding of people who suffer from various types of emotional distress. In a black mood, the normal longing for loved ones is amplified, and it was especially difficult on weekends and around the holidays, when I missed everybody at home.

I missed Mam most of all, of course. She and I had been joined at the hip for so much of my life—in sync the way I was in sync with no other human being. I carried with me her drive, her ambition for learning and for improving my life—for achieving the kind of education that no Dowling had ever achieved. I carried with me an ability I had inherited from her to block out distractions and remain focused on the mission at hand.

I missed my siblings as well. I had been away from home the vast majority of the time since I was seventeen—that summer when I traveled to Crawley, England, to work in the steel factory. I had returned from Crawley in the fall and gone off to college right away. Throughout my four years at University College Cork, I had traveled each summer to New York to work, and then after graduation I headed for graduate school at Fordham. All of this meant that my time home involved a week or two here and there at Christmas and the end of summer. By the age of twenty-five, I had been living away from Knockaderry for eight years. I was gone so much that to my two youngest siblings, I was in a way someone very much removed from their lives.

As a result of all this, my trips home were rare, yet immensely joyous occasions—sort of a Christmas and birthday rolled into one. Nothing excited me more than landing at Shannon Airport and making my way home. The anticipation of seeing the family was thrilling. And according to Mary and Pat, they felt just as excited as I did. They told a family friend about the preparations that went into a Christmastime visit I made from New York.

"Oh, my God, it was amazing," Mary recalled. "It was just the same as how I felt when I was a small child when Santa Claus was coming. Pat and I would be in our best clothes and Mam would send us up the road to wait in front of the school to see him when he was coming from the Shannon airport. We would walk the short distance from our house to the school, and we'd be in our best clothes and I remember my mother saying, 'Don't get dirty now until he arrives.' And we would sit on the wall waiting for him, and the excitement was huge. I think I was a little in awe of him in ways because, at that stage, America, it was just the other side of the world."

My brother Pat recalled my trips home as "major events in my childhood. He would come home once a year or once every two years and it was a major event—my eldest brother coming home from the states. I do remember it was always morning time we'd expect him to come because we didn't have contact with the airport. There was no Google. You couldn't check the flight arrival times or anything like that, so we'd go up the road and we'd wait in front of the school because we wanted to see him coming in the car and we'd sit on the school wall and wait for him to come. The excitement was great. And our mother would have the house cleaned, and Daddy would have the front walls painted, the house would be done up because Mike was coming. It was a big event."

Mary recalls that I would always bring home gifts for her and Pat and that one year I brought Pat a battery-powered model Volkswagen car. I recall those trips with great fondness, and while I recall buying gifts for Mary and Pat, I don't recall the specifics in the vivid way they do. I did my best to bring gifts that they couldn't get in Ireland, and I remember thinking, *Well, if I bring them this thing, nobody else in Knockaderry will have this.*

But the most important thing for me to bring when I went home was always money for my mother. That was my number-one priority. I knew my mother would paint the house, paper the walls, spending money as though there was a Yank coming who hadn't been home in fifty years! I always knew she would spend money to make the house look the best it ever looked—because I was coming home. So I made sure to more than compensate her for all of the stuff that she did, which, of course, I didn't think she had to do.

At home I would catch up on what and how everyone was doing. I would get a sense of Dad's health, and I would be brought up to date on Knockaderry village gossip—always a fruitful topic while sitting around the fire at our house. I would stroll through the village exchanging greetings with old friends and neighbors and attend Mass with Mam. One of the comforting things about going home to Knockaderry was that it never really changed. The village itself was the same as I had always known it—the church, the Carnegie Library center, the post office, the blacksmith's shop, Hanley's Pub, and the hurling pitch. It was the same as it had been for as long as I could remember. I always made a point of walking down to the hurling pitch to check out its condition and, sometimes, to reflect upon games played there in years gone by. These would be the sweetest days and then, suddenly, it would be time to leave with the knowledge that it would be a long time—a year or as long as two years—before I would be back.

After a summer visit while I was teaching at Fordham, I wrote a letter to my parents upon returning to New York that read in part: "Dear Mam and Dad, I want to say a sincere thanks for giving me such a great time when I was at home. It was the best time of my life. I did many of the things which I always wanted to do but never did. It convinced me beyond any doubt that Ireland is where I am returning (for good) very soon. There is much more I could say but words do not really express it. Let me just say that it is a pleasure to go home and thanks for everything . . . This trip home I think is the turning point in my life. It won't be long before we are all together . . . I hope Dad is feeling good. It was great to see him in such good mood and I really appreciate all of you coming to the airport. Give my regards to everybody around and keep an eye out for jobs. The quicker I get out of this stinking hole the better. Until next week. God bless, love, x M."

Chapter Nine

Hugs All Around

"Did I consider it a terrible loss at the time? I did not."

WHEN I WAS TEACHING AT Fordham and working on my doctorate, I injured my back. The pain was so severe that there were times when I could neither sit nor stand and could only find temporary relief by lying down on the floor. I had suffered from periodic back pain for years, a combination of hurling injuries, the toll of physical labor from a very young age, and genetics. My mother had back pain periodically and my siblings and I all had back problems at one time or another. Through the years I received a variety of treatments, including traction, acupuncture, and visits to a chiropractor, but none afforded more than temporary relief.

At one point when I was working up in the Bronx, I was in a plaster cast from my neck to my hips to immobilize my trunk and relieve pressure on the nerves. But I had to work, and the heat and humidity of the summer was bad enough without a plaster cast on, and intolerable with it. Mobility was a problem with the cast on, but the incessant itch was the worst. I carried an unwound wire coat hanger with me to reach down inside the cast and scratch the near-constant itching. It drove me crazy. It got so bad that one day I asked my friend Mike Fitzgerald to take his Skilsaw and cut the cast off me. We were at his house in the Bronx and I lay face down on the grass in his yard. He measured the thickness of the cast, set the saw blade, then began to cut. The blade couldn't have been more than a tenth of an inch, if that, from my skin. As he was leaning over me, cutting with the saw, his little daughter came out of the house and thought he was sawing a man in half.

At the same time, the lack of childhood dental care caught up with me. My remedy for the acute pain in my mouth was to soak a cotton ball in whiskey and place it against the tooth. This was during my black period. I was depressed, living alone after the divorce in a dingy Queens apartment. I missed my family. I missed Ireland. I missed Mam in particular, of course, but I also missed my siblings. In a way, I even missed my father. I felt very much separate and apart—so far away from everyone. The occasional letters and rare visits home certainly helped, but it wasn't enough. I felt I was missing too much of the life of the family.

This was during the mid-1970s, and my family still didn't have a telephone. In my letters, I tried to schedule calls to the phone box in the center of Knockaderry village—sometimes that worked, other times not. In one letter home, I note that I had "tried and tried to call but could not get through." I got lucky with a call I had scheduled in the days before Christmas when I was feeling particularly down. This required everyone to walk from our house into the village where Mam, Mary, and whoever else was home would huddle around the phone box waiting a turn to say hello to me. These calls were never very long—the expense was outlandish—but hearing everyone's voice comforted me as nothing else could. This particular time I got through and talked with everyone—Mam, Mary, Patrick, Joe, and Sean—and it was apparent to all that I was not in the best of spirits.

Sean got off the phone from talking with me and said, "He sounds sad and lonely. It's Christmastime." A moment later Sean got back on the line and told me, "I'm coming over!" And he did. He borrowed money from a friend and came to visit me for a week. This was vintage Sean. He wanted to help, and when he saw my need, he swung into action. His visit cheered me up greatly. He even helped reduce my pain by sitting on my back as I lay down and we watched television. I still had terrible tooth pain, and Sean urged me to go to the dentist, but I vowed that nothing would ever persuade me to darken the door of a dentist office—not after suffering the kind of pain I had experienced back in Newcastle West. Fortunately, as time passed, the pain in my mouth subsided, but two surgeries were required to fix my back.

Sean was instrumental in saving me that Christmas. So was my wife-to-be, Kathleen Butler. A mutual friend of Kathy's and mine, Paula Hunchar, had been telling Kathy for a couple of years that she wanted to introduce her to me and vice versa. Paula had been a college classmate of Kathy's and a graduate school classmate of mine, and she knew us both well. Although Paula thought Kathy and I would be a great match, she delayed introducing us for a couple of years because she kept telling me that I wasn't ready to meet Kathy. "You're too wild, Mike," Paula would say to me. "If I introduce you now, Kathy will have nothing to do with you. When you settle down I'll introduce you."

By Christmastime 1975, when I was at a low point, Paula decided the time was right. She introduced us at a Christmas party at a beautiful Manhattan apartment owned by our good friends Susan and Leland Vandiver. Kathy and I got along right from the start. As I got to know her, I found her to be exceptionally intelligent and career-oriented. She was energetic and clearly on a professional fast track, earning far more money at the time than I did. She had dipped her toe into business school at Harvard, found it wasn't for her, and pursued a master's degree at the New School in New York City. When we met, she was working in the personnel department at Beth Israel Medical Center in Manhattan, where she specialized in labor relations. I asked her out on a date to attend a Rangers game.

"Do you like hockey?" I asked.

"I love hockey," she lied.

We went to the game at Madison Square Garden, and when players started throwing punches at one another, she found it too violent a spectacle.

Meeting Kathy changed everything for me. She introduced me to a world where people were emotionally healthy and available, well-adjusted and rational, kind and caring—*always* kind and caring, thinking about others. Meeting her also brought the two-year period of depression I had suffered to a close. She brought me a sense of peace and stability I had never before experienced and remains one of the great blessings of my life.

When Kathy introduced me to her parents and siblings at their home in New Jersey, I initially found their behavior toward one another jarring. Life in the Butler household seemed like one big hug fest. No one ever seemed to raise his or her voice to anyone else and everyone acted as though they genuinely liked everyone else. They were openly affectionate!

I asked Kathy, "Don't you guys argue?" and she looked at me like I was nuts. "Why would we do that?" Her father, Ed, would come downstairs in the morning and the first thing he'd do was hug his wife, Barbara, and then they would all hug each other. Every morning. Having never seen anybody hug anybody in my family—ever—I was stunned. *Is this real?* I wondered. *Are these people really like this?* And I learned over time: It was real.

Her family welcomed me. Kathy's father was outgoing and positive, the opposite of my own father. I had never known a man like that, and he definitely had an influence on me, because after I got over the fact that it was strange, I realized that this was actually the right way to live. In my household in Knockaderry, you would never show emotion, because emotion was a weakness. In Kathy's family, emotion was a strength. Telling somebody that you cared for them was strength.

I would sometimes think, *you know, it would be nice if I had a little bit of that in my past*, but I didn't. I never saw my father hug my mother—ever. I had never seen any outward display of emotion between my parents. My mother would've fit in beautifully in Kathy's family. My father would've thought, *What the hell?*

It took me a while to get used to it. Meals at the Butlers' were important social occasions when everybody was relaxed and enjoyed a leisurely conversation. They were all lively conversationalists—including Colleen, Kathy's twin and soulmate, as well as her other siblings Ed, Mark, and Peg. My father's attitude about mealtime was *Shut up and eat and get back to work.*

Kathy and I were married on November 26, 1977 in the living room of her parents' home in Middletown, New Jersey. A small number of family members and close friends joined us while a judge who happened to be a neighbor married us in a civil ceremony. The only member of my family to attend was my brother Sean, who brought a priest friend of his with him, but Father Mossie was not permitted to marry us under Church rules due to my having been divorced. After the ceremony, we hosted a big party at a neighbor's country club, where we danced all night with friends and family. We have turned out to be a great match, even though we are very different. Kathy is open with her emotions, whereas I tend to be more reticent. While there is a lot of my mother in me, there is surely some of my father as well, and that part can be aloof, even cold. It is very difficult for me to share emotions. Kathy will say to me, "You look nice," and of course I should say, "You look nice too," but I don't, and she gets upset. Recently we were leaving to go to an event, and she said to me, "You look great." And I said, "Yeah." And then she said, "So?" I said, "So what?" And she said, "Well, what about me? Use your logic." I still have a hard time. It's not in me. And she is puzzled by this because being outgoing and complimentary to others comes so naturally to her.

Kathy recalled those early years in our relationship: "My family was totally different in how the parents interacted. My father was also Irish American and unlike many Irish men, he was publicly affectionate. He would hug my mother, he would hug us, he would show us that he loved us this way, and you always knew he loved my mother by the way he treated her. He appreciated her, he was grateful for her—and vice versa. The first time Mike was at my house he felt that it couldn't be real, it had to be fake because he had never seen a family react this way. We like each other," Kathy says of her own family. "We don't fight. Certainly, there have been times when we wanted to, but we chose not to. Because of Michael's upbringing he never knew if he was going to be hit by his father. Early on in our relationship if I would come up and touch him, just touch his shoulder, he would turn around, ready to defend himself; it took years for him to stop doing that."

I remained distracted by the thought of what was going on in Knockaderry. In one letter home during that period, I told my parents that I had read about Joe's Army Pressing Out Parade—a type of graduation ceremony—in the *Knockaderry Notes* (a local paper that came to me in New York by mail) and was so pleased for him. I recall receiving photographs of Joe in his uniform and he looked so fit and impressive. In another letter I note that "I had a letter from Joe yesterday and he told me that he is staying in the army, if he likes it then it's the best thing for him to do." I added that I would soon write to Mary away at boarding school and "send her a few dollars."

After graduate school, when I was teaching at Fordham, I wrote:

> Dear Mam and Dad,
>
> The summer is nearly over again and I was just remembering that I was at home this time last year. I am already looking forward to Christmas. I plan to book my flight next week—that way I will get it a little cheaper. I am writing this in Washington. I am sitting in a park just alongside the White House where I have a meeting in thirty minutes. The past five or six weeks have been very, very busy. I have been working at my regular job but also teaching each night from six to nine at Fordham University. I taught two courses at the undergraduate level (those going for a BA degree) in September and I go back teaching in the graduate level (those doing their MA). I enjoy the teaching very much and I am quite a bit in demand . . . I was sorry to see that Limerick were so badly beaten last week. They seem to be able

to go so far but that is it. Give my regards to everybody. It won't be long now before I am home again and this time I plan to hang around Knockaderry. Hope Dad is feeling okay. I will call home on Aug 21 (Sat) at 6pm your time. Hope you can all be there to say hello . . .

God bless, Love, Mike

One of the hard parts of going home was seeing my dad's declining health. He would be sitting near the fire or he'd be across the street next to a stone wall, enjoying a cigarette and a precious glimpse of sunshine. He'd have his cane and he would just be sitting there, all but immobile. It was painful to see. I vividly recalled him as a younger man, fit, powerful, possessed of limitless energy, and here he was now, a skeleton of the guy I used to know.

One good thing about his later years was that he mellowed a little bit. He'd still lose it occasionally, of course, but he grew calmer and more at peace. He'd sleep a lot, and he couldn't do any damage at that point because he couldn't move, so he was no threat to hurl a paint can at my mother or hit me in the head with a shovel. My mother took care of him completely. In her religious world, that was her duty.

Dad's arthritis was so painful that he required regular treatments at a doctor's office in Cork, which was fifty miles away. Accompanied by Pat or Mary or my cousin Vincent, who had previously been in the Irish Christian Brothers and had left the order, they would take a bus to Limerick and then another bus from Limerick to Cork and repeat the process coming home. In all it would take up the better part of a day, but it was worth it. The shots into his joints—the "golden injections," he called them—provided significant relief.

After a while Vincent, who accepted a teaching job my mother helped him get in Newcastle West, came to live with our family. Mary, Pat, and Vincent were enormously helpful to both my parents. Vincent bought a car, a new Mercury, and now instead of bus trips to Cork, he would drive my parents to the medical appointments. This was luxurious for them—riding in a new car rather than taking the bus.

Pat was thrilled when Vincent came to live at our house and became like another older brother to Pat. He and Pat played such an important role in helping Dad. Even almost incapacitated by arthritis, our father still had a magic touch growing vegetables. "He was a wonderful man to grow stuff," Pat says. "He had the biggest potatoes, the biggest heads of cabbage, the biggest heads of lettuce. He cultivated the ground and he nurtured it like it was human."

According to Vincent's recollections, our father was still a taskmaster at heart, although a gentler one than in prior years. "One year, when I would pick Patrick up and drive home from school in the evening," Vincent remembers, "Jack said that Patrick and I had to get out and dig the potatoes. This was October so the time had come. And Pat and I would say, 'Oh, yes, we will do it tomorrow' and tomorrow would come and Patrick and I would come up with some excuse and it would be fine. But this went on for three days or so and one evening Pat and I came home and we saw Jack sitting in a chair, bent over the garden digging potatoes. He had somehow gotten a chair down to the garden because he couldn't stand up on his own and he was digging out the potatoes himself. Our excuses were over and we went down right away and dug out the potatoes with him. He was very determined."

Dad enjoyed Vincent's company. They would sit around in the evening after supper and talk about all sorts of things—local news and politics and especially sports, including hurling and Irish football. By then, my father was sleeping in the living room, where a bed had been placed next to the fireplace. And of course Dad smoked, as he had done since his teenage years. He preferred the Gold Flake brand—short, unfiltered cigarettes. Sometimes he would fall asleep holding a lit cigarette and Mam, Mary, Pat, or Vincent had to put out the spark of fire on a chair or in his bed.

Even as he mellowed a bit in old age, Dad's edginess was never too far away. One evening, when Mary arrived home from her job working as a receptionist in a doctor's office in Newcastle West, she said she had plans to go into the village a bit later to meet friends. "There was a fellow in the village who sold cabbage plants and our father asked me to get him some plants and I said, 'I will. I'm going in an hour and I'll get them.' He said, 'No, don't bother. I'll get them myself.' I would have gone straight away, but he didn't need them until the following day, but my saying I would do it later he kind of took as, 'I'm not doing it at all.' And he went out and got on the bicycle which he could no longer ride and fell and hit his head. He just got on the bike and fell off. He couldn't cycle, but he was getting those plants. It's like a black rage that you can't make sense of anything. There is no logic in it. Logically, you're not functioning at all when you've gone that deep into this anger."

In December 1978, Dad suffered a heart attack and was taken to the hospital, where he received treatment and recovered. In early January he checked himself out of the hospital and took the bus home by himself. Throughout the winter and into the spring he was tired, and it was clear he had even less mobility or energy. After a scheduled checkup on May 15, he returned home complaining that the medical staff had not listened to him. He was angry and asked Mary to help him write a letter of complaint to the health board.

She did as he asked. Three nights later, Friday, May 18, 1979, he suffered a stroke and died. He was sixty-three years old.

I go back sometimes and look at the letters I wrote home from New York. In every one, I write something like, "I hope Dad is feeling better and give him my love." I had gone home to see him a month or so before he died, and it seemed clear he would not live much longer. When I got the call that he had passed away, I wasn't surprised. I packed and headed back to Ireland. Everybody came to the house for the wake and everybody talked about how great a guy he was, *best guy we ever knew!* which is what an Irish wake is all about. I've always thought that the only way to get a lot of compliments in Ireland is to die. It was good to see my siblings gathered together.

Patrick had broken his ankle playing Irish football and he was on crutches for the wake and funeral. He was only seventeen years old, but there is a tradition in Ireland that sons of the deceased carry the casket on their shoulders. Pat was so insistent on doing this that he persuaded Sean to take him to the hospital to have the cast removed and he went ahead and hoisted the casket with Joe, Sean, and me. He was in terrible pain, and having borne that weight on a broken bone almost certainly worsened the fracture. He suffers with pain in that ankle to this day. "I wanted to go under the coffin to carry it," Pat recalled. "I didn't want to be hobbling along with crutches and seeing the guys do it. Sometimes you do things . . . When you really feel like you need to do it. I was very sad. I used to bathe him. I used to brush his hair. The lads [meaning Joe, Sean, and me] never did that, you see. If he had difficulty with toilet I would help him. I did that stuff with him so I had a different kind of a bond with him."

My father worked as hard as, if not harder than, anyone in Knockaderry village. He was one of the most respected men in the area for his work ethic and his knowledge and was a very intelligent man. All of that was true, but there were other things that were true, too. He caused a lot of pain for all of us. At the time, did I overly grieve his passing? I did not. Did I consider it a terrible loss? I did not. Is this coldhearted of me? I don't think of it that way. I think of it more as being pragmatic because I knew my mother would be freed to enjoy her life. And I suspect that Joe and Sean may have felt as I did. Mary and Pat, who were close to our father during the time when he was sickest and therefore less angry and violent, felt the loss more acutely.

I have always believed that my mother's life really began when Dad died. She would go on to live an additional twenty-two years— two decades free of tension, anger, and violence. She finally had the joyous life she deserved.

Chapter Ten

The Mario Cuomo Years

"We had to help people help themselves."

I WISH MY MOTHER COULD have heard the eloquence and humanity I witnessed from Mario Cuomo when I first saw him in action. I
did not know at the time that I was about to spend the next twelve
years working side-by-side with Governor Cuomo, nor did I know
at the time that he and my mother would develop a mutual admiration society and become pen pals. All I knew that first time was
that he was different from every other politician I had ever seen. He
was real and human. He was *authentic*.

The setting was a conference in Rockland County, New York, in
1982, where I was a member of a panel discussion on welfare policy. After the panel came the main event—dueling speeches by Ed
Koch and Mario Cuomo, who were running against each other for
governor. Cuomo was lieutenant governor at the time, while Koch
was mayor of New York City. The topic of the debate was the death
penalty—Koch for, Cuomo against.

I wish I could quote in detail what Mario Cuomo said that day.
All I remember is that he spoke about the inequity of it, the racial
injustice inherent in such punishment. He spoke about cases where
men on death row for decades had been exonerated through new

evidence; of cases where a man was executed, only to have evidence of his innocence emerge afterward. It wasn't exactly what he said that captivated me, but rather how he said it. I was struck by the authentic humanity of the man. This was not political posturing, and he was certainly not appealing to the popular sentiment. This was what he *believed*. The hall was packed with law enforcement officials and others, and Cuomo was speaking against the interests of many in the room, but he was so eloquent that he was cheered by the audience, a standing ovation. Koch was the favorite in that campaign, but I recall going home and telling Kathy I thought Cuomo would be the next governor.

After Cuomo won the election, his team was being assembled in the winter of 1983. I received a call asking whether I might be interested in joining the administration. I was surprised, for I had not been at all aware that I was even on the radar of the people around the new governor. I later learned that Father Joe Sullivan, the leader of Catholic Charities, with whom I had done some work, recommended me. The call came while I was working at Fordham, and though I was flattered, I was hesitant to pursue it. Albany seemed a million miles away, and I was happy where I was.

That reaction was hasty, and fortunately, just weeks later, the Cuomo folks came back to me and we set up an interview at the New York State offices at the World Trade Center. It was an eye-opener for me. These were serious people talking about consequential roles, and I came away amazed that they were really interested in me. The job they were offering was Deputy Commissioner of Income Maintenance in the Department of Social Services. It was a huge jump in terms of responsibility—from teaching courses at Fordham to managing billions of dollars, serving hundreds of thousands of people. I knew little about Albany—had been there only a few times—but in a way, I had been preparing for this job my whole life.

Growing up in Knockaderry certainly gave me a visceral understanding of people in need, and I had been studying and teaching various elements of welfare policy for a decade. As I considered the offer, it seemed like a perfect opportunity to put into practice the principles and policies I had been learning and teaching for some time. But I was still hesitant. I liked the work and people at Fordham, as well as the security the job provided. Before deciding what to do, I consulted with Kathy's father, who said it sounded like an opportunity I should take. I also went to the president of Fordham, Fr. James Finlay, SJ, and asked his advice. He said I should take the job, and that if for some reason in a year or so it did not work out, I would always be welcomed back to Fordham. Having that safety net made all the difference, and I accepted the position.

I headed the one hundred fifty miles from New York to Albany late in the spring of 1983. From the moment I started, it was the most exhilarating intellectual experience of my life. I was just thirty-three years old, and I was doing work that directly affected the lives of hundreds of thousands if not millions of people who had been dealt a tough hand in life, most through no fault of their own. During my time in government, I served in various capacities, including the Income Maintenance division of the Department of Social Services, as Deputy Secretary of Human Services within the governor's office, and as Director of Health, Education, and Human Services for the state of New York, and finally Commissioner of the Department of Social Services, which required Senate confirmation. Over the years, my portfolio included programs on health care, welfare, nutrition, mental health and addiction services, food stamps, foster care, employment, adoption, and more.

When I arrived in Albany, I invested time in learning more about the details and nuances of government, including the legislative process. I went out to meet with key players in human services, including legislators, as well as officials in regional offices around the state, from Buffalo to Rochester and down to New York City. I made it a point to go out for beers with legislators and staff members and began building what became a network of strong relationships. I spent time learning about foster care and the adoption system.

I also made it a point to get out of the office and see firsthand the challenges that people we served faced in their lives. I went out to homeless shelters in the middle of the night to see the conditions and the people with my own eyes. Often, the first thing that captured my attention was the number of elderly women taking care of their grandchildren; women huddled with one or two toddlers. There was a particular detail that struck me then and stays with me to this day. These women would typically have a large green or black trash bag—often a Glad bag—stuffed with the family's possessions. The cruelty of life was captured for me in these scenes. An elderly grandmother, perhaps not in the best of health, caring for toddlers and, in some cases, infants, lugging a trash bag containing all she had in the world. The kids' parents were drug addicts or dead or gone.

The crack houses I visited were some of the grimmest places imaginable. I went into abandoned buildings where people had smashed holes through the plaster or concrete to sneak in and retreat from the elements. There were men and women who had resorted to injecting themselves in the eyelids, in the genitals, anywhere they could find a vein, anywhere, because their other veins were gouged from the countless injections. Discarded needles were scattered on the ground, surrounded by young men and women completely out of it.

It was important for me to be there, to witness the reality of those whose addiction had caused them to lose everything. It's one thing to sit in an office a hundred miles away thinking about the problem and quite another to see it up close so you understand the tragic human dimensions of the issue—so you can *feel* the suffering. When you see it firsthand, the grim reality is indelibly imprinted upon your memory, and you go forward working on policies always reminded of the real mission: to help people in trouble. I made a point of stopping to talk with people, asking about their lives and struggles, and it became clear to me over time that the addiction plague was an equal-opportunity scourge. There were some from the poorest neighborhoods in the city who had tumbled down this hole, and there were others from stable, affluent backgrounds whose lives had been overtaken by drug addiction.

I remember going into a place upstate where the men and women, developmentally disabled, were packaging soaps and things for hotels. These people had terrible disabilities, but they would do the work with precision and pride, including a woman without arms sitting at a typewriter and typing with a pen in her mouth.

My responsibilities included foster care and adoption. I remember monitoring the child abuse hotline where state workers took one call after another, day after day. It takes a special person with a deep well of compassion to do that job for any length of time. The horrors were unimaginable—a baby cooked in an oven, a baby dying because she had been burned a hundred times with a cigarette butt. One of the frustrating things, from my perspective working for the state, was that I would see the dedication of these social workers doing their best for children and families, and yet when a mistake was made—and mistakes were surely made—the press and public were quick to criticize. These state employees on the front lines were for the most part very caring and did a terrific job.

Sometimes we had disgruntled clients in the system. I remember being in an office in upstate New York when somebody set fire to the building while we were having a meeting. It was a long, one-story structure in a rural community with a central hallway, offices on either side. I was meeting with the local commissioner and staff members in a conference room toward the back of the building when a man whose child had been taken away because of abuse came into the building with a gasoline can, ran through the hallway, poured gasoline, and lit a match. We escaped through the windows and were in the parking lot when the fire engines arrived.

One of my two major focus areas during my time with the governor was health care. In pursuing the idea of an integrated health care delivery system, we were ahead of our time. We had the benefit of an outstanding team, and our work was inspired by Dr. David Axelrod, who had served as state health commissioner for a number of years before Governor Cuomo was elected. Dr. Axelrod was a brilliant man, recognized throughout the nation as a leading health care pioneer. In the early 1990s, Governor Cuomo outlined a vision, heavily influenced by Dr. Axelrod's thinking, in a special message to the state legislature calling for a shift from a focus on sick care to greater focus on providing preventive and primary care. We called for more comprehensive cost control to ease the cost burden on families and their employers, and we called for rigorous new approaches to measuring and delivering quality care.

What is remarkable about this is that these policy initiatives are among the leading goals within the industry in the United States today, more than twenty-five years later. In New York, we were in the vanguard of a new movement aiming to disrupt the health-care status quo by focusing on prevention and wellness and improving quality and safety, all while making care more affordable. We believed back in the 1990s that an integrated system would have the ability to control quality and cost across the enterprise while making sure all patients got the care they needed. We were one of the leaders in the US, working to reduce the uninsured. We strengthened Medicaid so that more poor people gained coverage. We grappled with the AIDS crisis, working to protect the privacy of patients suffering from the disease. We mounted anti-smoking initiatives and promoted vaccinations for children.

Among our most significant advances was the creation of an innovative child health program that provided universal primary care coverage to every child in New York State under the age of thirteen, regardless of family income. This was a game-changer. Primary care is where pediatric issues can be diagnosed and, very often, treated effectively before they progress to more troublesome stages.

Welfare reform or, more specifically, welfare-to-work initiatives was my second major area of focus. To me, welfare and work were interrelated. When I was in Albany, a welfare reform movement had been growing both nationally and within New York for several years. This had long been an issue dominated by Republicans, but the work Governor Cuomo did in Albany as well as efforts by President Clinton brought the issue into focus for Democrats arguing that a life without work, dependent upon government largesse, was destructive to individuals, families, and whole communities.

Much of what I needed to know about welfare reform I had learned growing up in Knockaderry—that work was the essential element that made everything else in life possible. Throughout the decade I worked on the welfare issue, I was guided by the idea of making sure that we supported people in need, while at the same time not promoting dependency upon the state—a delicate balance that states had rarely gotten right in the past. One of our initial policies in the mid-1980s was notable enough to make the front page of the *New York Times*. Under the headline "New York Plans Job Requirement for Welfare Aid," the article noted that about 220,000 people on welfare would be "required to take a job or enter a job-training program." I was quoted in the article saying that the state would take a number of measures to make sure recipients were spared a "financial shock" from the policy. This meant mainly that those on welfare who went to work would not lose all of their benefits. This was really important. From my perspective, there was a troublesome gap in this new policy, for it would exempt "mothers with children under age six, a group comprising 80 percent of the 1.1 million New York participants in the federal and state program."

This was crazy. Exempting 80 percent of the participants in the program meant that even if the program was perfectly executed—and needless to say, human services programs rarely achieved perfection—it would only help 20 percent of the people. My view was somewhat controversial at the time, but I believed that the state *should* require mothers of children under age six to participate. I made a case to the governor—successfully, as it turned out—that countless mothers of young children held down steady jobs, and that if they could work and find quality care for their kids, then why couldn't women on welfare do the same? We subsidized daycare costs and helped mothers train for jobs.

My belief, as I stated to the governor, was that our welfare reform proposals should be built upon a few key principles, including that "jobs and employment must be the central goal of the welfare system—not just the distribution of cash assistance; all work is good and all efforts to work must be supported and rewarded; if you're on welfare you should be doing something in return for your check." This approach was embodied in our most innovative policy, known as the Child Assistance Program (CAP), which created effective incentives for welfare recipients to find work. This was destined to become one of the most effective welfare programs in the United States and, in many ways, a model for both states and the federal government.

Throughout this period, when those of us in the human services arena tried to figure out how to move people from welfare to work, I was much more of a pragmatist than an ideologue. I worked with Republicans in the state senate as comfortably as I did Democrats in the Assembly. I was comfortable with liberals, moderates, and conservatives because I never wavered from a simple guiding proposition: Whatever we did had to help people help themselves. I stuck to basic themes: that the state had an obligation to help people in need, and that individuals had a responsibility to work toward self-sufficiency and to take responsibility for their families.

As I worked to promote our policies with legislators, the public, and the press, I was aware that my background in Knockaderry gave me a certain degree of credibility on the issue. Who knew that an impoverished upbringing in rural Limerick County would become an asset? In Knockaderry, I had seen the role the safety net played in my family's life—with my father's disability pension and the government's construction program for our new house. These were enormously impactful government supports in our lives.

Imagine if the government housing program had not existed and we had been forced to stay in the old house.

While we were grateful for the support, my parents, siblings, and I also recognized the need to work as hard as possible to make whatever contributions toward the family that we could. We all worked—my father until the arthritis crippled him. My mother always worked, as did all of my siblings. And we all contributed in meaningful ways through the years.

In New York, we wanted to make sure that while people were receiving assistance, they would also work, and that meant reducing or eliminating disincentives to work. Why would someone get up every morning, take their child to day care, and then go to work if she could make the same amount of money staying home and receiving a welfare check? We spent a lot of time trying to figure out how to change the incentive components of the system to allow people receiving welfare to work and gain ground. It was complicated and not easy to pull off, but we came up with an approach based on the core principle that made our program work, which was one I had been promoting for some time: Welfare recipients should not be punished by the state for trying to work.

I argued in a note to Governor Cuomo for a more understanding policy to help welfare recipients find and keep jobs: "The current welfare system has built-in disincentives. If you go to work and earn $1 you lose a dollar in benefits—no gain. If you work you can lose medical coverage and if you save money (for a rainy day) we take it away in reduced benefits. So while we encourage a client to go to work, the system has built-in penalties. The [Child Assistance Program] program tries to solve that dilemma. That is why it is such an innovative initiative and is the direction national welfare reform should be moving."

Part of my job was to educate people about our proposals, which meant meeting with legislative leaders, civic and community groups, and the news media to explain our programs and the reasons behind them. I spent a lot of time on the road speaking to various groups, and it seemed that every speech led to two more invitations. Most of my appearances went reasonably well, but occasionally I faced off against crowds hostile to our policies. One night in Manhattan, a tough audience berated me for a couple of hours, denouncing me for some of what we were proposing. People were so angry that even after the meeting ended and I was leaving, people shouted at me. As I exited, a reporter from the *New York Times* asked, "How do you feel after a meeting like that?" And I said, "You know, there are days when I feel like the state's fire hydrant." And he looked at me and said, "Fire hydrant?" And I said, "Yeah, everybody is pissing on me all the time!" It was in the *Times* the next day. The governor said to me, "Fire hydrant, huh? You roll with the punches. Every fight is fifteen rounds and you may lose a couple of rounds, but don't worry about it. Just make sure you know where you are going."

I worked to keep the news media informed of what we were doing, which led to many meetings with reporters, editors, and editorial boards of newspapers. The press takes a bad rap these days from many sides, but I have to say that the reporters, editors, columnists, and editorial writers I dealt with were smart men and women who cared about the issues just as much as I did. I generally found interactions with reporters enjoyable, and there were quite a few editorials and columns in papers from around the state that cited the work I was doing. A *New York Times* editorial, for example, began: "All those concerned about babies infected with the virus that causes AIDS can be grateful to Michael Dowling, New York's Commissioner of Social Services. He, at least, has had the decency and common sense to guarantee that all AIDS-infected babies in the foster-care system will be identified and cared for."

Occasionally, reporters would cover ceremonies we held for men and women who had completed an eight-week jobs program. The graduates would come in and receive a certificate and you would swear, based on their reaction and the pride of their relatives, that they were getting a PhD. They'd dress up in their best clothes and bring friends and family and introduce them to me. They were in heaven. A job can change someone's life as almost nothing else can, and this is particularly true for men and women who have struggled in life, who lack a quality education and may have grown up in a challenging home situation.

One of our programs, Jobs First, required people who applied for welfare benefits to actively search for work before any benefits were granted to them. The push to shift welfare recipients out of dependency and into jobs was gaining momentum across the country at the time, but many state programs were more punitive than not. The *New York Times* noted the contrast with how we were approaching it: "The Governor says New York will not place a two-year limit on welfare benefits, as Florida does. It will not deny increased benefits to mothers who have additional children, which is New Jersey's new policy. It will not eliminate its welfare program for able-bodied adults without children, as Michigan recently did. And unlike Oklahoma, which reduces welfare benefits for families whose children skip school, New York is proposing both to cut benefits in cases of chronic truancy and to increase them for good attendance."

We were proposing other ways to help people get into and stay in the work world. Some of these were hardly earth-shattering, but other states weren't doing them. For example, we wanted to provide welfare applicants with certain expense payments that would help them keep a job. Let's say a person's car breaks down, preventing him from getting to work in the morning. We wanted to make grants to people to get the car repaired. We recognized that many poor people live on the edge, and that the difference between being able to keep a job and get off welfare might mean a $300 car repair or a hundred dollars for emergency childcare. Sometimes in government common sense comes across as radical, but when you see men and women moving from dependence on government support to the freedom of engagement in the world of work, you know that these commonsense measures make a difference.

When I started work in Albany in the spring of 1983, our son Brian had just turned a year old. Kathy was working in human resources at Beth Israel Medical Center in Manhattan, and we were fortunate to have my sister Mary come from Ireland to live with us for a year to care for Brian. Over time, my job in Albany proved to be a significant disruption for our family.

We were living in Westchester County, outside New York City, but I was rarely home. I drove up to Albany on Sunday night, stayed in a rented room near my office during the week, and returned home on Friday night. As Brian got a little bit older, depending upon what time I would arrive Friday night, I would take him to buy a toy. "Whatever we could do to be a family, we did," recalls Kathy. "And by the way, it wasn't terrible: I was happy, he was happy."

But everything changed the day Brian was injured at nursery school when he was four. Kathy was at work when she got a call from the school that Brian had fallen off a playset and hit his head. Kathy recalls, "The babysitter brought him to the hospital and he had a concussion. It took me an hour and a half to get to the hospital from my office in Manhattan and I arrived as he was being wheeled into the CT scan. In that minute, I knew I was quitting my job and moving to Albany." That is exactly what happened.

It was also clear to me that after four years of a commuting life, we had to change. The hard truth is that you lose something when you are not home with your wife and child. At one point, when Brian was six or seven, he asked Kathy, referring to me: "Why do we need him?" It was a perfectly reasonable question for a child to ask. Another time, when I was home for the weekend, I'd brought Brian to a toy store, and he wanted something quite expensive. I said I was sorry we could not buy it because it was too much money. He looked up at me and said, "You've got plenty of money, Dad. You work all the time."

Within six months of Brian's concussion, we had bought a home in Albany for a fraction of what a comparable place in Westchester would have cost. And we could now live on my salary, since the cost of living in Albany was so much more reasonable. In Albany, Kathy met a lot of other women with children and was able to be a full-time mother, engaged with school activities and, most importantly, to be there for our son—which both she and Brian loved. I was very fortunate that Kathy was willing to put her professional career on hold in order to handle all the family work that freed me to pursue my workaholic tendencies.

In June 1991 Governor Cuomo promoted me from Deputy Secretary for Human Services to a new position as Director of Health, Education, and Human Services. He made clear at the time his desire for the administration to "place renewed emphasis on the state's human services policies." In May 1992, an article by reporter Kevin Sack was published in the *New York Times* titled

"Safety Net Savior." I quote it here at some length, not for self-promotion, but because I think it captures my work in that particular moment, when challenging fiscal realities forced us to make tough decisions about human services programs:

> It is a long way from that wee house in Limerick to Mr. Dowling's spacious office in the Capitol, where he is now Gov. Mario M. Cuomo's director of health, education and human services. In that job, he serves as the Governor's top adviser on everything from Medicaid to mental health and oversees agencies that spend almost two-thirds of the state's $30.8 billion budget.
>
> But Mr. Dowling's journey out of poverty left him with both a personal compassion for the disadvantaged and a pragmatic approach to government. And that approach, which emphasizes self-help over dependency and incremental progress over grand vision, has left a lasting imprint on New York's social policy during the difficult days of the recession.
>
> "Nobody knows the poor better than Mike or feels for them more than Mike," Mr. Cuomo said in a recent interview. "But he's a person who knows life too, and knows that you can't always have all that you want at the moment."
>
> That understanding has been critical to the 42-year-old Mr. Dowling's efforts to preserve New York's social safety net when there is increasing political pressure to shrink it.
>
> Many who work with Mr. Dowling, whose salary is $96,662, believe he is stretched too thin. As Mr.

Cuomo has expanded Mr. Dowling's portfolio in the last
year, it has fallen to Mr. Dowling to forge agreements
between the Democratic-majority Assembly, which is
highly protective of programs for the disadvantaged,
and the Republican-led Senate, which sees the recession
as an opportunity to cut social-service spending.

Last month, he brokered major components of the
deal that produced $1.1 billion in savings from the
state's Medicaid and welfare programs.

In the last year, Mr. Dowling directed the searches for
the state's new health and social services commissioners.
He worked with New York City officials to design new
programs to move homeless people out of shelters and
to fight outbreaks of tuberculosis and measles.

He helped design legislation to require Medicaid
recipients to seek care from health maintenance organizations. He had a heavy influence on Mr. Cuomo's
decision to keep private the names of health care
workers who are infected with HIV, the virus that
causes AIDS. And Mr. Dowling successfully pushed
to close underused mental hospitals in order to free
money for community mental health programs.

"There's an understanding in Albany now that in
the health and human services arena he is the most
important policy-maker, more important than any
commissioner," said Cesar A. Perales, the former state
social-services commissioner who is now New York
City's deputy mayor for health and human services.

"[Growing up] I basically developed the feeling
that families who are struggling need assistance, and

that the kind that is provided should recognize their struggle," Mr. Dowling said. "But I also developed a very strong sense that while the system should help you, it should never undercut the desire of people to help themselves." . . .

"Mike is not some academician," Mr. Cuomo said, "not some elegantly educated elitist type who, with heart pure as gold, turns the pages of his texts with uncalloused fingers and learns about life mostly by observing—albeit with great compassion—how poorer people live lives he's never experienced. That kind of person can become an intellectual zealot on a subject and be unbending. Mike knows what poverty is, knows what hard work is. Most of all he knows the give and take of life, the hard practicalities."

On a staff that is known for being all work and no play, Mr. Dowling does much of his most persuasive lobbying over a pitcher of beer at pubs near the Capitol. Tall and burly, he wears a scruffy beard that perfectly complements his ready smile and a lilting accent that Mr. Cuomo describes as one-quarter prose and three-quarters music . . .

But Mr. Dowling is also known as a no-nonsense negotiator whose face turns port-red when he grows impatient. His bouts of profanity, including those in the Governor's presence, are so common they are now dismissed as more endearing than intemperate.

"It's no big deal anymore when his cheeks turn red," said one colleague. "It's only when his neck starts to turn red that I get worried."

That side of Mr. Dowling's temperament may have been honed on the hurling field, where he was a championship player of the rugged Irish pastime that is part field hockey, part soccer. His philosophy on game day, Mr. Dowling said, was that "if your head gets in the way of my stick, that's your problem."

But for the most part, Mr. Dowling has become known as a conciliator who is forever seeking common ground. "I'm not a purist who identifies an ideal and says we can only accept success if we get what we've set in our dreams," he said. "The history of progress is taking continuous steps forward all the time."

One of the most satisfying developments while I worked in state government came when President Clinton drew a number of ideas for a national welfare reform from our practices in New York State, including some of the work requirements. In 1992, the *New York Times* reported on a study showing that our efforts were "having significant success in providing welfare mothers with the work incentives needed to wean themselves gradually from dependency, a long-awaited study of the program has found." The study, conducted by Cambridge, Massachusetts, consulting firm Abt Associates, found that "welfare recipients who were eligible for the program worked 25 percent more hours and earned 25 percent more in wages than those who were not." The *Times* article noted that the program "encourages welfare mothers to work by allowing them to keep a large proportion of their welfare grants even though they are working." The paper reported that "mothers of two who participated in the program in its first year received an average total monthly income of $1,045, compared with an average income of $765 for mothers of two who received Aid to Families with Dependent Children, the assistance program that would normally cover them." The *Times* also described testimonials to the Child Assistance Program "from its participants, many of whom said the program had given them both the financial means and the self-esteem to combat lifetimes of welfare dependency. 'CAP is like weaning a baby off the bottle or off breast feeding,' said Nancy K. Edwards, a 28-year-old mother of two from Kingston. 'Slowly but surely you wean yourself off the program. At first I was insecure about if I can really make it out here on what I make. But CAP is not only supportive financially. They treat you like a person.'"

Our team expected progress, but these results were more encouraging than anyone anticipated. In 1992, the Child Assistance Program received an innovation award sponsored by the Ford Foundation in collaboration with the Harvard Kennedy School. Our work drew the attention of policymakers in both Congress and the executive branch. Some of our staff members were recruited to work for the Clinton administration. In the summer of 1994, I was asked to testify in DC about our work before the Subcommittee on Human Resources of the House Committee on Ways and Means. I shared details about some of our work and said that I very much supported the idea of changing the system "from one focused on cash support and eligibility determination to one that promotes self-support, family life, and parental responsibility."

When I began working with Governor Cuomo, I was troubled by a nagging personal issue—that of citizenship. While working for the state, I held a green card, but I was not a United States citizen. By the mid-1980s, I realized that America had become my home— that I was not going to return to Ireland, not permanently, anyway.

I didn't face this reality until I had been working for the state for a number of months. While at Fordham, I had always planned on going back home to live, but not anymore. The differences in opportunities between the US and Ireland became just too stark for me. Now, when I visited Ireland, I was struck by how slow the pace of life was compared with New York. I remember walking in Dublin, and I'd be far ahead of everybody else on the sidewalk because I was walking New York speed. I knew I would never be able to walk at Irish speed again. *This is too slow, the city too quiet,* I thought. *There's nothing happening here. I have to get back to New York.* (For the record, Dubliners now walk very much at New York speed.) I felt I had to be in a lively environment with multiple opportunities for jobs and careers, and that definitely existed in New York—much less so in Ireland.

The citizenship issue had been in the back of my mind for a number of years. Once I started working in government at such a senior level, I actually wondered whether it was okay to not be a citizen. In the fall of 1983, about six months after starting work with the state, I went through the process and took the oath as a citizen of the United States. Not long after I became a citizen, I found myself in meetings in Washington with senior members of the Reagan administration, talking about some of the work-to-welfare initiatives we were considering. It seemed such a leap over time—from Knockaderry to the Manhattan docks to the Cuomo administration to citizenship to the White House.

Since we had moved from Westchester to the Albany neighborhood of Delmar, life had settled into a pleasant and predictable rhythm. Yes, I worked long hours and many weekends, but our family—by then we'd added a daughter, Elizabeth, born in 1989, when Brian was seven—was together and happy. And we were in good shape financially. I was making almost $100,000 a year, and that was a lot of money at the time in Albany, where the cost of living was so much lower than in the New York City area. I had enough money so that I could help out at home a little more—help my mother, Mary, and my brothers.

Working in a series of senior roles allowed me to spend increasing amounts of time with Governor Cuomo, and I came to admire him as one of the truly great men I had ever known. He was a brilliant, profoundly compassionate man serving in government not to amass power, but to help make society a better place for everyone, including those most in need. Working with him was also energizing and fun. He had a great sense of humor and we traveled the state together—often flying in the state helicopter from Albany to Buffalo or Manhattan or places in between. Sometimes we would use the ancient state airplane for longer distances. It was so old that the pilots told me several times that I really needed to persuade the governor to get something more modern. But he didn't want to spend scarce state resources on a new plane during tough times, so we continued to use the old one. One night after meetings in Washington, I looked out the left side of the plane as we were taking off and saw flames coming from the wing. I quickly informed the governor of the problem. He replied, "That happens all the time. The only worry is if it's happening in both wings at once."

The governor once called me in the middle of a Christmas Day when there were some urgent state budget issues to deal with. "How *was* your Christmas?" he asked, emphasis on the past tense. I spent the rest of the day with him in the office. Kathy loved the governor and described him as "an intellectual giant with workingman's hands." We were touched when, upon the birth of our daughter

Elizabeth, the governor wrote her a handwritten letter welcoming her to "the family of New York. You have chosen your parents well."

Through the years, when my mother was visiting, I would bring her to the office to show her where I worked and to meet the governor. On one occasion, he took her on a personal guided tour of the state capitol building. When she returned to Ireland, she wrote letters to him and he would always respond with personal notes to her. One time, Mam wrote a letter to him in which she said some very complimentary things about me. The governor passed her letter on to me with a cover note saying, "Mike, isn't it remarkable how you and I have been able to fool our mothers?"

Mario Cuomo and I bonded over a shared mission and a determination to make life better for the neediest people in New York State. We bonded, as well, over the immigrant experience. He was acutely aware of the sacrifices his parents had made coming from Italy, unable to speak English, seeking to establish a new life. He understood the difficulty of the immigrant experience, while at the same time recognizing the contributions immigrants have made and continue to make in all areas of life within the United States. The greatest thing Mario Cuomo did for me was provide me with opportunity. He took a chance on me, challenged me, pushed me out of my comfort zone into unfamiliar terrain. He forced me to push myself harder than I ever had before, and it changed my life.

During my years in Albany, I also had the good fortune to work with the governor's wife, Matilda Cuomo, who was focused on state issues related to children. We traveled the state together, promoting programs to support and encourage families in raising children in the healthiest possible environments. We were able to secure significant state funding for a variety of children's programs promoted by Mrs. Cuomo focused on adoption, foster care, and mentoring.

The end of the Cuomo era was a difficult time for the whole team. The governor had already served three terms. Against many people's advice, he decided to seek a fourth term, but in 1994, after a dozen years in office, he was defeated by George Pataki, a Republican. It was clear voters wanted a change.

It is interesting to look back at our work promoting reform in the health care sector. Working with the governor, I promoted policies aimed at providing care that was accessible, affordable, and of high quality. The issues we worked on during the 1990s—turning primary care to focus more on prevention and wellness as well as more rigorous measures of quality—remain enduring challenges in health care today. Perhaps at first blush, one might think that working on similar issues twenty-five years later suggests a lack of progress, but that is not the case.

It is certainly true that the American health care system has many faults, which have been exhaustively chronicled in the popular press and academic journals. A persistent and recurring theme has been the notion that in the United States, health care is inferior to systems in many other developed nations; that it is vastly more expensive here, even as outcomes in the US are lacking. Inherent in this narrative is the idea that there has been little progress in recent years.

In fact, there has been enormous progress since I was working on health care under Governor Cuomo. Our system now is far more aware of the need to go back upstream and focus on keeping people well. In the 1990s, provider organizations in the United States were largely focused on hospital-based care. Today we continue to provide care to the sick, of course. At the same time, there is a transformational shift toward aggressively going out and identifying patients at risk and taking steps to keep them healthy. This trend will only accelerate in the years ahead, to the benefit of society.

A final note about Mario Cuomo. He and I remained close after he left office and returned to the practice of law in New York. We would meet often for lunch. Sometimes he would show up at the restaurant wearing a Donegal tweed cap I had brought back from Ireland and given to him as a gift. As he grew older and his health declined, I would visit him at the Manhattan apartment where he and Matilda lived. We would talk about politics, issues, his children and grandchildren—any and all topics. Sometimes, near the end, when he lacked the energy to talk, I would sit there with him in silence, keeping him company. Mario's son, Governor Andrew Cuomo, paid me a high compliment when he recalled his father's description of me—"great mind, but great heart." Said Andrew Cuomo, "My father loved Michael Dowling." Mario Cuomo passed away on January 1, 2015 at the age of eighty-two.

Chapter Eleven

The Mission of Northwell Health

"The only way to serve yourself is to serve others."
—Mario Cuomo

FIVE YEARS AFTER MARIO CUOMO passed away, I found myself working side-by-side with another Governor Cuomo: Mario's son Andrew. Governor Mario and I encountered some difficult issues together, but nothing we faced approached the severity of the coronavirus pandemic. When this scourge struck New York State in early 2020, Andrew called and asked me, along with my team at Northwell, the health-care organization I'd helped build over the past twenty-five years, to work with him to try and save lives. With our work and Andrew's leadership, we were able to accomplish a lot.

How did it come to pass that a quarter century after Mario Cuomo left office, I was joining forces with his son in taking on a global pandemic? To tell that story, we have to go way back to the period immediately after Mario Cuomo left office. In late 1994, I was fortunate to have a number of job offers, and I came close to accepting a position in Vienna (which would have been a slightly different experience than Albany!) as director of the European Project, an effort to work with Eastern European nations after the fall of the Soviet Union. I passed on that opportunity and instead joined Empire Blue Cross of New York, but it didn't take long for me to see that the insurance industry was not the kind of mission-driven work I loved doing. After less than a year at Empire Blue Cross, I received a recruiting call from North Shore University Hospital in Manhasset on Long Island. I had met North Shore CEO Jack Gallagher in Albany, and I later learned that Jack had told a number of people that he viewed me as his possible successor as CEO of North Shore Hospital. I also later learned that Ralph Nappi, a member of the hospital board, had consulted with Governor Cuomo, who had given me a glowing recommendation. After a series of interviews at North Shore, I accepted a position as chief operating officer and joined the organization in the spring of 1995. Kathy and I sold our house in Albany and bought a new home in the town of Northport, not too far from my new office.

My new job presented an opportunity to continue working on the kind of integrated system I had envisioned as a Holy Grail when I worked for the state. While working in Albany, I had come to believe that large, integrated health systems, able to serve any and all patient needs, would be the way care would be delivered in the future. I carried that conviction with me to North Shore. There were examples in the US, such as Kaiser Permanente in California, which owned hospitals, directly employed physicians, and owned its own insurance company. But there was nothing comparable to Kaiser in the northeast.

An integrated system would be capable of providing all of a patient's medical needs from birth to death—primary and specialty care of all kinds, including world-class care for stroke, heart disease, cancer, mental health, and more. The ideal would serve all patients, irrespective of circumstance, with a focus on prevention and wellness, while providing care in a coordinated way.

Constructing such a system would be something of a Herculean task, particularly in the 1990s, when the managed-care movement was in full swing. This period saw unprecedented intrusion from insurance companies, overruling the judgment of doctors regarding what care was most appropriate for patients. For decades, doctors had been at the top of the health care pyramid, but in the '90s, insurers seized a significant degree of control over what medical interventions were appropriate for patients and squeezed reimbursements to physicians and hospitals. The whole trend was infuriating—good for insurance company profits, but detrimental to patients and doctors.

Before I joined the organization, Jack Gallagher, along with board members Saul Katz and Ralph Nappi, had begun laying the groundwork for the creation of a health system, the first substantive effort to do so in New York. They'd brought a number of hospitals into the new alliance and were in discussion with others. This was one of the main reasons I was interested in coming to North Shore. Assembling the pieces of a health system requires an ability to understand finances and politics, but it also demands an ability to work with an array of constituents—doctors, administrators, unions, community groups, elected officials, regulators, and more. That was exactly what I had been doing in state government for twelve years—working with often conflicting constituencies to try to reach consensus.

During that time, I had built a reputation in Albany as a person who could work constructively in a partisan atmosphere without making enemies. This proved particularly valuable at North Shore Hospital when we went through a contentious merger with our neighbor and fierce rival, Long Island Jewish Hospital. We were able to join the institutions within a single organization, which helped strengthen our growing system—not merely a collection of individual entities, but rather an interconnected network of hospitals, ambulatory sites, and every conceivable specialty capability, including mental health.

I took over as CEO of the newly named North Shore-Long Island Jewish Health System (which would eventually be renamed Northwell Health) at the end of 2001 and accelerated the growth strategy, purchasing or merging with additional community hospitals in the region and expanding our footprint into Manhattan. We were moving quickly and aggressively, and while many of the decisions early on worked out well, I make no pretension that things were perfect. It was an exciting time, but when you are trying to build something new, you invariably make mistakes, and we made our share. In one painful case we tried to micromanage a local hospital, essentially taking away its identity and undermining its local culture and sense of independence. Blowback from the local community was both intense and warranted. Community hospitals spend many years building reputations and developing confidence within their communities. To come in and start to dictate policy, as we did in this case, wasn't very smart. We quickly changed course.

Mergers and acquisitions in health care have gotten a generally negative reputation in recent years. Some studies show that many health care mergers do not result in any quality improvement and often cause prices to rise. That is not sustainable over the long term. There is, however, another side to the consolidation story. As Northwell has expanded, we have acquired a number of hospitals that might not have survived had we not brought them into our network. When community hospitals fail, cities and towns not only lose access to care, they also suffer economically. Many people lose good jobs. We have invested heavily in New York area hospitals that were in decline, nursing them back to health for the benefit of patients and the communities served. These community hospitals are important links in our growing system.

I recalled Mario Cuomo often speaking about the US as a mosaic, and I adopted that analogy for our system, describing it as a "collection of organizations, each with their own individual history, culture, and personality, that are bound together by a common set of beliefs, goals, and values. The system, like a mosaic, is made up of unique individual pieces, but when placed side-by-side, the whole is more impressive than any one piece."

By the time Governor Andrew Cuomo called at the start of the COVID-19 crisis, Northwell Health had grown exponentially, expanding across Long Island into Brooklyn, Staten Island, Westchester, and Manhattan to include twenty-three hospitals across the New York region along with 800 ambulatory sites, making us the largest health care system in the state as well as the largest private employer in the state. Our 72,000 employees care for patients with cancer, heart disease, diabetes, schizophrenia, and every other imaginable mental and physical malady. We provide the full continuum of care from birth to end of life, as well as home care and everything in between. We transplant kidneys, livers, hearts, and lungs. We bring babies into the world—almost 40,000 a year—and we comfort the dying. Our scientists conduct research into some of the most difficult diseases in the world. We are also one of the largest academic teaching systems in the United States, with one of the most innovative medical schools anywhere (the Zucker School of Medicine at Hofstra/Northwell). In a time of crisis, an integrated system plays a crucial role. In 2020 we were selected as one of *Fortune* magazine's top 100 best places to work in America.

But for all that we do *within* our own walls, we also feel called to work outside our walls to help solve broader societal problems. Health is affected more by social determinants—housing, food, income, etc.—than by medical care, and that inspires us to work on the larger social issues that affect the health of communities we serve. This is a historic shift in the health care industry. Just a few decades ago, medical organizations such as ours were focused entirely within our own walls, caring for sick people who came to our hospitals and physician offices. In the new world of health care, in addition to caring for the sick, our mission is to venture into our communities to prevent illness and to highlight social conditions that have an impact on the health of our patients. We have evolved over time from a medical organization to a health care delivery organization and social service agency, a direction consistent with having spent my entire professional career in the nonprofit world—academia at Fordham and Columbia, working with United Church of Christ and the Urban League, government with Governor Cuomo, and now in medicine.

In a commencement address at Iona College some years ago, Mario Cuomo asked the audience "whether we are the ones to tell [graduates] what their instructors have tried to teach them for years? That the philosophers were right. That Saint Francis, Buddha, Muhammad, Maimonides—all spoke the truth when they said the only way to serve yourself is to serve others; and that Aristotle was right, before them, when he said the only way to assure yourself happiness is to learn to give happiness." Mario Cuomo defined his core philosophy, saying that "We believe in a single fundamental idea that describes . . . what a proper government should be: the idea of family, mutuality, the sharing of benefits and burdens for the good of all, feeling one another's pain, sharing one another's blessings—reasonably, honestly, fairly, without respect to race, or sex, or geography, or political affiliation."

At Northwell, we try to live this vision by taking care of our people, including paying special attention to employees who serve in the military. We have been recognized as one of the best employers in the country for military members and veterans, and we aggressively recruit and hire veterans and provide them with an array of benefits, from educational opportunities to behavioral health programs. We also make sure that employees who return from deployments do not lose money because of their service. When employees return from deployment to Northwell, we present them with a check for the difference between their military pay and the regular salaries they would have received had they not taken military leave. In many cases, this runs to tens of thousands of dollars. Finally, we operate a Unified Behavioral Health Center in partnership with the Veterans Administration Medical Center to assist veterans dealing with mental health conditions.

Our caring for people throughout the communities we serve takes different forms, including getting involved in divisive political issues when necessary. The US gun epidemic is an example. There is no question in my mind that the 40,000 gun deaths in the US each year constitute a public health crisis. At Northwell, our EMTs, paramedics, nurses, and emergency room physicians see the devastation firsthand. I believe that if major health systems join together, we can make a powerful case that lives could be saved by taking a few commonsense steps, such as stricter background checks and a ban on the sale of assault weapons.

An increasingly important part of our mission within our communities is the epidemic of mental illness—to help those suffering from anxiety, depression, and other emotional conditions.

This issue is personal with me in light of my childhood in Knockaderry and my own bout of depression after my divorce. I have made a major commitment to treating patients with these conditions, including in a primary care setting where behavioral health specialists are now part of the primary care team. We not only treat patients with mental illness, we also work to reduce the stigma attached to it. If a person has cancer, others are empathetic. But too often, if a person is diagnosed with mental illness, others may judge or even shun them.

In early 2020, we opened a clinic near a populous school district where the incidence of mental health challenges among students had been growing alarmingly. Through our clinic, we are able to help with identification and treatment of emotional challenges for students. I cannot help but wonder whether mental health services in Knockaderry in the 1950s and '60s might have helped my father. With the right intervention, could his life have been a happy one? Could he have learned to bring lightness and joy into our house instead of darkness and anger? The idea that my dad suffered from depression for much of his life yet went entirely untreated is incredibly sad.

In January 2020, I was serving at Governor Andrew Cuomo's request as co-chairman of a committee with the responsibility to reform the New York Medicaid program. (I had served in a similar role a number of years earlier, also at Andrew's request, when our committee helped get Medicaid on solid financial footing.)

I take these kinds of assignments deadly seriously. I know from firsthand experience in government how critical these programs are for people in need, and Medicaid in New York covers about six million people who face very difficult circumstances in life—homelessness, poverty, addiction, mental and physical illness, and much more. But rapid growth had made it necessary to curtail the growth of spending to ensure sustainability over time. A big part of the problem was that in recent years, the state's payments to private insurance companies for homecare for Medicaid patients, rather than nursing homes, had increased by nearly $5 billion annually. Leading a committee charged with cutting the Medicaid budget brings an avalanche of criticism. I certainly did not relish cutting, but I knew it was necessary, and I was in the midst of leading this initiative when I first heard about an obscure new virus in Wuhan, China.

Our team at Northwell is always scanning the horizon for potential threats to the health of our communities, and while we were aware of what was happening in Wuhan at a very early stage, its disastrous potential was not yet clear to us. Reports at the end of December 2019 focused on an outbreak of sick people, but it wasn't until doctors there discovered that the cause was a new virus that we began to be concerned. Even then, it was unclear whether the virus was easily spread by humans.

But in January everything changed at warp speed, with the virus making its way to Japan, South Korea, Thailand, and into America, when a man in the state of Washington returned from Wuhan. In mid-January, China confirmed that some people were dying from the virus. The city of Wuhan, larger than New York with a population of eleven million, was closed off. A week later the World Health Organization declared a global health emergency, even as some American leaders downplayed the severity of the situation. The speed of the spread was stunning, and we began to brace for an inevitable assault on the New York area.

One of the advantages of having spent years constructing the largest integrated health care delivery system in the state is that we stand ready to handle emergencies of all kinds. When Hurricane Sandy slammed into New York, we were able to transfer hundreds of vulnerable hospital patients from one of our facilities to another to keep them safe. We had been through other challenges—the SARS epidemic, the Ebola crisis, H1N1, 9/11—but obviously we had never seen anything like what was about to hit us. We activated the Northwell emergency team led by Gene Tangney, one of the country's leading emergency management professionals. Eighty people convened in our Operations Center, including experts in the areas of supply chain, clinical, emergency management, legal, human resources, etc. Key leaders in the room also included Mark Solazzo, chief operating officer, and Dr. Kevin Tracey, head of the Feinstein Institutes for Medical Research at Northwell. Our physicians and epidemiologists, along with our emergency management professionals, scoured reports out of China, Iran, and Italy.

By the end of February, when the virus landed in our own back-yard, it was clear we faced a crisis. Earlier that month, a lawyer in the town of New Rochelle in Westchester County, where we have facilities, joined a large number of people at temple services and also attended a wedding and a bar mitzvah. He traveled in the greater New York area, including commuting via the Metro North rail system. In other words, he was living a normal life. Unbeknownst to him, the lawyer had been infected with the coronavirus, and all of his interactions with crowds occurred when he was asymptomatic. Near the end of February, the lawyer got very sick and was hospitalized. On March 2, he tested positive for the virus. By that point the virus had spread widely throughout the community, and New Rochelle was identified as a hot spot where a wide variety of institutions shut down as residents went into quarantine.

Governor Cuomo, while isolating New Rochelle, asked me whether I could put together a team to begin rapid testing for the virus within the New Rochelle community. Working with the state, we were able to set up drive-through testing centers to identify carriers of the virus, then isolate and treat them.

One opportunity that came during the crisis was the chance to help make the governor and others more familiar with our capabilities at Northwell. We had built a very large enterprise piece by piece, without much fanfare along the way, and our laboratory was an example of the scope and quality of what we had created. Over the years we have made significant investments in our system—billions of dollars—to improve and update facilities, equipment, and capabilities. Well before the crisis hit, we knew we needed a much larger and more modern laboratory for conducting an array of tests, and toward that end we acquired the property that formerly housed the Sperry Gyroscope Corporation, which played such a central role in producing gyroscopes for Allied aircraft in World War II. After the war, the same site became the first home of the fledgling organization known as the United Nations. It was on this site that we built one of the largest and most sophisticated labs in the United States.

Part of my responsibility throughout the crisis was to serve as an authoritative voice of information in the press. The governor had me at his side for many press events. Interviews with virtually every major television network and the major newspapers took time, but I thought it was important for me to convey accurate information while remaining calm and professional. This was not difficult for me because, in fact, I felt perfectly calm throughout. I knew that the situation would be bad, but I also knew that we had the people and equipment needed to get us through. Health care organizations and the professionals who work within them are incredibly resilient. Doctors and nurses adapt rapidly to even the direst situations, and that is exactly what occurred during the crisis.

Once we began to test in our system, the numbers exploded, and we set about a series of urgent tasks: increasing the number of beds in our hospitals; locating personal protective equipment, especially masks, for our staff; increasing our ability to test more rapidly; and locating ventilators to save the lives of the most gravely ill patients.

One of the uplifting things about the whole experience was the willingness of just about everyone in New York to work together. Governor Cuomo led us with a spirit and focus that would have made his father proud. In fact, I must say that during the crisis, Andrew reminded me of his father in his calmness and in his sustained focus on facts and science. Like his father, Andrew also displayed an uncanny ability to communicate the reality of the situation with clarity and precision. He pulled no punches. He called upon New Yorkers to sacrifice for the greater good, and tens of millions of people complied.

I do not mean to suggest that every day was perfect. Far from it. With municipal, county, state, and federal agencies, as well as private health systems, interacting moment-to-moment, there were periods of confusion and chaos. But that's part of leading your way through a crisis—figuring out how to get through the fog and move toward clarity. In working with the governor, Northwell's sheer size proved valuable. We have capabilities, equipment, and personnel unmatched elsewhere in the state.

As a leader, I felt few constraints. I knew, in any given situation, that I had experts within my system to help guide us through. Over the years, we have hired and promoted people accustomed to working cooperatively in teams, their egos set aside. This is not altogether common in health care, but it is the essence of our culture. From day one, my colleagues and I understood that, like anything in life, it's not how hard you get hit, it's how you respond. The two toughest challenges involved ventilators and sufficient staffing. The ventilators were essential. There was much talk in the press during the crisis about the need to increase the number of ICU beds, but the reality is that in this sort of crisis, when you add a ventilator to a standard room, you have the essence of an ICU bed. Because of our size, we had a fair number of ventilators in reserve, so we started out in a strong position.

The governor asked me to work along with Ken Raske, president of the Greater New York Hospital Association, to develop "surge capacity" within all hospitals by increasing the number of beds by 50 percent. Other health system leaders responded wonderfully to this call to action, and some smaller hospitals were even able to increase beds by 100 percent. The state supplemented this with portable setups at a variety of other locations, including empty dorms at state colleges, as well as convention centers in different locations around the state. Along with increasing the number of beds, we were also able to find suppliers from whom we purchased huge quantities of N95 masks and gowns. The personal protective equipment (PPE) was essential. Without it, our doctors and nurses would be unable to care for patients. With it, they were still taking risks, but making sure that we had sufficient quantities of PPE not only to protect our staff, but also to help sustain staff morale in a frightening time, was essential.

Keeping up morale in an organization such as ours is always an important role of the CEO, but in a time like this, when everyone is under tremendous pressure, when fear runs through the frontline workers, it becomes massively important. I have always been a hands-on leader, going out and meeting with staff members in our facilities so I could fully understand their point of view and so I could thank people for their work. During this crisis, what I saw when I met with staff members at our hospitals was an incredible level of courage and commitment. We have many staff members who are older and more at risk in the face of the virus. We also have thousands of young mothers and fathers, with small children at home, who were willing to come in every day and care for sick patients. It was an inspiring thing to see. It was the clearest proof of what we like to say within our organization—that we are made for this. It has never been clearer that our 72,000 people were made for this moment, including the scientists at our Feinstein Institutes for Medical Research, where we began enrolling patients in three clinical trials aimed at finding treatments to improve recovery for hospitalized patients with COVID-19. Because of our size and influence in the world of medical science, we have developed strong relationships with a number of biopharmaceutical companies through the years. In this instance our researchers worked with scientists at Gilead Sciences, Regeneron Pharmaceuticals, and Sanofi.

In April, after the virus had reached its peak in New York, we acknowledged our gratitude to our frontline employees in many ways. One of the most meaningful was to provide each person with a $2,500 bonus as well an additional paid week's vacation. We did this despite the massive financial losses we sustained, because what our clinical teams accomplished was as majestic as anything I have ever seen in my entire career.

As I reflect upon the pandemic and our response to it in New York, I am struck by the selfless way in which doctors and nurses, their own health and even lives in jeopardy, showed up shift after shift to care for very sick patients. In light of this, how do we judge the health care system in the United States? I raise this question particularly because I have been concerned about the narrative that has taken hold in the US in recent years: that American health care is lagging behind systems in other industrialized nations. I don't believe it for a minute. When you see these men and women working every day, putting themselves on the line for other people, it is magnificent.

However, there is no doubt that significant changes are needed if we are to be prepared as a nation for the next time—and there will be a next time. It is obvious that we will need a greater stockpile of PPE and ventilators. We will need to reduce our reliance upon the Chinese supply chain. I suspect some American manufacturers will increase their output to supplant some of the Chinese production and that major organizations such as Northwell will be willing to pay the premium required to support domestic manufacturing. Other changes will be needed as well, and these will be difficult. At present, emergency preparedness is not a priority for most major health systems. This must change. Having an excellent emergency response capability is as important as having a quality oncology or cardiology department. All of this will demand a change in culture, where leaders of health care organizations truly value and promote the importance of emergency preparedness in saving lives.

The lessons that emerge from this crisis will surely change how we live, work, and behave—and, in health care, how we prepare. Going forward, we and every other medical group in the state will have a much larger stockpile of protective gear, including N95 masks. We will have greater reserves of ventilators. The state government will have its own stockpile as well, ready for the next invisible killer when it arrives—and it is a question of when, not whether.

One result of this event will be more people working remotely. There are some jobs—analysts huddled over data all day—where remote work sites are well suited. We will also see much more application of the telehealth technology we already have up and running in the United States. The fact is that any person with a smartphone is potentially capable of getting in touch with a doctor in seconds, but only if the system enables that contact. The technology is certainly there and ready. Until now, however, the red tape of government and private insurance plans prevented most of that contact, or, if not prevented it, certainly paid so little for those contacts that it actually caused doctors and hospitals to lose money.

During the crisis, however, the federal government, along with a number of commercial insurance companies, agreed to pay for telehealth services at the same rate they pay for in-person visits. It is hard to overstate the importance of this breakthrough. Telehealth will never replace in-person visits, but there are countless conditions which doctors could easily diagnose and treat via smartphone. Think of the convenience for both patient and doctor. Think about how this might well enable doctors to interact with more patients. The possibilities are exciting—in the years ahead, in part thanks to the coronavirus crisis, we will see the use of telehealth flourishing.

One thing that could have helped in the crisis would have been clearer leadership from the White House—something like the calm, fact-based presentations by Governor Cuomo. As the crisis was building, on March 10, I was interviewed live on the set of CNBC, the financial network that I knew going in was closely monitored at the White House. I certainly knew that one of the hosts would ask what I thought of the response from the federal government, and when that question came, I replied, "I do think that the federal government was slow to respond. We activated our emergency management system six weeks ago when at the federal level people were talking about, 'Don't worry about this; it's going to go away.'"

In fact, as we look back upon the whole crisis, the government failed at the highest levels to take the situation as seriously as was warranted. Could we as a nation have done a more effective job of containing the virus with stronger, more effective leadership from the White House? In my view, absolutely.

I have been fortunate in my role at Northwell. We have been able to build one of the most innovative health care systems anywhere in the country with a supportive board and world-class staff. We have broken with many traditions and disrupted the status quo of health care in the process—with a different type of leadership team, an in-house educational system, broadening the scope of our mission and social responsibility, creating from scratch a radical new way to educate doctors, and more.

But there is a price to be paid for all of this. When I worked for Governor Cuomo, I was never home. I'm reminded of what my son, Brian, asked Kathy: "Why do we need him?" I am my father's workaholic son in some ways. Mary once wondered aloud whether our family would have actually been worse off if our dad had inherited the farm. Maybe, Mary suggests, if we had owned the farm, he would have had us all out there working night and day without respite. Families suffer when workaholics indulge their obsession. I love my son and daughter, but I wasn't there for them in the way some other fathers were when their children were growing up. I wasn't with my kids much in the early years at all. I missed a lot.

Being CEO of a large health care system can, ironically, have negative effects on your health. There are world-class workout facilities available to me, as well as some of the leading physicians in the country in their specialties. But there are also many social responsibilities—dinners with donors, board members, and others. And the schedule is demanding—fifteen-hour days are not at all unusual. This too often has meant that I get lazy and fail to exercise enough.

In 2014, I was exercising in a gym near my home when I felt chest pain. It was pretty intense, so I sat down and took a break and it went away. The chest pain was an obvious signal to seek medical care immediately, but when you are a stubborn Irishman, you don't always follow the rules.

I went home and did not feel well. I thought it was because I was out of shape and hadn't been exercising regularly. That night I was lethargic, and Kathy told me that I looked gray. She said I should go to the hospital. I did not go. The following morning, at a staff meeting, Gene Tangney said to me, "You don't look right." Gene is a paramedic with an extensive background in emergency medicine. He said I had to go to the emergency room. I said later. He said *now*.

In the hospital, on a treadmill, hooked up to heart monitors, I had barely taken a step when the doctor ordered me off and had me wheeled into the OR, where surgeons discovered that my main artery was 90 percent blocked. They inserted two stents. Afterward, the surgeon told me that if I had not gotten off the treadmill when I did, I would probably not have made it. He called my condition "a classic widow-maker." That day I was, as I have been throughout my life, very lucky.

Chapter Twelve

Gun Violence and Climate Change: Two Major Public Health Crises

Not so long ago the mission of a medical organization was straightforward: Take care of sick and injured people who show up in your hospitals and medical offices. During the past couple of decades, however, American medicine has awakened to the idea that the great majority of a person's health depends upon many factors having little or nothing to do with doctor visits or hospital stays.

Research suggests that 80 to 90 percent of a person's health is determined by lifestyle and what are known as the *social determinants of health,* including the availability of fresh food, a steady income, clean air and water, safe housing, reliable public transportation, and other factors in the socioeconomic rather than the strictly medical realm. The World Health Organization has a concise definition of social determinants as "the conditions in which people are born, grow, live, work and age. These circumstances are shaped by the distribution of money, power and resources at global, national and local levels."

This thinking is relatively new in the medical world, but the broader public health issues were our bread and butter when I worked in New York state government for Governor Mario Cuomo in the 1980s and 1990s. Many of the great advances in human health have come from public health investments in sanitation, clean water, and air.

Much has been written about the obvious social determinants such as quality food and safe housing, but there are two other issues that deserve attention—gun violence and climate change. These are political, social, and scientific issues that I see as *medical emergencies*.

In health care, we are inundated with statistics to such an extent that sometimes the numbers blur. But when researching the crisis of gun violence, I came upon a statistic that stopped me in my tracks. It is well known that that gun violence disproportionately harms communities of color, but looking a bit deeper, I found that it is the leading cause of death for young Black men in America. Here is how dire the situation has become: Among the top ten killers of young black males, gun violence is not only number one on the list, it actually takes more lives than the next nine causes of death *combined*. And while the rate of US deaths from heart disease, cancer, motor vehicle accidents, and other major contributors is declining, deaths from firearms in this country increased more than 30 percent from 2014 to 2021. Firearms are the *leading* cause of death among all children and teens (ages one to nineteen), surpassing motor vehicle accidents for the first time in sixty years.

How can we as a society tolerate such carnage? I believe that as guardians of the young people in our society, we have a responsibility to take extraordinary action toward reducing the bloodshed. And one extraordinary step, in my view, is to bring the issue into the medical realm where the concern for the health of patients transcends the bitter partisan divisions about guns.

In 2019, I was talking with one of our newly-hired physicians, Chethan Sathya, MD, a young pediatric surgeon. Before coming to Northwell he had trained in surgery in Chicago. On his third day of training, a thirteen-year-old child was rushed to the emergency room with bullet wounds to the chest. Chethan cut the boy's chest open but the wounds to the heart and lungs proved fatal.

"That same night," Dr. Sathya told me, "I treated the teenager's six-month-old sibling. The baby had bullet wounds through the chest, two holes on either side of the belly, blood gushing out. I had my fingers on the bullet holes. This child looked very similar to my own child, born just a few months earlier. This baby was struggling and there were the parents in the trauma bay breaking down, hysterical."

A surgeon's job is to save lives. Chethan described this heart-breaking surgery: "Cut open the baby's abdomen, and you look to see organ damage and you repair the liver. You repair the bowel, the intestine that's been injured. You repair whatever's been injured. And then you close that baby up and the hope is that you can do it quick enough that you stop the bleeding and you give that baby a chance to survive." And although the baby did survive, his spine was shattered by a bullet and the child will never be able to walk.

This is tragic for the child and parents and horrifying for a civilized society. We are a nation of about 330 million people. And yet there are more guns, about 400 million in the United States. Violent acts with guns harm people throughout the nation in cities, suburbs, and rural areas, but there is no question that a disproportionate share of harm comes to people in urban neighborhoods where guns are so readily available. How can older people or children—or anyone for that matter—enjoy the peace of mind essential to good health in an area where shootings are a regular occurrence?

As someone who grew up in rural Ireland in the 1950s and '60s, this gun epidemic is mind-boggling to me. Most of the violence I encountered growing up was confined to the hurling pitch. I am very much in favor of peaceful solutions to conflict, including inter-personal conflict, but I also understand that sometimes tempers get the best of people. In my hometown of Knockaderry, there were times when a couple of men, typically alcohol-fueled, would square off over some dispute. A few punches would be exchanged, the issue was settled, and everyone moved on.

In America, however, the ubiquity of guns—often illegal hand-guns—means that disputes are increasingly settled with deadly out-comes. Traditionally, discussions about gun violence have come in the political realm, but that has changed and one of the most hopeful developments is that doctors, nurses, and other clinicians are step-ping up and adding the credibility of their voices to the discussion. When I hear the stories from trauma surgeons like Dr. Sathya and ponder the enormity of the statistics—nearly 45,000 dead and more than 40,000 injured in the United States every year—it becomes clear that gun violence is much more than a political problem; it is as nothing less than a national medical emergency.

One of the bumps in the road toward tackling the social deter-minants of health is a belief among some people in medicine that social issues such a housing, poverty, education, etc. are not the responsibility of doctors. Public policy instruction about income, education, housing, transportation, gun violence, and climate change have never been part of medical school curriculum. At the same time, however, if we look back at the power of the anti-to-bacco campaigns in the United States, we know that physicians were on the front lines fighting for change. Who knew better than doctors how truly damaging smoking cigarettes could be?

I believe gun violence is analogous. In 2018 it became clear to me and my colleagues at Northwell that we needed to act. That action meant trying to understand why there is such an epidemic of gun violence in our country and, secondly, figuring out a way to harness the collective power and credibility of the medical community on this issue. And that is what we have done.

Since 2019, we have been hosting annual gun violence prevention forums, which attracted medical and other experts from throughout the country, including former Congresswoman and gun violence survivor Gabby Giffords; former New York Mayor Michael Bloomberg; Dr. Daniel Webster, director of the Johns Hopkins Center for Gun Policy and Research; President Biden's national policy advisor Ambassador Susan Rice; Dr. Mark Rosenberg, former head of the Centers for Disease Control & Prevention's National Center for Injury Prevention and Control; and many others prominent in medicine and public policy.

Soon after our inaugural forum, we established the Northwell Center for Gun Violence Prevention in early 2020, with Dr. Sathya as director. Because there was no regular venue for health systems and practitioners to share best practices and galvanize their colleagues to call for broader policy change, we've taken some small but important steps forward. In early 2021, we convened what we call a "learning collaborative" where more than five hundred health care professionals from thirty-five states are having monthly discussions, sharing ideas on how to mitigate accidental shootings, suicides, and street violence.

The medical movement to reduce gun violence is in its infancy, but the fact that it is now recognized as a public health crisis among health care providers is a breakthrough. When politicians shout at one another about the issue, it most likely hardens positions on both sides of the gun control issue. But when doctors step in with measured tones it's possible to transcend political bias and say, *Hold on. Let's look at this not from the hardened positions of the political left and right, but from the evidence-based view of health professionals trying to protect the well-being of individuals and communities.* I think the timing is right for this initiative and it's clear that many medical professionals have been looking for exactly this type of opportunity.

We walk a fine line as we approach the issue from an apolitical position. It's not about the second amendment, but it is about control and safety. We are not trying to engage in unproductive political discourse. The work we are doing in the medical community is on a separate pathway. We bring the credibility of healers to this initiative. We are in the business of collaborating with law enforcement, gun owners, community organizations, and others to reduce the 45,000 firearm-related homicides, accidental shootings, and suicides that occurred in 2021.

One thing we know for certain is that this is among the most pressing public health issues in the country and it will take a concerted effort of thousands of doctors and nurses many years to make real progress. That is not pessimism—it's an acknowledgement of reality.

But we have already been able to make important progress. The best place to start is always within the trusting, one-on-one space where doctor and patient meet. At present, doctors routinely talk to patients about their weight, nutrition, whether they exercise, smoke or use other substances, etc. In spite of the potential danger of firearms, fewer than 10 percent of adults who live in homes with firearms have ever discussed firearm safety with a clinician.

We are changing that. We have added a new standard screening on gun safety, thanks to a $1.4 million grant from the National Institutes of Health—the first round of federal dollars awarded for gun violence research in more than twenty years. This first-of-its-kind protocol screens all patients for gun injury risk at three of our hospitals.

Our clinicians now ask patients basic questions like, "Do you have access to a firearm within or outside your household?" or "In the past six months, including today, how often have you heard guns being shot or had someone pull a gun on you?" Teens are also asked if they have gotten into serious physical fights, or if their friends carry knives, razors or guns. Thus far, many of these conversations have resulted in patients saying that they will take action to store guns in the home in a more secure fashion. By asking every patient we are aiming to make discussions about firearms an accepted, normal part of interactions between clinicians and patients—no different than asking about their personal lifestyles and how it could be affecting their health.

We have also been fortunate to receive a grant from the state of New York to establish violence intervention programs at the three Northwell hospitals involved in the gun safety screening protocol. We have hired social workers and other clinical staff to partner with community-based organizations to develop interventions aimed at curbing the cycle of violence, and keeping patients and communities safe.

There is one additional statistic that stopped me in my tracks: Nearly half of patients treated for a violent injury are reinjured within five years. In other words, these patients have been to our emergency departments before after being victimized. We are now using this opportunity to intervene with victims during their first visit and explore whether we can help them avoid future violent interactions.

I have always been an optimist. I have always believed that with clear thinking and hard work anything can be improved. It is thrilling to see the progress in medical science in recent decades. The creation of COVID vaccines in record time has likely saved millions of lives. The success of the Human Genome Project advanced the ability of scientists to fight disease as never before. Human beings worldwide have benefitted from enormous strides against heart disease and cancer. The combination of statins lowering cholesterol levels, coronary stents holding open heart valves, medications stabilizing blood pressure, pacemakers and other devices have made heart disease less deadly than ever before. Age-adjusted mortality rate for cardiac disease has been reduced by about 50 percent in the past thirty years. We have witnessed similar progress in treating cancer. Early detection and improved therapies drove down the cancer death rate by 27 percent between 1999 and 2019, according to the CDC. Targeted therapies and immunotherapies are saving lives and prolonging the lives of patients with metastatic disease.

This sort of progress is in sharp contrast to one of the most daunting threats to human health in the history of mankind—climate change. It is jarring for me to think about this planet-level deterioration. I cannot help but contrast the new reality with the world in which I was raised in the southwest of Ireland, where the environment could not have been more pristine. We had little in the way of material things, but we lived in a land blessed with environmental purity and some of the most enduring natural beauty anywhere on earth. It seems incomprehensible that during my lifetime, while human health has advanced exponentially, our planet's health has steadily declined.

Nearly every day there are reports of scientific advances that improve human health, and nearly every day there are reports sounding an alarm about the health of the Earth. In early 2022, a United Nations panel of 270 researchers from sixty-seven countries issued a report that, in the words of the UN general secretary, is "an atlas of human suffering and a damning indictment of failed climate leadership. With fact upon fact, this report reveals how people and the planet are getting clobbered by climate change."

If there is a greater long-term risk to the health of humanity I am unaware of it. Consider just some of the impacts:

- More frequent and severe heat waves lead to more heat-related illnesses and deaths.
- Seasonal changes can shift the geographic area where disease-carrying insects, such as mosquitoes, ticks, and fleas transmit West Nile Virus, dengue fever, Lyme disease, and malaria to humans.
- Rising exposure to pollen due to increased plant-growing seasons, to molds due to severe storms, and to air pollution due to increased temperature and wildfires, can all worsen lung diseases such as asthma.
- Rising temperatures can cause poor air quality that affects the heart and worsens cardiovascular disease.
- Flooding events can contaminate water with harmful bacteria, viruses, and chemicals that cause foodborne and waterborne illnesses.
- More frequent and severe extreme weather events can cause injuries, deaths, and illnesses, and can also harm mental health due to damage to property, loss of loved ones, displacement, and chronic stress.
- Extreme climate events can place added stress on hospitals and public health systems and limit people's ability to obtain adequate health care during crises.[1]

---

1 Bulleted information courtesy Donna Drummond, senior vice president, Northwell Health.

I believe that just as gun violence is a medical emergency to our country, so, too, is climate change. And that makes it imperative that we do everything in our power—no matter how small an act it might seem—to treat the planet with greater reverence than ever before. With a concerted effort our team at Northwell was able to reduce our health system's carbon footprint by 15.6 percent from just 2009 to 2011 and continue reducing it each year. We pursue U.S. Green Building Council guidelines in renovations and new construction. And in an initiative similar to our efforts to collaborate with others on gun safety, we convened a conference in 2021 to explore best practices in health equity, women's health and reducing damaging impacts on the climate.

Optimism is a powerful thing. The belief that things will get better is wired throughout my DNA. As an eighteen-year-old, I set out from Knockaderry to make the money I needed to continue my education, which I believed would lead to more opportunities, a better life. As they age, some people seem to grow progressively less optimistic—about their lives and the world around us. But I am very comfortable holding tight to my optimistic nature. I do this partly because it is who I am and have always been. But I also do it because my experience over the past fifty years has proven that even the problems that seem most insurmountable can be tackled with some success. Because I live in the world of health care, I am reminded every day of the historical improvements over time. As professionals, as a society, we can make progress against the most intractable problems, including gun violence and climate change. With the medical community more actively involved in both of these issues, I am convinced that better days lie ahead.

Chapter Thirteen

Mam's New Life

"Is that you?"

MY MOTHER'S NEW LIFE BEGAN the day my father died, when she was "liberated," as my brother Sean put it. It was a time, as Mary recalls, when my mother experienced a kind of freedom that was entirely new to her. "The freedom, the sheer lack of stress, of not having to walk on eggshells all the time," says Mary. "Freedom from fear of a blowup at any moment."

Mam was living a new life, and she did not hold back. A few months after Dad passed away, Mam and Mary came to the US and stayed with me and my family for two wonderful weeks. Soon thereafter, out of the blue, Mam said that she wanted to go to the beach in Ballybunion, a town in County Kerry, about forty-five minutes from Knockaderry. She said she had learned about people renting mobile homes and staying there on the beach, and she said she would like to try that. Mary had a new Mini Cooper that Sean had purchased as a gift for her, and she drove Mam over to Ballybunion and helped her get set up. Mam rented two mobile homes so there was enough space to have visitors during her two-week stay. It became one big party, with her sister and brother-in-law coming to stay, along with various nieces and nephews, as well as Mary, Sean, and Pat. "She just loved it," Mary recalls. "It was absolutely wonderful to see her so free, like a weight had been lifted from her. It was like she discovered this part of her that was just pressed, hidden, kept under wraps. She could never be that person when my father was there. She just blossomed." She would put on a swimsuit and walk the few hundred feet along the sand and swim in the ocean for the very first time that any of us could recall.

And then she discovered the card-playing circuit. I suppose she knew about the different card games held each night at someone's home or at a social club in the greater Limerick area, but she had never talked about joining the circuit before. She had always loved playing cards and had done so for a night each week at our house, but always in my father's looming presence. When he was gone, she joined a sprawling card-playing community throughout the area and began going out three or even four evenings a week to play, and then, over time, she would be out as many as seven nights per week. Sometimes she would also play Sunday afternoon! And she loved every minute of it.

The games, with modest prizes for the winners, were mostly held in community centers in nearby towns such as Granagh, Ballingarry, Coolyroe, Rathkeale, and Shanagolden, as well as Knockaderry. Mary would drive her to the games some nights, while other nights she would get a lift from one of the neighbors. Around Christmas and Easter, different groups would host big card games where the prizes would be large, and the crowds were also much larger than the weekly ones. Mam was a skilled player of a popular game called Forty-Fives that derives from the Irish game Spoil Five, which in turn derives from a game called Maw, popularized by Scottish King James VI in the seventeenth century. At the weekly games, she would often win prizes, such as dishes or small amounts of money. At some of the bigger events, you could win as much as one hundred euros.

As much as she enjoyed her evenings, she also loved the freedom of her days, when she would start the morning by walking into the village and going to Mass and then visiting neighbors on her way home. She was a faithful friend to Phil Meehan, the woman who had lost her legs in a farm accident. Phil lived a few houses away, and Mam frequently visited her, often bringing groceries. My cousin Vincent and his wife Catherine lived next door, and our mother was like a surrogate grandmother to their two children.

She was a gifted baker and would frequently bring baked goods to friends and neighbors. She would clean the house, making sure everything was perfectly tidy. Every afternoon, she would take a nap. Sometimes after that she would get out her brushes and do paint-by-numbers pictures, a hobby she enjoyed. She spent many hours at her Singer sewing machine making clothes for friends and neighbors. She was expert at all kinds of alterations for pants, skirts, jackets, and coats. Sometimes she would get a request on Saturday afternoon from someone who needed a rush job in time for Sunday morning Mass. She always said yes. In the evening, when Mary would come home from work, she and my mother would have supper together, and then she was off to a card game somewhere in the area.

She began traveling as well, coming to New York every summer to visit me and my family. I always purchased her a round-trip airline ticket with an open return so that she could stay with us for as long as she wished. She would make brown bread, Irish soda bread, and scones. Sometimes she would stay for two weeks, other times more than a month. Sometimes she would come over with Mary, but usually she came alone. Kathy and the kids and I moved around a bit—from Manhattan to Westchester to Albany to Long Island—and it didn't matter to my mother whether we were living in a cramped Manhattan apartment or a spacious Long Island home. It was all grand to her.

When we were living in Northport, Kathy would drive her to daily Mass at St. Philip Neri parish in Northport Village. When visiting, she would get to know neighbors, and she would go into town and visit the library to check out books. She and I would talk at home in the evenings and every once in a while I would bring up those not-so-pleasant days when Dad was at his worst, but she never, ever said a bad word about him, even many years after his death. She preferred to focus on the good in everyone. "Oh, it wasn't that bad," she would say. "He was a good man." And that was it. She much preferred to talk about her children and grandchildren and how happy we all made her.

She was very proud of my brother Sean—as we all were. He had worked within the Mental Health Association of Ireland setting up programs that did a world of good, and followed that by shifting to work in the pharmaceutical industry, where he organized the first all-Ireland meeting to coordinate efforts on breast cancer. He also organized sessions aimed at improving care for patients with lung, colorectal, and ovarian cancers, as well as lymphoma. As proud as Mam was of Sean, she was equally proud of Joe, his career in the Army, and his having conquered alcoholism. Joe had become a successful builder, showing impressive skills surely inherited from our dad. Mam was also proud of Pat, who graduated from University of Limerick and went on to serve in a series of major governmental roles in different parts of Ireland, rising to chief executive of the Clare County Council.

And then there was my sister Mary, a special case. How do you describe someone so loving and selfless that she devoted years of her life to caring for our mother and helping Mam care for our father? To this day, Mary still lives in the house we moved into after the roof caved in; it's the only place she's lived since she was two. Pat was home during Dad's decline, and he also played a big role in helping Mam. When Pat married and moved away, Mary remained at my mother's side. In a way, Mary became an extension of Mam, always there to drive her to card games, take her for medical appointments, or drive her up to Dublin to visit Sean or over to Clare to visit Pat.

When Pat went through a rough divorce, all but prevented from seeing his five children, Mam was as heartbroken as he. She had always gravitated toward the child most in need, and when Pat was suffering through his most difficult days, Mary, Joe, and Mam would rush to Pat's side. When Sean's children were born, Mary and Mam were there to welcome the new babies, and the same for Joe's two kids as well.

Things changed a bit when Mary met her future husband, Patrick Geaney, a terrific guy who worked as a teacher. Mary had been entirely focused on our mother, and did not meet Pat until she was thirty-seven. The following year they married, and the question became where they would live. Pat had a plot of land picked out on which to build a new home for them, but if Pat and Mary moved into a new house, what would Mam do? But then Mary did what she'd always done—put Mam's well-being above all else. "I can't leave her," Mary said. "I can't." To Pat's eternal credit, he understood. Pat moved into the house and he and Mam got along well, although it surely required an adjustment period for both.

The house was much as it had been when our family had moved in more than thirty years earlier, and when Mary became pregnant with her son Simon, Pat and Mary wanted to renovate—with

204 • After *the* Roof Caved In

a substantial addition. Mary could tell that such change was up-
setting to Mam. She had been paying a weekly amount to the
county council for the house for thirty years and had only made
her final payment about a year before Mary and Pat were married.
Mam didn't say anything, but Mary was so close to her that she
could read her emotions, and could tell that the renovation plan
upset her. I thought that what Pat and Mary were planning for the
house sounded absolutely great and I knew that Mam would come
around at some point.

One summer, Mam came to stay with me and my family in
Albany, and I could tell when she arrived that she was not in good
health. Kathy took her to the doctor, and it turned out that she
was suffering from internal bleeding. After several tests, it was
determined that she had colon cancer. She went back to Ireland
for treatment, and Sean swung into action, as he had so often done
through the years for every member of our family. The thing about
Sean is that if there's a tough time or a crisis, he responds with full
force. Sean was by then well known and influential in the health-
care community. He was able to connect her to a surgeon in Dublin
who performed a major operation which, fortunately, went well,
and she recovered nicely.

In the summer of 2000, we had a family reunion in honor of
Mam's eightieth birthday. Mary and my brother Pat did a brilliant
job planning and organizing, and dozens of her card-playing
friends, neighbors, and family members gathered in the town of
Rathkeale for the celebration. We started the event with a Mass for
the immediate family, which pleased her, of course. Afterward, we
told her we were going to dinner in the local hotel in Rathkeale.
When we arrived she was greeted by dozens of friends, neighbors,
sisters, nieces, nephews—a huge surprise. We had a celebratory

meal, a magician entertained everyone, and then a band struck up and there was dancing. Later she even played cards with her friends. Kathy's family joined us, combining the tribute to Mam with their annual Butler family reunion. Two of Mam's sister's children traveled from England to be there; children whom Mam had brought from London back to Glenroe during the war, where she cared for them.

The September after the July reunion/birthday celebration, there was some bad news. Mam had not been feeling well, and the diagnosis was bone cancer. The doctors did not give her much longer to live. She deteriorated in November, and I flew home to spend time with her. She was stable for a time, and then rallied and found strength that surprised the doctors. Throughout that winter and spring of 2001 she was quite ill, but stable. Mary's son Simon was four years old, and Mary had the challenge of caring for both an active little boy and a sick mother. A friend would come by sometimes to take Simon to school or sit with my mother to allow Mary to go grocery shopping. Mam declined throughout the summer of 2001, and then in September, a year after her diagnosis, she took a turn for the worse. She was frail, confused, and in pain.

One morning Mary awoke to find Mam packing her suitcase. Mary asked what she was doing, and Mam said that she was going to a neighbor's house to help deliver her baby. Mam's weakness and confusion alarmed Mary, who took her to hospice for pain medication. Mam never came out. During the eleven weeks she was in hospice, Mary tried twice to bring her home, but Mam became agitated and confused and had to remain.

I visited during this period, when Mam was in a beautiful hospice facility in Limerick that seemed to me a model of how people in the final stages of life should be cared for (I set up a similar hospice facility at Northwell Health when I returned to New York). The last time I'd been home she was in very bad shape. She'd lost much of her vision and she hadn't recognized me at first. But I sat by her bed holding her hand, and after a moment, squeezing my hand, she said my name. "Is that you?" she asked me. I said it was, though of course she could not hear me, but I squeezed her hand, and I believe she knew it was me.

Mary spent every day with her during the eleven weeks while Mam grew increasingly confused, but the medication kept her pain at bay, and it was a relief that she was comfortable. Before she died, in a moment of clarity, she raised the subject of the house renovation with Mary, bless her heart. She told her, "I now know what you're trying to do and I love it." She died on December 29, 2001, twenty-two years after our father passed away.

It seemed as though everyone who lived within ten miles of Knockaderry visited our family during the wake. As is traditional, the wake was held at our family home—Mary's home now—and it was one of those occasions when the mourners' expressions of how truly wonderful the deceased was were actually heartfelt. The stories flowed.

She'd been known far and wide for her ability as a seamstress. She had been at it for going on a half century, and at some point people in every village around had heard about her skill, her speed, and her absolute reliability. And many had also heard that if money was tight, there would likely be no charge. I spoke at the funeral in the church she had visited thousands of times over the decades. She had found so much solace there, in that modest structure. For her, it was a place of peace—a refuge where she could reflect upon her faith, think about her family, and puzzle over the behavior of my father. This was her place, and I sought to treat it with the reverence it deserved. Family members brought gifts recalling Mam to the altar during the Mass. There was a copy of *Glenanaar*, the novel by Canon Sheehan that she loved. There was one of her paintings, as well as a soutane, the cassock worn by priests, in remembrance of the many garments she had made. Her passport was brought to the altar to celebrate her love of travel and adventure. A deck of playing cards was brought to the altar, along with her prayer book and rosary, the fifty-nine beads well-worn. Also at the Mass, a commemorative piece of writing was distributed with a picture of Mam, a drawing of a red rose, and a poem written by Mary which read, in part—

> Sometimes when I think of Mam,
> I think of what she took,
> A child . . . and set them on the road of life,
> And loved with just one look.

I wonder what might have become of me without my mother's love and guidance. Had she not encouraged me to read, would I have gotten an education? Had she not stood up for me at that pivotal moment in my life when she faced off against not only Mr. Burke, but my father on the question of whether I would continue to secondary school, what would my life have been? She gave me the gifts of ambition, of curiosity about the world, of open-mindedness to explore what was out there beyond the hills of Knockaderry.

I now realized clearly my duty to give her a gift she would find more precious than any other—the gift of love and unity within our family. We had frayed a bit over time, my siblings and I. There had been ups and downs and clashes and moments of contention and unpleasantness. There were many good moments, too. But the fraying over time had taken a toll, and I knew now that it was my responsibility as the oldest to do whatever I could to try and knit us back together. I knew that this was what she would want.

Chapter Fourteen

Grand Marshal

"The greatest incubator of opportunity the world has ever known."

PHYTOPHTHORA INFESTANS, THE MICROORGANISM THAT caused the Irish potato famine, altered the history of both Ireland and America. In the 1840s and '50s, *phytophthora infestans* mold destroyed half to two-thirds of the Irish potato crop, upon which millions of Irish tenant farmers relied for sustenance. Catastrophe ensued: a million Irish men, women, and children perished, while an additional million fled, some to England, many more reaching the shores of America.

Irish families were crammed into the holds of vessels known as "coffin ships," where 300 people huddled in a space that would normally accommodate a quarter that number. Entire families were jammed together, sleeping against and on top of one another, suffering for two months in below-decks squalor amid rampant sea sickness, diarrhea, and worse. Passengers were allowed on deck for only thirty minutes per day, spending the rest of the time awaiting meager portions of porridge and rationed water. Many passengers, weak from hunger at the start, died during the journey. Others, fatally weakened by the crossing, succumbed upon arrival. Some rickety sailing vessels never made it all the way, sinking in violent storms.

These desperate Irish immigrants accounted for nearly half of all newcomers to the United States in the 1840s. The men and women who migrated in the middle of the 1800s are long gone, of course, but their legacy is ever present in New York City. One manifestation of that legacy is the Irish Hunger Memorial in Battery Park City, at the southern tip of Manhattan. There, steps from where the World Trade Towers stood, sits an Irish cottage, shipped from Ireland, surrounded by natural growth. It is a humble scene, and all the more moving for its modest nature.

There is another structure in Manhattan that I think of as a memorial to those who fled to the United States during the potato famine. Saint Patrick's Cathedral occupies a city block between Fifth and Madison Avenues and Fiftieth and Fifty-First Streets. It sits in all its majesty across the avenue from Rockefeller Center, and the two structures, a religious cathedral and a civic one, serve as the epicenter of Manhattan. The cathedral is constructed of brick, white marble, and limestone, and stretches more than a hundred yards long and fifty yards wide. Beneath its Neo-Gothic spires reaching 330 feet into the sky, the cathedral can accommodate 3,000 worshippers. Saint Patrick's holds a place of pride on the National Register of Historic Places for its architectural significance and transcendent presence, but it is the beating heart within the cathedral that makes it a monument to tens of thousands of immigrants from Europe—many from Ireland—who built the church over a twenty-one-year post-famine period, from 1858 to 1879. When you pause to think about these workers who came to the United States in the nineteenth century, you realize the extraordinary nature of their journeys.

Imagine saying goodbye to your loved ones in a rural Irish village, knowing it's quite likely you will never see them again.

Imagine making your way to Foynes Harbor on the west coast of Ireland, New Ross on the east coast, or Kinsale in the south and boarding a ship, where you are placed in unthinkable conditions. You set sail across the Atlantic Ocean having very little notion of what lies ahead, only to arrive in New York City and face discrimination and hardship. At the same time, however, you are welcomed into an immigrant community of people who have come before you and done the hard work of paving the way for you and others. And these people who have preceded you, although they reside in slums, and although they are regarded by many citizens with disdain, have nonetheless begun to build lives for themselves and their families.

You can imagine these Irishmen, by the hundreds, making their way after dawn each morning from the crowded tenements on the Lower East Side up to the middle of Manhattan to work. For some, no doubt, it was just a paycheck, but I imagine that for many others, fresh from the deeply Catholic villages of home, this was not just a job, but a blessed undertaking. Over the two-decade construction period, these Irishmen worked as laborers, engineers, stonemasons, glaziers, painters, carpenters, and countless other jobs. The work of these immigrants was and remains the soul of this house of prayer.

There were immigrants from all over Europe in the mid-nineteenth century, but the Irish presence in the city made it natural to name the church after the Irish patron saint. Immigrants from Ireland, working alongside those from Italy, Poland, Spain, and other nations, helped build the modern industrial America. As time passed, immigrants and their descendants were educated and became engineers, doctors, physicists, artists, members of the US Armed Forces, and CEOs of large, complex health care organizations. I am proud to call myself an immigrant, knowing that I stand among the ranks of tens of millions of men and women who came to this country and found a chance at a new life.

Today, as anti-immigrant sentiment, recurrent throughout much of American history—against the Irish, Italians, Poles, Jews, Muslims, etc.—now once again rears its ugly head, it betrays ignorance on the part of those who espouse such views. As Mario Cuomo used to say of his ancestors and those of other immigrants: "We are the sons and daughters of giants who built this country." Amen. I believe that one reason so many first-generation immigrants have risen to prominent positions in the United States is that, by definition, immigrants do not fear risk. These people, who left their home countries for the unknown, were willing to do almost anything to seize an opportunity at a new life.

As a CEO, I'm often asked to get involved in community activities, from serving on university boards to helping the leaders of Ireland reform the health system. I serve on a number of boards of other organizations—including my alma mater, Fordham University. And if you happen to be Irish American or an Irishman who holds a prominent position, your name may be suggested for the role of Grand Marshal of the Saint Patrick's Day Parade in New York City.

A selection committee chose me for the role in 2017. The chairman of the parade, John Lahey, told the media that I had been chosen because he considered me "the true embodiment of the values we celebrate on St. Patrick's Day, a leader in a noble healing profession, an educator, a public servant, an Irish American who has made enormous contributions to his adopted country and who has made us all proud to be Irish." It was a great honor to be following in the footsteps (literally!) of people like US Senator

George Mitchell, Cardinal Timothy Dolan, New York mayor Robert Wagner, and New York governor Hugh Carey. Had I been asked a few years earlier, I would have felt obligated to decline, given the parade organizers' position at the time preventing gay men and women from participating in the parade. Thankfully, that had been resolved prior to my year, and I accepted the invitation with a great sense of excitement.

I have been fortunate to receive some awards through the years, including honorary doctorates from University College Dublin and Queens University in Belfast, and I was inducted into the Irish American Hall of Fame located in New Ross, County Wexford, where a replica of the famous coffin ship, the *Dunbrody*, is on display. In 2007, I was also awarded the Ellis Island Medal of Honor, given to "individuals who have made it their mission to share with those less fortunate, their wealth of knowledge, indomitable courage, boundless compassion, unique talents and selfless generosity. They do so while acknowledging their debt to their ethnic heritage as they uphold the ideals and spirit of America." Speaking to the gathering on the hallowed ground that is Ellis Island was an almost haunting experience. Although I had not come through Ellis Island, I had come to America with aspirations identical to those who had experienced their first steps on American soil on that plot of ground in New York Harbor.

But I have to confess that there was something about being Grand Marshal that was different and particularly affecting for me. I felt that it was my responsibility to embody the aspirations of all those Irish men and women who had come before me. Honoring them was a humbling thing for someone from the village of Knockaderry. I marched to represent the sick and desperate who had come in the coffin ships, family members dying in transit. I considered the position of Grand Marshal to be a sacred duty, and I did everything I possibly could to honor the lives and memories of *all* immigrants.

In the New York City area, there are numerous events celebrating Saint Patrick's Day in the weeks leading up to the parade. I had been told that these gatherings—in Queens, the Bronx, Westchester, and elsewhere—were not mandatory events; that past Grand Marshals attended some but not all. To me, these events, where Irishmen from the outer boroughs gathered to celebrate their heritage, were just as important as the parade itself. I attended every dinner, breakfast, and luncheon to which I was invited, and found that a number of them involved three or four hundred people, with prominent locals on the dais and bagpipers setting the mood. On the day before the parade, Kathy and I made our way down Wall Street to the New York Stock Exchange, where I rang the opening bell. That evening there was a gala at a hotel in Manhattan, with seven hundred people celebrating, among them Cardinal Dolan clutching a frosty bottle of Budweiser.

On Saint Patrick's Day itself, we began with an 8:00 a.m. Mass at the cathedral. Members of the 69th New York Infantry, known as the "Fighting 69th" or the "Fighting Irish," were there in uniform. This was the legendary unit of Irishmen who had formed to fight for the Union during the American Civil War, and fight they did at Bull Run, Antietam, and Appomattox, and later serving honorably in the World Wars, from Chateau-Thierry in World War I to Saipan and Okinawa in World War II. The presence of the Fighting Irish brigade, resplendent in their uniforms, was a tangible reminder that Irish immigrants had adopted this new land as their own and were willing to lay down their lives for America's hard-won freedoms. Tradition holds that these soldiers lead the parade, with the Grand Marshal close behind. In the pews was a contingent of police officers who had traveled to New York from Limerick for the event. There were elected officials, civic and business leaders, and many of the prominent men and women of Irish descent in the city. Hundreds of my friends and colleagues from Northwell Health were there. A number of bishops celebrated the Mass, along with Cardinal Dolan. Kathy and I entered the church when everyone was in place, walked down the center aisle, and were greeted at the altar by the cardinal, then seated in the front row along with the mayor of New York.

I had not been to Mass in some time. As jaded as I am about Catholicism in some ways, I confess that I was moved by the pageantry of it all, by the music, soaring and beautiful. As I sat through the celebration of the Mass, my thoughts, as you might expect, turned to my mother. Throughout her life, she had found solace and joy in church. She had taken the Eucharist—the body and blood of Jesus Christ—many thousands of times through the decades, and the experience of being in the presence of the Mass, even though she was unable to hear the words, enriched her life. I imagined she would have been beyond happy to have been here with us—with Kathy and our kids, and with Joe, Sean, Mary, and Pat—all of us here as an expression of support and love for one another.

I wish I was one of those people who could have gotten through the Mass without my mind somehow finding its way back through the years to Knockaderry and those moments when the priest would announce the amount each family had donated; the priest who, it seemed to me at the time, took a certain satisfaction in conveying to the people of the village what a modest sum Jack Dowling had donated. But the truth is that I am a Dowling, an Irishman, and it is not easy to let go of those painful memories and the resentment that goes with them.

The best part of the experience was having the entire family there for the festivities: Joe; Sean and his wife, Bernadette; Pat and his wife, Rose; and Mary and her husband, Pat, all traveled to New York to celebrate with me. Each of my siblings had visited me in the states before, and some had stayed for a while. Sean, for example, worked construction in the Bronx one summer and lived with me. One year, I was able to help Pat get a summer position at the United Nations. Having them visit individually was great, but there was something special about having them all here together. It made it doubly special to have Kathy's family there as well—her twin sister Colleen and her husband, Ron, along with her other siblings Peggy and Mark, and Mark's wife, Debbie.

The most affecting personal moment for me came the day after the parade, when my family, Kathy's family, and close friends gathered in Manhattan at the New York Athletic Club for brunch. We were joined by Paula Hunchar, who had introduced Kathy and me so many years earlier, convinced we would make a good match. Also joining us were Susan and Leland Vandiver who had hosted the Christmas party at which Kathy and I met. We were entertained that day by the amazing Irish violinist, Greg Harrington.

After Mass the morning of the parade, as the hundreds of bands and groups were gathering at the start, Kathy and I had breakfast with Cardinal Dolan. Then it was on to the parade, where I was quite conspicuous, attired in a dark suit and gray overcoat with a wide sash proclaiming me as the Grand Marshal. Following tradition, I wore a tall, black, formal top hat. After only a few blocks, I was awed by the experience of striding up Fifth Avenue with tens of thousands of people lining the street cheering as we went by.

The parade starts off at Forty-Fourth Street and proceeds up just a couple blocks shy of the American Irish Historical Society on East

Eightieth Street. After finishing walking the length of the parade, I caught a ride back down to the reviewing stand, where I was able to see hundreds of my fellow employees from Northwell march by. Throughout the course of the day, I was interviewed by a dozen or so reporters for print, radio, and television. I told them all the same thing: that I was proud to be an immigrant and that America is a better country for being a beacon to immigrants from throughout the world.

As I walked up Fifth Avenue, waving to the crowd, I thought not just of the Irish men and women who had come here. I thought as well of the others from across Europe who, like the Irish, had come to America in the later part of the nineteenth century, settled in one of the variety of ethnic enclaves, and gotten up early every morning to head over to Manhattan and shovel the sand, lay the bricks, apply the mortar, climb the scaffolds, and build this monument to God and to the immigrants whose calloused hands, as Mario Cuomo would have put it, had brought this glorious structure to life. I wondered about the immigrants who marched in or witnessed New York's first St. Patrick's Day parade in 1762.

Those immigrants possessed rare courage. They left everything behind, virtually certain they would never again see their homeland, and journeyed what must have seemed like halfway around the world to what was, at best, an uncertain new life. I was marching in the 256th parade, and I was struck by that number and by the passage of so much time—two and a half centuries during which Irish immigrants had been celebrating our heritage in the New World. I walked in the footsteps of these pioneers, and I have benefited throughout my life, following the path they created for millions of Irish men and women like myself. Those Irish pioneers became Americans, and I am deeply proud to be an Irishman and just as proud to be an American. There is pride for all of us of Irish descent in the fact that nine of the signatories to the Declaration of Independence were Irish; that 190,000 Irish-born men fought for the Union in the Civil War.

As an immigrant, I confess that I have grown increasingly uncomfortable with the anti-immigrant rhetoric in the political realm. There have been prominent voices asserting that the United States has become a dark, forbidding place—a nation in decline. People who say such things do not know the America I know. In fact, the United States has been and continues to be the greatest incubator of opportunity the world has ever known. Imperfect? Absolutely. But at the very same time, truly great in so many ways.

The story of the United States is an immigrant story. It is about the talent, perseverance, and dedication of immigrants and their descendants. At Northwell Health, I work with more than 72,000 people, most from the United States, but many from around the world. In fact, within our organization are men and women—some of them on the parade route that day—from Africa, Asia, South America, Europe, everywhere. In our hospitals and ambulatory sites there are doctors, nurses, and technicians who grew up speaking Mandarin, Russian, Portuguese, Arabic, and a half-dozen other languages; who were raised as Hindus, Muslims, Jews, Catholics, and more. At meetings I hear wonderful accents from all over the planet from doctors whose names I initially struggled to pronounce. We have a medical melting pot, and it is a beautiful thing.

As my colleagues up in Albany noticed, when I got upset or angry, my face would turn red, and when I got really angry, my neck would turn red as well. Few things in this modern American cultural and political moment turn my neck redder than bias against immigrants. Unless you are Native American, your people came from elsewhere. How the national dialogue about this issue has reached such a depth of malicious ignorance, I do not know. What I do know is that anti-immigrant hostility has been all too common throughout American history. In my life I do everything I can to combat this ignorance, and I see all around me the immense benefits of an immigration policy that does not discriminate based on ethnicity or religion, and that welcomes those fleeing the worst kind of violence and oppression.

It seems there are always conflicts of one kind or another within families, and clearly ours is no exception. Mitigating the joy of Saint Patrick's Day for my siblings and me was our concern about Sean. Many years after Sean swung into action to help get Joe into rehab, it was now Sean himself who needed help. Though he'd worked as an alcohol counselor, Sean observed, "It didn't teach me a lot, as it turns out."

This time, it was Joe who provided help and support to Sean, but the effects on Sean's body have been severe. "His liver is shot from the drink," says Joe. Sean has done so much for all of us through the years, and it's painful to watch him suffer. Mary has tried to help him. "It is very difficult to see a brother whom you love harm himself and his family because of alcohol," she says. "He will be upset reading these words and I am very sorry about that." The good news is that Sean has been making progress lately which we are all very glad about.

Helping people and organizations in Ireland has been a big priority for me. Years ago, I established two scholarships for University College Cork students (members of the hurling team, in fact), and each year I create openings within the Northwell system for paid summer internships for students from UCC, University of

Limerick, and University College Dublin. A couple of years ago, I donated money to the Aughalin School—the primary school I went to in Knockaderry—for musical instruments, and the boys and girls performed beautifully for me when I visited. I have donated to a variety of causes and organizations in Ireland, and I have provided funds to individuals who were in need as well. I derive immense satisfaction from sharing what I have.

My involvement with Ireland goes beyond the financial, of course. At a University College Cork alumni gathering in Manhattan, I was honored to give the keynote address. When the Limerick hurling team traveled to New York, I met with them and they presented me with a framed photograph of the team that had just won the all-Ireland championship. I have made arrangements numerous times through the years for people in Ireland who needed excellent medical care to come to one of our Northwell hospitals, particularly for highly specialized surgeries and other treatments. I have served and continue to serve on various committees working to reform the Irish health-care delivery system. I currently serve on the strategic planning committee for the University of Limerick Medical School.

My connection to Knockaderry, in particular, lies within my DNA, as do memories of life in the old house where the roof caved in. So much of life then was about work, and work is still what I spend the overwhelming majority of my time doing, even trimming the tall hedge in my yard—I scale a ladder and do the work myself, not because I have to, but because I want to. It is who I am.

I was reminded of the old house not too many years ago, while I was speaking at a conference held at Mount Vernon in Virginia, the residence of George Washington. It is a spectacular place, vast farmland with a stately home set along the Potomac, and it is quite moving to imagine that the great Washington once walked this property, lived within these very rooms. We had just about completed a tour of the house, built in 1734 by Washington's father, when we entered the kitchen. I was dumbstruck. To my eye, the kitchen was a replica of the main room in the old house in Knockaderry! Simple, basic, a large open fireplace with bellows, steel pots and pans for cooking over the open flame, plain table in the center of the room. No running water or electricity. The reality was that we had grown up in in the 1950s and 60s in a house with a kitchen that looked very much like something constructed two hundred years earlier.

In the 1990s, I thought so often about life in the old house that I took on a project to build a small-scale model of it—including all the furniture—in my basement at home. It took about a year of work here and there on evenings and weekends, but I completed it and proudly display it in the house in which I now live—a home that is approximately twenty times the size of the old house. When we moved into our new house in Northport, we had quite a spacious yard, but it was overrun with high grass, bushes, and brambles. I spent weekends clearing it all out myself. It was important to me that I do the labor on my own. I could have hired a landscaping company, settling on the porch with a cup of coffee instead of doing the work. But as I reflected upon my life during the Saint Patrick's Day experience, I realized what I had long known—I am who I have always been.

I have grown through the years, but I don't think I have really changed all that much. Maybe that's both a good and a bad thing. I am the same Mike Dowling from Knockaderry as I was many decades ago. I had to do the work in my yard by myself because I am my father's son and the work had to be done the right way. I have worked all my life, since I was a little boy. I confess I love to work. And I am thankful for the experiences in Knockaderry that taught me the value—on many levels—of an honest day's work.

Chapter Fifteen

A Good Ending

"We're lucky we've gotten closer as we've gotten older."

It is nearly sixty years since the roof caved in. Sixty years since a thousand pounds of wet straw and soaked canvas came crashing down in the room I shared with Joe and Sean; sixty years since, working with our father, we rebuilt that section of the roof, perhaps not quite as well as a master thatcher would have, but well enough to keep most of the weather away for a bit longer. The old house has been gone for a couple of generations, but we all carry its image in our minds.

As I was working on this memoir, a new book was published by Lewis Hyde, the American scholar. *A Primer for Forgetting* "explores the many situations in which forgetfulness is more useful than memory." As one reviewer put it: "What if forgetfulness were seen not as something to fear . . . but rather as a blessing, a balm, a path to peace and rebirth?" While I understand the potential appeal of forgetting—of careful editing within our memory bank in order to soothe or calm—the truth is that I don't want to forget. I want to remember everything. Time blurs certain memories, but what my siblings and I remember is a rich mix—of sadness, joy, fear, regret—all of which make for hard-earned wisdom.

I turned seventy as I was writing this, a milestone that naturally makes a person reflective. What happens when you look back, remembering? I have been aided immeasurably in my recollections through conversations with Joe, Sean, Mary, and Pat. And part of remembering involves examining the journey each of us has taken. I think that the closest I can get to characterizing our lives, individually and collectively, is that we have persevered. We have weathered the various storms through the years, and we remain standing together. We have all faced adversity along the way, and I wonder sometimes: How much of that adversity was rooted in the old house? Was there a predisposition toward alcoholism within the family? Toward violence? Fear? Toward a lack of warmth or an inability to express emotions?

Members of the Dowling clan tend to hold strong opinions, especially the brothers. Sean never backed down from anything in his life, including his current battle against declining health. I have my own stubborn views, as do Joe and Pat. Mary has opinions, of course, but she has something more valuable: an innate peacemaking ability. It is not an overstatement to suggest that Mary was traumatized as a child by the tension in the house, including the arguments and violence between and among the brothers and our father. Mary seeks to play the role my mother played—that of peacemaker—and she does it brilliantly.

Relationships among siblings, especially those who grew up in a traumatic environment, can be complicated. While in Knockaderry I recalled the famous scene in the classic novel *Portrait of the Artist as a Young Man*, by James Joyce, when the Dedalus family gathers at Christmastime for a festive holiday dinner amid warmth and good fellowship. At dinner, Mr. and Mrs. Dedalus entertain Aunt Dante, Uncle Charles, and a friend, Mr. Casey. What starts as a joyous event takes a tense turn when Mr. Dedalus criticizes the Catholic Church for its involvement in politics. To Dante, this is heretical. With sharp disagreements and increasingly heated language, the goodwill and warmth are chased away by anger and recrimination. In no time at all, Dante storms out as Mr. Casey breaks down.

In the Dowling family, even after the death of our father, we had our share of these moments through the years, times when arguments had spiraled out of control before you could apply the brakes. Most normal siblings have conflicts, but too many such events over time wear down the family fabric. My brother Joe is a devout Catholic, and there have been more than a few heated conversations among Dowling siblings who disagree with Joe. He takes the position that the priests are all right, while I tend to take the opposite view, probably out of bitterness about how my family was publicly humiliated by the priests. I confess that I'm still infuriated by the Church when I recall the old hurt. And now with the unspeakable pedophilia scandal and, what's more, the denial and the coverup, I'm even less tolerant of anyone who tries to defend them.

For a time, it seemed that disagreements, however mild, would turn into conflicts. Why? Because our default setting leaned toward confrontation. We grew up amid conflict just about every day. We grew up in an edgy environment where people did not react with thoughtful analysis, but rather with intensity inappropriate to the occasion. Sean, for example, can be highly opinionated and domineering, and his conversations can degenerate into arguments.

By no means do I exempt myself from criticism. I have had a tendency to play the annoying role of the all-knowing oldest sibling. We are all guilty to one degree or another, with Mary the sole exception. Pat and Sean have had their difficult moments, and as mentioned, if you're around Joe, you'd better not talk about religion. For all our conflicts, however, not long after Mam passed away, Joe, Sean, Mary, and Pat traveled to the states to stay with me so that we could all spend time together.

I feel guided by Mam's example in life. There are families where, after the parents die, the siblings drift apart. My siblings and I were determined not to let that happen. We evolved an informal agreement—*let's make sure we connect on a regular basis*—and we have done just that.

When we were together in Knockaderry, Patrick summarized it well: "We're lucky we've gotten closer as we've gotten older. We didn't really like each other very much for a long time. Typical family, different things going on, growing, fighting, people expressing opinions and other people having a different view, like any family, and maybe as time goes on everybody was doing their own thing. We may not be in contact as much, whereas now, for the last ten years, we're all in contact weekly, which is great, so it's a good ending for our family."

Kathy and I land in the gray light of dawn, a night flight from JFK, rain streaking the plane's windows. We touch down as Dublin is waking up to what will become a sparkling October day in 2019. We check into the Westbury Hotel in the heart of Dublin city center, steps from Grafton Street and blocks from Trinity College Dublin, an easy walk to the post office building where the martyred rebels challenged British occupation in the 1916 Easter Rising and all the leaders, save De Valera, were executed (most shot, one hanged). I like wandering around Dublin, taking in the sights. It is so cosmopolitan now, so much part of the modern world, in sharp contrast to the way it was in the 1950s and early 1960s.

Later that morning, I head out to an appointment with the new head of the Irish Health Services Administration. I had been involved in advising the leaders of the Irish national health system on how best to overhaul the system to improve quality and efficiency. I recruited a couple of other executives from Northwell, and we volunteered our time to share the sorts of approaches we thought worked best at Northwell and that also might suit the Irish system. Subsequently, I chaired an international advisory group charged with bringing ideas and best practices from other countries to Ireland. I had met previously in New York with the minister of health, as well as the Irish prime minister.

The Irish central bureaucracy is a stubborn creature and change is difficult. There is an impulse among bureaucrats to set up studies and commissions to make recommendations that end up being debated more than they are implemented. In past visits to Ireland, I had done some field work, making it a point to meet with doctors and nurses on the front lines, and I had been impressed by their knowledge and commitment. I'm hopeful, even optimistic, that the new leadership will take a more assertive role in pushing for improvements within the system—because that system clearly could be run far more efficiently and with a much greater focus on the well-being of patients, which is exactly how workers on the front lines want it.

It is cloudy off and on as we make our way through Dublin's crawling traffic and head west along the M7, a smooth ribbon of highway unlike any roadway that existed when I was growing up. We wind through Kildare, Tipperary, and on down to the southwest and into Limerick County. As we drive, some of the clouds part and a ray of sun shines through, illuminating the rolling hills and valleys.

The farther west we travel, away from the traffic and commerce of Dublin, the more the countryside reveals its simple beauty—farms beyond farms, cows and sheep grazing, the land much as it has been for centuries. I find that the deeper I get down into the southwestern part of Ireland, the more relaxed I become. These towns and villages, the hills and valleys, the tapestry of multiple complementary shades of green—they get a hold of you in childhood and never let go.

Since Mary's house in Knockaderry is too small to accommodate the whole crew, Kathy and I stay at the Adare Manor in the little town of Adare. The Manor is perched on the banks of the meandering River Maigue and features a vast landscape that includes a golf course, magnificent gardens, farmland, falconry, and a variety of outbuildings. The heart of the property is the neo-Gothic manor house, complete with gargoyles, constructed in 1832. It is interesting to note that construction jobs provided sustenance for laborers and craftspeople during the potato famine. Adare Manor is a few miles and a million light years from the Knockaderry in which I was raised. The old house had no plumbing or electricity, rats in the roof, mice on the floor, and water seeping through the walls. Adare Manor is perhaps the finest resort in all of Ireland, and could not possibly be more luxurious.

But I have to say that as much as I enjoy Adare Manor— and we have spent many family vacations there—my heart is in Knockaderry. When I think of growing up in Knockaderry, I invariably find my thoughts making their way to the idea of adversity as a powerful and sometimes positive force in life. Adversity can smother hopes. It can crush people. But it can also inspire and motivate. I was never smothered or crushed. I was always inspired and motivated.

I feel lucky in that respect, because I know there are many people whose natural disposition is to go in the other direction. I often come back to my father's life story, because I think it is so instructive. I suspect that my brother Sean is correct that our father suffered from depression, that he had a terrible time fighting his way out of black moods, out of the quicksand that was his anger. When Mr. Sullivan said those memorable words to me—"Isn't it too bad that someone like you could never go to college?"—I could have reacted any one of a number of different ways, including self-pity. He was, after all, telling me what had long been the reality—that boys like me in the lower social echelon of a rural Irish community really did not typically go to college. I took his comments as a put-down, as reminding me that my family was well below his on the socioeconomic ladder.

But, reflecting on it more than five decades later, maybe that was unfair. Maybe Mr. Sullivan was honestly lamenting the fact that someone like me didn't have an opportunity to go to college. Whatever his intent, the comment was rocket fuel, and I believed that no matter the adversity, I could work hard enough to make a serious attempt at improving my position in life. So, too, when Mr. Burke and my father said there was no point in my proceeding to secondary school.

I always believed, from a very young age, that my ambition to go beyond what I saw around me in Knockaderry was legitimate and well grounded in reality, rather than a matter of whimsy. This came from my mother, no doubt. She established in me a foundational belief in myself that I had the brains, ambition, and work ethic to rise above the dismal side of life.

The adversity of my life propelled me to where I am today. I don't recommend it, but for those who have difficult circumstances, you can turn the adversity into fuel. I sometimes wonder whether our kids have missed out on knowing so little adversity in their lives.

Where I came from is never far from my mind. Every once in a while, I encounter successful people who seem to believe they got where they are on their own. I don't buy it. And it is certainly not the case in my life. Yes, for sure, I worked hard and faced obstacles, but at every pivotal point, I received help.

My mother, first and foremost, made the life I now have possible. My friends at University College Cork, especially Willy McAuliffe, encouraged me to overcome my natural reticence and run for student government, which eventually brought out my ability for leadership. Without Willy's encouragement, I might have been too timid to run. Without the support and mentorship of the college president, I might not have prospered in college as I did. My mentors at Fordham and Columbia encouraged me and taught me how to navigate academia. Governor Mario Cuomo, entrusting me with leadership of health and human services programs for the state, allowed me to learn and grow as we worked our way to some important innovations that helped needy people. My wife Kathy made it possible for me to follow the professional pathway I chose, while my children, Brian and Elizabeth, brought joy to our family.

Both Brian and Elizabeth have chosen the health-care field—Brian as the manager of an imaging center, and Elizabeth as an oncology nurse. I love seeing their professionalism and commitment to serving patients. And my siblings Joe, Sean, Mary, and Pat, individually and collectively, supported me in many ways at crucial points in my life.

When I think about the journey I have been on, I trace so much of it back to Knockaderry, to the things in the village that shaped me—in one way or another—and prepared me for what lay ahead.

Fifty-two years after leaving Knockaderry for America for the first time, I walk through the village with Kathy, Joe, and Mary, along with her husband Pat. In appearance, Knockaderry is essentially unchanged in the years since I lived there. Buildings in the village remain largely the same. The farms extend out into the hills and valleys, just as they did when I was a boy. In other ways, it has been transformed—affluence, cars in driveways, electricity in homes, kids going off to college, more secular than religious. In this modern age, the all-day trek to Cork is a short drive. Dublin is easily accessible, and America is no longer far away.

It is a blustery October day, billowing clouds, crisp air, a sharp breeze. As Mary puts it—I have come home. Though I have lived in New York for forty-plus years, I have never traveled to Knockaderry. I have always *come home*. I embrace this description.

We stroll from Mary's—the new house—along the roadway, past where Mam's good friend Philomena Meehan lives, and turn right to St. Munchin's Church. This spare building remains mostly unchanged. The only significant new addition inside is a marble baptismal font, which my siblings and I donated, bearing a plaque in memory of our mother. Past the church is the building where Mike Guiry once plied the blacksmith's trade, and beyond is the Carnegie Library hall, where the concert was held the night that Joe disappeared.

There is an inescapable melancholy in the air when I exit the church. I recall sitting with Mam in that place countless times, every time knowing that she was unable to hear a word of the Mass or the sermon, but that she was there because she believed in a benevolent God. I had to make a choice when I was seventeen years old—to stay in Knockaderry to help Mam, or to leave and help Mam in a different way. And help myself, of course.

I don't often get this way, but the emotion of the moment clutches me. I have been thinking lately of keeping the family together in later years and beyond. Our kids—the cousins—need to strengthen relationships so when my siblings and I are gone, our kids will be together. This is massively important to me. Thankfully, it has already begun to happen. My daughter Elizabeth is very close to Sean's daughter Laura. Elizabeth has visited Laura in Ireland and Laura has come to the states, and they have had weekends together in London as well. This makes me very happy.

We make our way to Hanley's Pub, which is much as it was eons ago, though Sean Hanley and his sister Peg are long gone. We stop in and a couple of us have a beer. Joe draws our attention to pictures on the wall of old friends from past generations. Joe knows what happened to just about every one of them, and he tells us about their children and grandchildren. He is a marvelous storyteller and the only thing he does not do in Hanley's that day is drink. He has not touched the stuff now for thirty-seven years. I don't tell him, but I know for sure—that my siblings and I love Joe for having quit; we love him for regaining his life and bringing so much to our family.

Beyond the pub, we make our way down a long pathway to the hurling pitch. It is in the same location, but everything about it has changed. There are modern stands for spectators and locker rooms for the players—no need to stash clothes under furze bushes to keep them dry. And the whole enterprise is surrounded by a fence, locked tight now to keep the field in the best possible shape for whenever the next match is to be played. Joe and I recall players from days gone by. These are some very sweet recollections.

I'm known within the family for my emotional distance. I am, in that respect, my father's son. But I realize as we slowly make our way back to Mary's for dinner that I am a lucky man. I have these people who have meant so much to me, and as I reflect upon this, I realize what I have really always known: that everything that has happened to me—everything I have achieved in life personally and professionally—can be traced back to lessons I learned in this tiny place, a place that was at times harsh and unforgiving, at times loving, and remains to this day one of the most beautiful places on earth.

We walk down the road and follow a winding path up the hill where my father used to stand and wave to me, his cane extended towards the sky. I do not recall the slope being so steep, and it strikes me that it must have required quite an effort for Dad to make his way up this hill, through the gate, and up to the summit. I think that I understand now, as I never did before, that he appeared up on the hill when I was leaving for America because it was too painful for him to be with me, to look me in the eye, shake my hand, and bid me farewell. He likely feared that he was losing me and could not bear to see me go. I realize now that his waving from the top of the hill was not a rejection of me, but rather an expression of his love for me; an expression in the only way he could convey to me.

The portrait of my father in this book is not a flattering one, and that pains me. I have written honestly about him and his nature. But I find as I get older that perspectives change over time, and I now have a deeper understanding of the difficulties my father faced in his life—challenges and setbacks that I never fully understood growing up. In many ways, he was a product of circumstances he could not control.

We ascend the hill slowly, carefully avoiding the sting of the furze bushes. There is a gate separating the pasture where cows graze, and we climb over it to continue our ascent to the top of the hill. I have not been up here for many years, and I am struck by the panoramic view. Everything I can now see is just as it was back when I was a boy. There in the distance I can see Limerick City and the Shannon estuary beyond. There is Foynes Harbor, and as I turn there are the Galtee Mountains, Knockfierna, and the village of Ballingarry.

I feel for a moment that I am watching a shot from a movie filmed long ago, for I can see that very little, if anything, has changed in the past couple of generations. There are farms and cottages in every direction, and I am struck by the realization that many of them were abandoned years ago by people who felt they had no other choice but to migrate to England and America.

Back at Mary's house, there is a wonderful dinner that she and her husband, Pat, have prepared. Joe tells stories from the old days, and we laugh about what it was like living in the old house. Mr. Burke's name is mentioned, and the context is not favorable. We recount harrowing stories about visits to the infamous dentist in Newcastle West and get updates from Mary on some of the neighbors. My brother Pat and cousin Vincent recall some of the days with Dad, and we all laugh at the stories about his cigarettes nearly setting the house on fire. There is food and wine, and much fretting over the fate of the Irish national rugby team. We watch a game on television and cheer loudly when our boys score.

This is when my brother Pat says what strikes me as so true: "We're lucky we've gotten closer as we've gotten older . . . so it's a good ending for our family." Yes, it is. Not perfect by any means, but good. Better than many days in the past. Mam would be happy about it, and I am sure my father would be, too.

As Kathy and I depart Mary's house for Pat to drive us back to Adare Manor, we all bid goodbye to one another. If this were

Kathy's family, there would be hugs all around. As I leave, no hugs. That's not me. I do not tell my siblings that I love them, but I think they know.

Afterword

A Lifelong Love of Learning

THANKS TO MY MOTHER'S INFLUENCE and my own innate curiosity, I have been focused on learning since I was a child. Reading and learning have brought insight, knowledge, and joy to my life. I cannot imagine a life without books. Learning is a joyous pursuit that is part of every day of my life. At Northwell I learn from brilliant colleagues and their expertise in every conceivable field of science and medicine. Learning remains as central to my life now as it did when I was listening to stories from my parents and their friends in the old house before the roof caved in. I believe that learning is a lifelong pursuit for an individual and that learning should be an essential part of the DNA within any organization. My colleagues will tell you I am a bit obsessed by the idea of continuous learning throughout life—for professional and personal growth. I regularly post lists of recent books that I find interesting and informative in the hopes that a number of our employees might consider reading them. I have included a number of these titles from recent years below. I have also included a summary of the various stops along the way of my professional learning journey.

Within our organization here at Northwell, my learning obsession has tangible expression in our medical and graduate nursing
schools as well as in an internal learning facility inspired by the
world-class GE corporate university at Crotonville, New York.
Our Northwell Center for Learning and Innovation allows our
workers time away from their daily pursuits to step back, reflect
on their work, and learn new ways of delivering better care for
patients. Educational programs at the Center have improved the
safety of our care, the quality of our care, access to our care, and
the overall experience of care. While I have focused on continuous learning throughout our organization, I have also worked to
improve the quality of learning for medical students. I remember
the day it became clear to me that there was something wrong
with the way we educate doctors in the United States. I was
speaking to an orientation session with medical students and residents, and I was talking about the importance of identifying the
right ways to measure quality. This was back around 2005, and it
was clear that they didn't really understand what I was talking
about. I thought maybe they couldn't understand my Irish accent,
but that wasn't it. I figured out that they only had a vague sense
of quality metrics—sepsis, medication errors, infections, overall
mortality—everything. I said, "You learned about this in med
school?" They said *no*. "Did your school ever tell you about quality
outcome metrics?" *No*. "What about community-based care?" *No*.
"What about the integration of behavioral health with primary
care?" *No*. I thought, what are they teaching them? *What in hell is
going on here?* I could not help but wonder why they were so out of
sync with the reality of modern health care. It seemed obvious to
me that we needed to train these doctors differently. I was always

perplexed by medical students heading from school to training in a hospital where a declining percentage of care is being delivered, certainly not where the bulk of the care will be delivered in the future.

Our idea was to build one of the most radical and innovative medical education institutions in the world, and that is what we have with the Donald and Barbara Zucker School of Medicine at Hofstra/Northwell along with the Hofstra Northwell School of Nursing and Physician Assistant Studies. In traditional medical schools, students don't see patients until year three. We start students out in a rapid EMT course and send them out in an ambulance so that from just about day one they interact with patients in their homes in a variety of stressful situations. We learned through research that medical students are turned off by lectures and prefer to learn through modern technology on their own. We eliminated lectures in our school. We took a cue from leading business schools, where students are relied upon to learn collaboratively in teams through studying real-life cases. Assessments in medical school traditionally relied heavily upon a student's ability to recall a variety of facts. The doctors who led the innovation work on our medical school—Lawrence Smith and David Battinelli—developed a method to determine not who had the best memory but which students could process a complex set of medical facts and come up with an appropriate treatment. The focus is on critical reasoning rather than memorization. By any measure, the medical school has been a huge success and stands as something of a model for where medical education is headed in the years to come.

Every year, I recommend books to my colleagues at Northwell Health. Here are some of those I recommended in recent years.

2022

The Warmth of Other Suns by Isabel Wilkerson
If you like history, this is for you. It chronicles the migration of black Americans from the South to the North and West between 1915 and 197—a total of six million. This is an exceptional piece of the American story and is told through the lives and struggles of three spectacular individuals.

Dying of Whiteness by Jonathan Metzl
This is worth reading and will help provide perspective—a unique perspective on recent politics and elections. It focuses on the issues, health, guns, schools and racial resentment in three states, Missouri, Tennessee and Kansas. He poses the question—why do people support those policies that eventually hurt them? This book is provocative and enlightening.

You Bet Your Life by Paul Offit, MD
This is an enjoyable and informative book. It chronicles the stories and risk taking that resorted in major scientific and curative discoveries—heart transplants, antibiotics, anesthesia, etc. Beautifully written—you learn about the people and the circumstances that led to such amazing progress. Entertaining and informative.

Killing Reagan by Bill O'Reilly and Martin Dugard
I thank Mark Solazzo for introducing me to the books by Bill O'Reilly

—they are exceptional in their storytelling—vivid, informative, and educational. This book tells the story of Ronald Reagan from beginning to end in a unique engaging way. It will add to your knowledge.

Killing Lincoln by Bill O'Reilly
This, in my view, is one of the best informative and entertaining books I have read on Lincoln and the details of his death. Worth reading.

No One Wins Alone by Mark Messier
This of course is for hockey and sports fans but it has wonderful lessons for those interested in leadership. Messier tells his story from his youth to his unbelievable success as one of the best hockey players of all time. He helps understand what it takes to be successful—as an individual and as an organization.

Oscar: A Life by Matthew Sturgis
This is, up to now, the most detailed and complete book on the life of Oscar Wilde, the famous Irish poet and playwright—the good, the bad, and the ugly.

San Fransicko—Why Progressives Ruin Cities by Michael Shellenberger
Given current discussions on the plight of some cities (including New York City) this is an informative book. It analyzes issues of crime, homelessness, housing, and the policies that exacerbated them. He does propose some solutions that might work. It will get you to rethink and think anew.

2020

Just Mercy by Bryan Stevenson
A terrific book based on true stories about defending those trapped in the criminal justice system, including inmate Walter McMillian, who had been sentenced to die. Bryan Stevenson founded the acclaimed Equal Justice Initiative.

Call Sign Chaos by James N. Mattis and Bing West
James Mattis was Trump's secretary of defense, who subsequently resigned. This is his story, his background, his ideas on leadership, and his view of the world we now live in—its challenges and opportunities.

These Truths: A History of the United States by Jill Lepore
If you like history, this book is for you. In my view it's a classic that will enhance your knowledge and perspective. Its final sections are a wonderful analysis of recent developments and their implications.

That Will Never Work: The Birth of Netflix and the Amazing Life of an Idea by Marc Randolph
How do successful organizations begin? Not how you may think. An interesting analysis and history of an idea that many said would never work.

The Great Pretender by Susannah Cahalan
Cahalan's first book was *Brain on Fire*, about her own personal circumstance, and which highlighted Northwell's Dr. Souhel Najjar. This book is a terrific follow-up that delves more into mental illness, the use of psychiatric hospitals, and the history of research.

Learning to Lead by Ron Williams
Ron Williams is the former CEO of Aetna. This is a very good
book on what it takes to be successful. He also provides the history
of his own personal journey.

Kochland by Christopher Leonard
This is an excellent history of Koch Industries and their corporate
and political influence. It provides an inside look at business acu-
men, entrepreneurship, grit, and at times ruthlessness. A great read
that will add to your understanding of the many angles to success.

The Big Nine by Amy Webb
This is a book about technology and the influence—positive and
negative—of the Big Nine: Amazon, Google, Facebook, Tencent,
Baidu, Alibaba, Microsoft, IBM, and Apple. A great read.

The Good Doctor by Tom Lee, MD
Tom Lee is a very insightful thinker. He did much of his training
at North Shore. By profiling certain physicians, he addresses issues
of empathy, commitment, burnout, and focus. It emphasizes the
benefits of optimism and inspiration—a great read at this time.

Chronicles of Old New York by James Roman
If you want to learn more about New York City, this is a great little
book. It describes Manhattan's landmark neighborhoods—history,
geography, people, etc. A wonderful read.

2019

More than Medicine: The Broken Promise of American Health by Robert M. Kaplan
A very readable and timely book. It focuses on the need to re-prioritize and deal with social, behavioral, and environmental issues, not just on treatment of disease. Very informative and readable.

The Culture Code: The Secrets of Highly Successful Groups by Daniel Coyle
You know the saying—"culture eats strategy for breakfast." This excellent book is about culture—what it is, how to sustain it, and what it means for leadership.

Capitalism in America: A History by Alan Greenspan and Adrian Wooldridge
This traces the history of economic development, discovery, innovation, and productivity. Well written and readable. It focuses on change and creative destruction—a relevant topic as we discuss health care reform.

The Fifth Risk by Michael Lewis
There are many books written about the current federal leadership. This one, I believe, gets at a core issue of the dangers of putting people in power who do not understand the organizations they have to lead and the long-term dangers that potentially result. Brief, a great read, and provides great data about some of the federal agencies.

Say Nothing: A True Story of Murder and Memory in Northern Ireland by Patrick Radden Keefe
This is a book that, once you begin, is difficult to put it down. It's about the history of the "troubles," but it brings you inside the events so you feel like you are there. You will connect with the characters and the environment—and be so glad you were not there. A true story.

The Age of Surveillance Capitalism: The Fight for a Human Future at the New Frontier of Power by Shoshana Zuboff
This book is one of the best in discussing the implications of the new technology business and the impact on control, behavior modification, inequality, privacy, and human interaction. A powerful but large book—over five hundred pages. If you wish to understand the future, read this.

The Four: The Hidden DNA of Amazon, Apple, Facebook, and Google by Scott Galloway
This is an important read about the history, power, practice, and implications of the Big Four. The author is not shy about challenging many of their intentions and practices and reminding us of what is at stake. A great beach read.

Radical Inclusion by Ori Brafman and Martin Dempsey
A small book but full of leadership tips on influence, power, control, and focus. Full of examples from many different fields—enjoyable.

The Enlightened Capitalists: Cautionary Tales of Business Pioneers Who Tried to Do Well by Doing Good by James O'Toole
This is a wonderful book about business people who, as the subtitle

states, do well by doing good—an important subject in today's environment. You will read about people you may know nothing or little about and their contributions: James Penney, Robert Owen, Milton Hershey, Levi Strauss, Ken Iverson, etc.

The Jungle Grows Back: America and Our Imperiled World by Robert Kagan
A wonderful little book on the importance of America's role in a changing and more complicated world and the dangers inherent in a retreat. Very relevant in light of current events.

2018/2019

Frederick Douglass: Prophet of Freedom by David Blight
This is the story of an extraordinary individual. Born a slave, he became a national and international orator (one of the greatest of all time), writer, and abolitionist. This is a large book but a must-read for those who wish to understand history, gain a broader perspective, and have an appreciation for what's possible.

The Coddling of the American Mind by Greg Lukianoff and Jonathan Haidt
Are we becoming intolerant, unaccepting of conflicting ideas, creating destructive entitlements, making things too easy, etc? These issues are discussed and, in my view, necessarily so if we are to prepare individuals for the often harsh reality of life. This will make you think. Worth reading.

Grit: The Power of Passion and Perseverance by Angela Duckworth
This great work focuses on character, persistence, and refusal to

quit as core ingredients in success. Titles, position, what school you graduated from—these alone don't do it. This analysis is captivating—you will enjoy it.

The Restless Wave by John McCain and Mark Salter
If you are interested in politics, the power of leadership, recent political events, and history, this book is for you. A great read about a remarkable individual—who could have been (in my view) a good president—somebody to emulate and admire, even if you disagreed with some of his ideas. Enjoy.

Devil's Mile: The Rich, Gritty History of the Bowery by Alice Sparberg Alexiou
Many of you remember the Bowery of half a century ago; others heard stories about it. This book gives you the history and its many transformations. A fascinating story, much of it very different from what you know. It's a major part of the history of immigration and therefore of New York.

The Corrosion of Conservatism: Why I Left the Right by Max Boot
Max Boot was a staunch right-oriented conservative. This book is about his transformation as a result of the growing alt-right ideology—his view that current thinking and policy is toxic, tribal, and dangerous. This is well written, enjoyable, and a must read for those interested in current political discourse.

Nine Irish Lives by Mark Bailey
This brief, enjoyable book chronicles the lives of nine Irish people whose lives made a difference. A quick informative read—even if you are not Irish.

Leadership: In Turbulent Times by Doris Kearns Goodwin
A very good book focusing on the leadership attributes of four presidents—Lincoln, Teddy Roosevelt, Johnson, and FDR—their strengths, weaknesses, and how circumstances dictated or informed their actions and decisions. If leadership interests you, read this— Goodwin's special talent as a writer is very evident.

21 Lessons for the 21st Century by Yuval Noah Harari
His previous book, *Sapiens*, focused on the past—this focuses on the future, on such issues as work, liberty, war, justice, and education. This gets you to think.

Presidents of War: From 1807 to Modern Times by Michael Beschloss
An account of leaders and their involvement in various wars—their struggles both physical and emotional, their battles with other institutions of government, their success and failures, and their impact in the world. It's a history from another perspective. It's a large book but worth it.

Turncoat by Stephen Brumwell
This is the story of Benedict Arnold and his transition from hero to traitor—with a more balanced perspective. A good history—well written and very enjoyable.

Fascism: A Warning by Madeleine Albright
For those interested in current political trends—both here and abroad— this is definitely worth reading. Beautifully written with a lot of historical context. It will educate you and force you to think and worry.

Anti-Pluralism: The Populist Threat to Liberal Democracy by William Galston
Another political book. Only 135 pages but provides an informative analysis of current trends and political divisions with suggestions on what should be done.

Enlightenment Now by Steven Pinker
Negativity, pessimism, and cynicism abound. This is a great read on progress, optimism, and hope. It takes a broad look at multiple areas across the globe and outlines what has been accomplished and how fortunate we are to live in this time. Meticulously researched and well written. A large book but worth it.

The Inevitable: Understanding the 12 Technological Forces that Will Shape Our Future by Kevin Kelly
A look to the future with predictions of what we should expect. Want to become an amateur futurist? Read this.

Dagger John by John Loughery
This is a biography of Archbishop John Hughes, one of the most influential figures in New York City's history. He was the founder of Fordham University (originally St. John's College) and the builder of St. Patrick's Cathedral. This book will place you in the midst of the turbulence and success of the mid-nineteenth century.

Lincoln and the Irish by Niall O'Dowd
A terrific book on the relationship between Lincoln and the Irish and their influence on his presidency. Very informative—full of important things you did not know, but should.

How Democracies Die by Daniel Ziblatt and Steven Levitsky
This is an enlightening book about the dangers facing democracy, using examples from current situations around the world. If you are interested in current affairs, this is an important read. It's brief—only 230 pages.

The Tyranny of Metrics by Jerry Muller
While we are all proponents of metrics and their many forms, this book is informative and can get us to rethink how we proceed. It emphasizes how metrics can be gamed and manipulated. A very useful read.

The Everything Store: Jeff Bezos and the Age of Amazon by Brad Stone
We talk a lot about Amazon—its potential and its dangers and threats. If you want to understand how it began and developed and to appreciate its strategy and culture, read this. It will make you think.

Killers of the Flower Moon: The Osage Murders and the Birth of the FBI by David Grann
This will teach you new history—disturbing but very informative. You may not have heard of the Osage Indian Nation—read this and you will be surprised and shocked, and learn about why the FBI began.

Prescription for the Future: The Twelve Transformational Practices of Highly Effective Medical Organizations by Ezekiel Emanuel
Twelve trends that the author sees as transformational in the process to improve quality and promote reform.

The Efficiency Paradox: What Big Data Can't Do by Edward Tenner
A thoughtful book about the need to be wary about the networked world and overreliance on algorithms and digital platforms. He questions the assumption that they automatically lead to more efficiency. A worthwhile read.

Broadway by Fran Leadon
A history of New York in thirteen miles. If you are interested in New York history, read this. The next time you are on Broadway your perspective and understanding will be different.

The Soul of America by Jon Meacham
This is terrific and puts current disturbing developments in historical context—difficult to put aside once you start.

Acknowledgments

THIS BOOK IS A PORTRAIT of my life and my family's life. During the past seventy years, many people played important roles in my life. Many of the people who helped me when I was growing up in Knockaderry have long passed away, but I want to acknowledge a few who were special to me in important ways, including Sean Hanley, Coach Paddy Hennessey, Mr. Sullivan, and Ned Fitzgerald. I owe much to my teachers in secondary school, including Mr. Breen, Tim Murphy, David Hayes, Dennis Murphy, and Neel Ruddle, who succeeded Mr. Breen as headmaster. I owe a debt of gratitude to all my hurling teammates, most notably Jim Begley, Sean and Mike Maloney, Moss Walsh, Paddy and Jack Hennessey, Gerald and Tom Frawley, Paddy Lyons, Donal and Liam Sullivan, and Johnny Corkery.

University College Cork opened up a whole new world of learning and opportunity to me. I am especially grateful to my UCC and lifelong friends Mick Bond (also a hurling teammate), Mick Lane, and Willy McAuliffe, and to all the hurling stars I was so privileged to play with. To UCC president Dr. McCarthy and all my professors, a special thank you.

I benefited greatly from my years at Fordham as a student, an administrator, and a faculty member, and I thank in particular Jim Dumpson, Mary Ann Quaranta, former presidents Father James Finlay and Father Joseph O'Hare, and current president Father McShane.

Working in Albany for Governor Mario Cuomo for twelve years was a defining experience in my life. It was a privilege to work with caring and talented people, including Jerry Crotty, Hank Dullea, Maryann Crotty, Drew Zambelli, Liz Moore, Rick Cook, and so many others. I am deeply grateful to the entire Cuomo family, including the late governor himself, of course. He was the best mentor I ever had. I am grateful to Andrew (the current governor) for his continuing confidence in me, as well as to his siblings, Maria, Margaret, Madeline, and Chris. To Matilda Cuomo, the family matriarch, I pay the highest compliment possible: She reminds me of my mother.

On a personal level, I am grateful to Paula Hunchar, the matchmaker who believed, correctly, that Kathy and I were just right for each other, and to Susan and Leland Vandiver, special friends who hosted the party on Manhattan's Upper East Side where we first met. I am grateful to my friend Niall O'Dowd, a fellow Irishman and New Yorker whose counsel I highly value. I am grateful to my cousin Vincent, who has done so much to help our family through the years.

For more than twenty-five years, I have had the privilege of working with a remarkably talented group of people here at Northwell. During the coronavirus crisis, the 72,000 men and women of Northwell performed extraordinary life-saving work. It is an honor for me to be part of this group of compassionate, caring, and skilled people. I feel blessed to work alongside those friends and coworkers, including board members Ralph Nappi, Saul Katz, Roy Zuckerberg, Bill Mack, Mark Claster, Michael Epstein, Jeff Lane, Don Zucker, Paul Guenther, Richard Goldstein, Roger Blumencranz, and Lloyd Goldman.

Our executive leadership team is second to none, in my opinion. I am grateful to Mark Solazzo, Howard Gold, Jeff Kraut, Joe Moscola, Dr. Larry Smith, Dr. David Battinelli, Gene Tangney, Ramon Soto, Terry Lynam, Kathy Gallo, Michele Cusack, Dr. Kevin Tracey, Sven Gierlinger, Maureen White, Deborah Schiff, Dr. Mark Jarrett, Donna Drummond, Rich Miller, Dr. Tom McGinn, Dr. Ira Nash, Brian Lally, Larry Kraemer, Kevin Biener, Dr. Jason Naidich, Merryl Siegel, Rita Mercieca, Steve Bello, John Bosco, and all the other employees, managers, and leaders throughout the organization. A special thanks to a special assistant, Jeanne Gabriel. Thanks as well to Susan Marelli, Jason Philip, and to a special friend, Dr. Angelo Acquista.

I am grateful to my colleague, Charles Kenney, who has been my partner throughout the process of organizing and writing this memoir. Without him this book could not have been done.

Finally, my deepest gratitude to the most important people in my life—my family. My mother and father, my siblings, Joe, Sean, Mary, and Patrick, freely shared their experiences and recollections which helped me recall many important events. Sadly, Sean passed away on November 12, 2021. A special thanks to Kathy's family— her wonderful parents Ed and Barbara, her twin sister Colleen and her husband Ron, brother Ed (deceased way too young), Mark and his wife Debbie, and younger sister Peg.

My children Brian and Elizabeth bring immense joy to my life. And finally, to my wife Kathy for her love, wisdom, guidance, and steadfast support. She makes every day better than the day before.

About the Authors

Michael J. Dowling grew up in Limerick, Ireland. He earned his undergraduate degree from University College Cork (UCC), Ireland, and his master's degree from Fordham University. He served in New York State government for 12 years, including seven years as state director of Health, Education, and Human Services and deputy secretary to former governor Mario Cuomo. He was also commissioner of the New York State Department of Social Services. He is the president and CEO of Northwell Health and lives in Long Island, New York, with his wife.

Charles Kenney serves as chief journalist at Northwell Health and executive editor of the Northwell Innovation Series. He is the author of many books including *The Best Practice: How the New Quality Movement Is Transforming Medicine* (PublicAffairs 2008), which *The New York Times* described as "the first large-scale history of the quality movement." He serves on the faculty of the Institute for Healthcare Improvement in Cambridge, Massachusetts.